PERGAMON INTERNATION
of Science, Technology, Engineering anɑ ɔoᴄɪaɪ ɔτuuɪᴄɔ

The 1000-volume original paperback library in aid of education, industrial training and the enjoyment of leisure

Publisher: Robert Maxwell, M.C.

Early Childhood Autism

Clinical, Educational and Social Aspects

Second Edition

———————— Publisher's Notice to Educators ————————

THE PERGAMON TEXTBOOK INSPECTION COPY SERVICE

An inspection copy of any book published in the Pergamon International Library will gladly be sent ʷithout obligation for consideration for course adoption or recommendation. Copies may be retained for a period of 60 days from receipt and returned if not suitable. When a particular title is adopted or recommended for adoption for class use and the recommendation results in a sale of 12 or more copies, the inspection copy may be retained with our compliments. If after examination the lecturer decides that the book is not suitable for adoption but would like to retain it for his personal library, then our Educators' Discount of 10% is allowed on the invoiced price. The Publishers will be pleased to receive suggestions for revised editions and new titles to be published in this important International Library.

OTHER TITLES OF INTEREST

Early Childhood Autism

Clinical, Educational and
Social Aspects

Second Edition

Edited by

LORNA WING

*Member of Scientific Staff, Medical Research
Council Social Psychiatry Unit,
Institute of Psychiatry,
De Crespigny Park,
London, S.E.5*

PERGAMON PRESS

OXFORD • NEW YORK • TORONTO
SYDNEY • PARIS • BRAUNSCHWEIG

U. K.	Pergamon Press Ltd., Headington Hill Hall, Oxford OX3 0BW, England
U. S. A.	Pergamon Press Inc., Maxwell House, Fairview Park, Elmsford, New York 10523, U.S.A.
C A N A D A	Pergamon of Canada Ltd., 207 Queen's Quay West, Toronto 1, Canada
A U S T R A L I A	Pergamon Press (Aust.) Pty. Ltd., 19a Boundary Street, Rushcutters Bay, N.S.W. 2011, Australia
F R A N C E	Pergamon Press SARL, 24 rue des Ecoles, 75240 Paris, Cedex 05, France
W E S T G E R M A N Y	Pergamon Press GmbH, D-3300 Braunschweig, Postfach 2923, Burgplatz 1, West Germany

First edition 1967

Second edition 1976

Library of Congress Cataloging in Publication Data

Main entry under title:

Early childhood autism.

    First ed. edited by J. K. Wing.
    1. Autism. I. Wing, Lorna. II. Wing, John
Kenneth, ed. Early childhood autism. [DNLM: 1. Autism,
Early infantile. WM203 E12]
RJ506.A9W5   1975   618.9'28'982   75-17623
ISBN 0-08-017177-X
ISBN 0-08-017178-8 flexicover

Printed in Great Britain by A. Wheaton & Co., Exeter

"Each case of developmental delay forms an individual problem in which factors derived from the neurological status, the emotional reactions, the educational needs and the facilities for carrying on retraining must be evaluated and a program devised to conform to all of these. This point can scarcely be emphasised enough since we are all prone to search for a simplified and universally applicable formula, but no such general 'method' can be defined for any of these syndromes and any attempt to apply such a blanket prescription without thorough diagnosis of the individual case would assuredly lead to error and misguided effort."

(Orton, S. T. (1937) *Reading, Writing and Speech Problems in Children*, Chapman and Hall, London.)

CONTENTS

LIST OF CONTRIBUTORS   ix

FOREWORD   xi

PART ONE: CLINICAL AND PSYCHOLOGICAL

1. Kanner's Syndrome: A Historical Introduction   3
   JOHN K. WING

2. Diagnosis, Clinical Description and Prognosis   15
   LORNA WING
   Appendix 1: A Scheme for Clinical Description and
              Diagnosis   49
   Appendix 2: Case Histories of Three Young Autistic
              Adults   53

3. Epidemiology and Theories of Aetiology   65
   LORNA WING

4. Language, Communication and the Use of Symbols   93
   DEREK M. RICKS and LORNA WING

5. Coding and the Sense Modalities   135
   BEATE HERMELIN

6. Motor, Perceptual-Motor and Intellectual Disabilities
   of Autistic Children   169
   MARIAN K. DeMYER

PART TWO: EDUCATION, MANAGEMENT AND
               SERVICES

7. The Principles of Remedial Education for Autistic
   Children   197
   LORNA WING

8. An Approach to Teaching Cognitive Skills Underlying
   Language Development   205
   JOAN E. TAYLOR

9. Towards Reducing Behavior Problems in Autistic
   Children   221
   ERIC SCHOPLER

10. The Severely Retarded Autistic Child   247
    JANET CARR

11. Medical Management   271
    JOHN CORBETT

12. Provision of Services   287
    JOHN K. WING and LORNA WING

Index   335

LIST OF CONTRIBUTORS

CARR, JANET, Ph.D. Senior Psychologist, Hilda Lewis House, Bethlem Royal Hospital, 579, Wickham Road, Shirley, Croydon. Lecturer, Psychology Department, Institute of Psychiatry, London.

CORBETT, JOHN, MRCP, MRC Psych. DCH. Consultant Psychiatrist, Maudsley and Bethlem Royal Hospitals, Denmark Hill, London, S.E.5.

DeMYER, MARIAN K., MD. Director, Clinical Research Center for Early Childhood Schizophrenia, La Rue D. Carter Memorial Hospital, 1315, West Tenth Street, Indianapolis, Indiana, 46202. Professor, Department of Psychiatry, Indiana University School of Medicine.

HERMELIN, BEATE, Ph.D. Member of Scientific Staff, Medical Research Council, Development Psychology Unit, Drayton House, Gordon Street, London, WC1.

RICKS, DEREK M., MD. MRC Psych. Consultant in Charge Children's Department, Harperbury Hospital, Radlett, Herts. Hon. Consultant in Mental Handicap, Departments of Paediatrics and Child Psychiatry, University College, London. Hon. Consultant Psychiatrist, Wolfson Centre, Hospital for Sick Children, London.

SCHOPLER, ERIC, Ph.D. Co-director, Division TEACCH, Administration and Child Research Project, Trailer 18, Department of Psychiatry, N. C. Memorial Hospital, Chapel Hill, N.C. 27514.

TAYLOR, JOAN E., BA Hons Eng. Dip NCTD. Teacher in Charge, Language Unit, Charles Burns Clinic, Queensbridge Road, Birmingham 13. (retired)

WING, JOHN K., Ph.D. FRC Psych. Director, Medical Research Council Social Psychiatry Unit, Institute of Psychiatry, De Crespigny Park, London, S.E.5. Professor of Social Psychiatry, Institute of Psychiatry and London School of Hygiene.

WING, LORNA, MD. MRC Psych. Member of Scientific Staff, Medical Research Council Social Psychiatry Unit, Institute of Psychiatry, De Crespigny Park, London, S.E.5. Hon. Consultant Psychiatrist, Maudsley and Bethlem Royal Hospitals.

FOREWORD

The second edition of this book, like the first, has contributions from the fields of education, psychology and psychiatry. As in the first edition, a common point of view emerges from these different approaches. In the 8 years since the first edition was published, ideas concerning the impairments underlying autistic behaviour have become more sophisticated but there has been no fundamental change in emphasis. The present authors all regard early childhood autism and related conditions as resulting from a basic disturbance of cognitive development, the effects of which include abnormalities of language and communication and a variety of secondary behavioural and emotional problems. In recent years, a considerable weight of evidence has accumulated to support this view, although, as yet, no clear indication of the precise aetiology has emerged.

Some progress has been made in education, management and the provision of services. As a result of practical experience and evaluative research, the techniques of teaching are beginning to be better understood. These techniques are discussed in *An Approach to Teaching Autistic Children* (edited by Margaret P. Everard), published in conjunction with the present book. Since the Education (Handicapped Children) Act of 1971, all children in England and Wales have become the responsibility of the education authorities, whereas, when the first edition of this book was published, some handicapped children were still excluded from education in school. A number of special schools, units and classes for autistic children have been opened in various parts of the United Kingdom, both by the National Society for Autistic Children and local education authorities. Following the example of the British Society, parents' groups have been formed in other countries. Some have succeeded in opening their own special schools or have persuaded the relevant authorities to provide appropriate education. The problems posed by severely retarded and disturbed autistic children and by chronically handicapped autistic adults remain to be solved, although here and there in this and other countries a start has been made by a few dedicated pioneers.

Autistic children receive a great deal of attention and interest, perhaps because many of them have an attractive elfin appearance combined with their strange behaviour. Much of the interest they arouse has been of positive value, but it has also led to the proliferation of strange theories, which have, on the whole, been harmful to the children and even more so to their families. Many of these theories arise from the mistaken belief that autistic children are special and mysterious, because their behaviour is quite different from that found in any other condition. In contrast to this romantic idea, all the contributors to this book regard early childhood autism as an identifiable syndrome with characteristic features, but they also recognize its relationship to other childhood handicaps. Only when both these aspects are taken into account can the problems of autistic children be seen in perspective and realistic solutions found for them.

NOTE

The authors from the United Kingdom use the following definition of the grades of mental retardation:

Mild mental retardation—Intelligence quotient (IQ) 50 to 69
Severe mental retardation—Intelligence quotient (IQ) 49 and below

The authors from the United States of America use definitions which differ from the above. The details are given in the relevant chapters.

PART ONE

CLINICAL AND PSYCHOLOGICAL

CHAPTER 1

KANNER'S SYNDROME: A HISTORICAL INTRODUCTION

JOHN K. WING

The present generally accepted view that there is a set of recognisable behaviours, sufficiently often associated together to constitute a clinical syndrome of "early childhood autism", is due to Leo Kanner (1943). In the history of medicine, the recognition, definition and labelling of a syndrome has time and again proved of incalculable value, since it has provided a stimulus to the discovery of first and precipitating causes, methods of treatment, rehabilitation and prevention, and of an underlying pathology or pathophysiology. Possibly because of the success of this type of approach, it might be thought that medicine had come to rely too heavily on the elaboration of disease theories, to the neglect of other educational, sociological, psychological or pastoral techniques of investigation and treatment. It would be a mistake, however, to suppose that these approaches were alternatives, rather than complementary to each other. We hope to show in this book that to seek to recognise the various syndromes associated with "early childhood autism", each with its specific pattern of impairments, is not simply to undertake a sterile exercise in clinical classification but to lay a groundwork essential for any rational plan of remedial action, whether by doctors, occupational supervisors, psychologists, relatives, social workers or teachers.

The outstanding nature of Kanner's achievement can best be demonstrated by considering progress before he made his contribution. For example, two cases of the condition came to light in 1799 and both were written up by first-class clinicians. John Haslam described a five-year-old boy admitted to Bethlem Royal Hospital in that year. The child had suffered from severe measles when aged 1. At the age of 2, according to his mother, he was "more lively than usual and more difficult to control". He walked at the age of $2\frac{1}{2}$ but did not speak a word until he was 4. He wept only briefly on parting from his mother. He was noted to be in good physical health but in constant action, with a striking talent for mimicry. "To watch other boys gave him great satisfaction but he never joined them nor did he ever become attached to any one of them." He played in an absorbed but isolated fashion with toy soldiers. He remembered many tunes and could whistle them. He always spoke of himself in the third person (Haslam, 1809). This pattern of behaviour was sufficiently arresting for Haslam to publish it but that was all. It was not until Vaillant (1962) read Haslam's description more than a century and a half later that the *diagnosis* was made.

The other example is even more instructive because the author, Jean Marc Gaspard Itard, has written one of the most moving clinical documents of all time, well worth reading as much for its literary and human value as for its scientific interest, and magnificently translated into film by François Truffaut. Moreover, the methods of treatment devised by Itard began a new tradition in the field of mental retardation. In 1799, a boy of perhaps 11 or 12 years old was found in the woods of Aveyron, France. He was naked, and covered with scars, most of which were probably acquired because of the hazards of life in the woods. There had been reports of this wild boy for several years past. Various people had seen him searching for nuts, roots and acorns to eat, but he had always escaped capture. However, in 1799 he was caught and brought to Paris. Then, "a Minister of state with scientific interests believed that this event would throw some light on the science of the mind" and he was given into the care of Itard, who was physician to the new institution for deaf mutes. Itard describes his first impression of the child—disgustingly dirty, affected with spasmodic movements, swaying back and forth like an animal in a menagerie, biting and scratching those who opposed him. He showed no sort of affection and was attentive to nothing.

The famous physician Pinel came to the conclusion that he was a congenital idiot and that he had been abandoned for this reason.

Itard, on the other hand, was filled with the enthusiasm for new ideas and the feeling of intellectual liberation which were current at the time of the French Revolution. He saw his unprepossessing charge as the prototype of the natural savage; a human being who was completely untouched by education. To the modern reader there can be no doubt that the wild boy of Aveyron showed most of the diagnostic features of autism—whatever the original cause. The details of his behaviour are uncannily familiar. Itard describes how deficient he was, at first, in the use of his eyes and ears. He did not focus on objects or people. He showed no reaction to a pistol shot right behind his head but if someone cracked a walnut, however quietly, the boy would immediately look up in the hope of being given one of his favourite foods. He never played with toys, but laughed with great delight when allowed to splash and drip the water in his bath. He led people by the hand to show them what he wanted. When unwelcome visitors stayed too long he would hand them their hats, sticks and gloves, push them out of the room and shut the door firmly behind them. He resisted any change in his environment and had an excellent memory for the position of objects in his room, which he liked to maintain in precisely the same order. He loved the feel of things and would touch and fondle the clothes, hands and faces of the people he knew, but at first he appeared completely insensitive to heat and cold. He obviously inspired great interest and affection in the people who cared for him. Even the old man who brought him to Paris to hand him over to Itard said that he would look after the child if the Deaf and Dumb Institution felt that they could not keep him. Itard noticed his quality of innocence. To begin with he would take the things he wanted with no idea that he was stealing. He also shared with other autistic children an incredible ingenuity, drive and persistence in obtaining something he wanted.

The description of Victor's behaviour is interesting in itself, but more fascinating is Itard's account of how he set about educating the child. With no previous experience to guide him, he had to devise methods of educating Victor in the use of each of his senses, making all the teaching apparatus himself. He used the child's good memory and obsessionality, his fondness for certain foods, his developing attachment to the people he knew, as means of teaching him new skills, and described his methods in detail.

Victor never became normal and never spoke, but his social behaviour improved beyond recognition. He was even able to read some words and obey written instructions, and to communicate with others in non-verbal ways. This story illustrates some important points having a close bearing on the management of these children. Itard put himself in the position of teacher to Victor. He was also helped by a Madame Guérin—who looked after Victor, as Itard says "with all the patience of a mother and the intelligence of an enlightened teacher". The gradual development of Victor's affection for Madame Guérin is described very touchingly (Itard, 1801, 1807a,b,c).

Itard's recognition that there was something special about Victor was not lost, because he later taught Seguin who in turn influenced Montessori. The principles of remedial education which Itard discovered (as Montessori later observed, he was the first experimental psychologist), were preserved and developed (Montessori, 1912). However, the nature of Victor's condition, the differences and similarities between him and deaf-blind children or "idiots", were not understood. It was not recognised that certain aspects of Victor's behaviour constituted a recognisable syndrome, distinct from these other conditions. Itard's own theory, based on Rousseau out of Locke, was that the child was normal but uneducated; a theory in line with earlier ideas about so-called "wolf children". Itard's theory was wrong and when he finally became convinced of this fact he regarded his work, for all its partial successes, as a failure. He may well have accepted, finally, Pinel's opinion that the child was an idiot. This meant that the chance of helping other children with the same behaviour pattern had been missed. It was more than a century before a similar approach was recorded in any detail and then it had to be rediscovered from scratch.

In 1920, Lightner Witmer, an American psychologist, discussed his technique for educating a severely disturbed little boy who would nowadays be called autistic (Witmer, 1922). At the age of 2 years and 7 months Don spent most of his time absorbed in the contemplation of a card which he held in his hand, scratching the surface gently with his finger. He paid no attention to people or objects and appeared to be indifferent even to his parents, but if an attempt was made to remove his card he screamed with fury. He had practically no understanding of language and did not speak, but he loved music. Witmer at first thought that he was severely and hopelessly subnormal, but found encouragement in the amount of concentrated attention which Don gave to the few things which did interest him. This same attention and determination, however, proved one of the biggest problems which had to be overcome before any formal teaching could begin. Don angrily resisted every time he was bathed, dressed, fed, or involved in any activity, because this meant that he had to relinquish whatever object he had clasped in his hand. Neither kindly persuasion nor anger had any effect—if his special "toy" was removed he yelled and put up his hands to scratch his face, already scarred from previous self-injury. Finally the teacher whom he knew best held his hands while he raged and screamed. She remained calm and gentle but quite implacable. Don resisted for $1\frac{1}{2}$ hours and then gave in—he ceased to scratch his face, and he never again had one of these lengthy tantrums.

Witmer described how he encouraged the development of attention and interest in learning. To quote his own words, "The first task of teacher and parent is to gain and hold the child's attention by giving him something he can do, and after that, something he *can't* do . . .. I watch the child to discover what he does with interest and ease and from here I get him to take a step forward in the direction best calculated to bring him to 'the next highest level of attention'."

Don's teachers seem to have had endless patience, ingenuity and calm determination in the face of resistance. By the time he was 6 he was talking fairly well, he could read as well as other children of his own age, and was able to relate to other people. He was by no means normal. For example, he had many fears of quite harmless things, he was intensely absorbed by boats, cars, trains and other vehicles far beyond the usual interests of a child, and his speech seemed to be very repetitive. All these things are characteristic of autistic children. However, he had obviously improved out of all recognition, in a way which could not have been predicted when he was first seen.

After Witmer's time there was again a lapse because of the lack of recognition that the techniques he and Itard had used could be generalised to a whole class of children, who were not simply mentally retarded in a global fashion but had highly specific impairments. No distinction was made between what was irreducible in the syndrome and what was secondary. No flourishing tradition of remedial education could therefore develop. The situation was similar to that which obtained before it was recognised that children born deaf could nevertheless learn to use language. Deaf children were classed, for many centuries, with the severely mentally retarded and no efforts were made to develop special techniques to educate them. Even when this fundamental distinction was recognised by Cardano, in the sixteenth century, it was another three centuries before generally accepted teaching methods were developed. During this time, much writing on the subject was formless, speculative, anecdotal or based upon sheer prejudice (Pritchard, 1963).

Kanner pointed out that the history of medicine "has been marked by a gradual transition from the general to the specific, from the massive to the minute, from the ill-defined to the ever more concise and delineated" (Kanner, 1969). The "fevers" and the "plagues" were differentiated into more specific entities as bacteriology and virology advanced and provided the disease model which has served medicine so well during the past century and a half. These technical advances in turn led to better clinical differentiation. However, it must also be admitted that, as this kind of differentiated advance has been made in one field, new global and untestable assumptions have been put forward in others. During every historical epoch, scientific development has pursued a meandering path through a myriad of assertions and hypotheses; some credulous, some fantastic, some merely ignorant, some bold and inventive, most untestable or demonstrably false. Only a few proved able to withstand informed criticism over long periods of time. Terms like "mental retardation", "psychosis", "personality disorder" have been used as loosely and unhelpfully as the term "fever" was used in mediaeval times.

Theories of causation, whether involving the humors, or infantile sexuality, or interpersonal relationships, have been so over-generalised as to become discredited.

Kanner's first and major contribution on the subject of the severe disorders of childhood illustrates both the flash of clinical genius that perceives a syndrome worth separating from the amorphous mass of subnormality and psychosis, a delineation which proved useful when subjected to the test of subsequent informed criticism, and at the same time the adoption of a much more global concept, "autism", the theoretical overtones of which turned out to be vague and misleading (Kanner, 1943). Curiously, at virtually the same time, but quite independently, Asperger had also delineated a condition linked to Kanner's syndrome (though not identical with it) and had also used the term "autistic" in naming his syndrome (Asperger, 1944).

Kanner began his famous article as follows:

> Since 1938, there have come to our attention a number of children whose condition differs so markedly and uniquely from anything reported so far, that each case merits—and, I hope, will eventually receive—a detailed consideration of its fascinating peculiarities (Kanner, 1943).

After summarising the case-histories of eleven* children and pointing out the individual differences between them, he came straight to the point:

> But even a quick review of the material makes the emergence of a number of essential common characteristics appear inevitable. These characteristics form a unique "syndrome" not heretofore reported, which seems to be rare enough, yet is probably more frequent than is indicated by the paucity of observed cases. It is quite possible that some such children have been viewed as feebleminded or schizophrenic.

Kanner abstracted from the behaviour of his eleven children a number of behavioural features that seemed to him to be both *unusual* (i.e. not typical of other conditions such as schizophrenia or general mental retardation) and *characteristic* (i.e. present in most of the children). These traits included a failure during infancy to assume an anticipatory posture preparatory to being picked up, a

---

*Large numbers of cases and a sophisticated statistical analysis are not necessary for all advances in psychiatry.

failure to use speech for communication, an excellent rote memory, delayed echolalia, an inability to use abstract concepts, pronominal reversal, an anxious desire for the maintenance of sameness, a monotony of activity, a tendency to panic or to excitement in unusual situations, a seeming unawareness of other people, an inability to play imaginatively with toys or with other children, and with all this an impression of serious intelligence and a normal physical development. The course of the condition was towards improvement, particularly after the age of 6, but all the children remained severely handicapped.

The observation is brilliant and exact. Nearly all the behavioural characteristics in the list had been noted by Itard nearly 150 years earlier but Itard, like Witmer, had not realised that he was dealing with a separate syndrome. Kanner not only identified the syndrome but he labelled it, and thereby opened a new and fruitful era of scientific exploration; one which is by no means yet exhausted. Humanity has reason to be grateful to Kanner and to honour him among the precious few who have created new clinical beginnings.

The term "syndrome" used by Kanner is carefully neutral but it nevertheless implies rather more than a cluster of traits. In medical usage, the elements of a syndrome are called "symptoms" and there is always a suggestion of an underlying pathology or pathophysiology. This link is necessary for any fully-fledged disease theory (Wing *et al.*, 1974). Kanner did not suggest what it might be. Even without it, however, the usefulness of isolating the syndrome can be tested. Does it, for example, give rise to theories of aetiology which in turn can be used to suggest methods of prevention? Are there methods of treatment specific for this syndrome? At the very least, does the recognition of the syndrome allow a prognosis to be given? These tests of the value of isolating the syndrome are considered at greater length in later chapters. On the whole, Kanner's original views as to the innate nature of the condition, its distinction from other childhood psychiatric disorders and its progression toward improvement but not to cure, have been substantiated.

The other effect of Kanner's first paper was not so happy. He singled out one of the characteristics of the syndrome as basic to the others and labelled it "autism".

> The outstanding, "pathognomonic", fundamental disorder is the children's *inability to relate* themselves in the ordinary way to people and situations from the beginning of life .... There is from the start an *extreme autistic aloneness* that, wherever possible, disregards, ignores, shuts out anything that comes to the child from outside (Kanner, 1943, italics in original).

This formulation followed that of Bleuler (1919, 1950) who had singled out "autism" as one of the fundamental symptoms of schizophrenia (the other was a disturbance of associations) to which the rest of the phenomena described, for example, by Kraepelin, were secondary. For Bleuler, "autism" was an active withdrawal from contact with reality in order to live in an inner world of fantasy.

> The reality of the autistic world may also seem more valid than that of reality itself; the patients then hold their fantasy world for the real, reality for an illusion. They no longer believe in the evidence of their own senses (Bleuler, 1950, p. 66).

This kind of "autism" is similar to dreaming although the individual is awake. It is certainly possible to see how symptoms such as delusions and hallucinations could be manifestations of such a state. However, Bleuler also used the term "autism" in a much wider sense, to refer to mechanisms which might be present even in normal people (Bleuler, 1919). "The difference between this wider concept of autism and the autism characteristic of schizophrenia is obviously that while the normal person may experience all kinds of wishful 'autistic' thinking, he will also be able to correct the wishful aberrations, at least to himself" (W.H.O., 1973, p. 19).

Bosch (1962, 1970) has pointed out that there is yet a further complexity to the use of the term "autism", since there are at least two clinical varieties to be found in schizophrenia. These were called by Kretschmer the "hyperaesthetic" or Hölderlin variety, in which the individual is oversensitive to his environment and therefore retreats into an inner fantasy life, and the "anaesthetic" variety, in which there is a simple lack of affective response without any great inner experience. Both varieties could be present at the same time (Kretschmer, 1942). Moreover, as Gruhle suggested, there is no need to assume that "autism" is a fundamental symptom. It is just as likely to be forced on the patient by his cognitive disorder (Gruhle, 1929).

Bosch emphasizes the paradox implicit in applying the concept of "autisme riche" (Minkowski, 1953) to children with Kanner's syndrome whose inner life appears to be so poor. The logical conclusion seems to be that the concept of "autism" is too highly complex and controversial to be of much value in understanding schizophrenia, let alone Kanner's syndrome. It is one of those global concepts, like "fever" or "miasma", referred to by Kanner (1969), which explains so much that it is positively misleading. Nevertheless, Kanner did take it over, at the same time saying that his new syndrome was not related to schizophrenia.

He has himself explained how Despert wrote to him pointing out that he could not have it both ways (Kanner, 1949). If "autism" was fundamental both to schizophrenia and to Kanner's syndrome, how could the two be unrelated? Kanner was not able to resolve the dilemma and this confusion has been reflected in many of his subsequent articles as well as in the literature which he has so decisively influenced. The confusion depends on a failure, characteristic throughout the history of science, to see when terms are being used in different ways. The "autism" of Kanner's syndrome is the exact opposite of Bleuler's "autism" (that is, of Kretschmer's "hyperaesthetic" variety). The *lack* of fantasy and creative inner life demonstrated by children with Kanner's syndrome, and so clearly expounded by Kanner himself, cannot possibly be explained by an escape into fantasy. Kretschmer's anaesthetic variety of "autism" might perhaps be more appropriate but would carry little theoretical significance.

This is not the place to discuss which phenomena are fundamental, whether in schizophrenia (Wing *et al.*, 1973) or in Kanner's syndrome (see Chapter 2). The consequences for childhood psychosis of Bleuler's interpretation of schizophrenia, before Kanner had published his observations, may be seen in the criteria formulated by Potter (1933). These are based upon Bleuler's fundamental symptoms and include a generalised retraction of interest from the environment, dereistic thinking, thought blocking and other disorders, flattening of affect and a tendency to perseveration and stereotypy. The use of Bleuler's terminology has resulted in the presentation of a blurred syndrome, in terms which are difficult to define and which could be interpreted to include virtually any kind of abnormality.

It is refreshing to come across the crisp prose of Kanner's first paper, describing observations that owe nothing to Bleuler's theoretical speculations and marred only by the use of that fatal term "autism". Since that time theories have proliferated but there has always been an inescapable referent against which they can be judged. Even if it is found that Kanner's syndrome is not unitary or that some of its characteristic features are shared with other conditions, sufficient scientific progress has already been made, as will be sufficiently clear from the rest of this book, to justify its delineation. More than that, it is likely that further study will help not only the affected individuals and their relatives but our understanding of the development of normal children, particularly their acquisition of speech. Itard was conscious of this aspect of his work. In his original preface he wrote: ". . . Man can find only in the bosom of society the eminent station that was destined for him in nature and would be, without the aid of civilisation, one of the most feeble and least intelligent of animals;—a truth which, although it has often been insisted upon, has not as yet been rigorously demonstrated".

Itard's theory concerning Victor's normality was incorrect but the study of children with Kanner's syndrome has thrown light on processes equally fundamental. Indeed they may offer an opportunity of judging between the rival merits of those theories which suggest that language is an innate activity of the human brain (Brown, 1965; Popper, 1972) and others which postulate that it is entirely a matter of environmental conditioning (Skinner, 1973). We consider these matters in Chapter 4.

Meanwhile, we can amend slightly the paragraph which ended Chapter 1 of the first edition of this book. Part of the fascination of children with Kanner's syndrome lies in their resemblance to John Wyndham's *Midwich Cuckoos*. But the mystery and magic are illusory. For the romantic seeker after myths, the truth will be as disappointing as the decipherment of the Linear B script. The most exciting sentence in all the ancient tablets which had defied translation for so many centuries turned out to be, "How Alxoitas gave Thyestes the unguent-boiler spices for him to boil in the unguent"

(Palmer, 1965). Autistic children do have a fascination which lies partly in the feeling that somewhere there must be a key which will unlock hidden treasure. The skilled searcher will indeed find treasure, as Michael Ventris did, but the currency will be everyday and human, not fairy gold. In return for our attention, these children may give us the key to human language, which is the key to humanity itself.

CHAPTER 2

DIAGNOSIS, CLINICAL DESCRIPTION AND PROGNOSIS

LORNA WING

Despite all the work on childhood autism which has been carried out since Kanner first described and named the syndrome, no underlying pathology has as yet been established. This is hardly surprising, since so little is known about the relationship between brain structure and brain function, either in health or in disease. There are no physical or pathological tests which can confirm the diagnosis. The syndrome can be defined only by describing a pattern of abnormal behaviour, but there can be no certainty concerning which of the elements making up the behaviour pattern are of primary importance, although some formulations of the problem have more practical relevance than others. These difficulties are fundamental to all the issues to be discussed in this chapter.

Identification of the Syndrome

Kanner's diagnostic criteria

In Kanner's first papers on the syndrome that he named early infantile autism (Kanner, 1943; 1949) certain points were abstracted from the many behavioural abnormalities listed, which he considered to be of basic importance in making a diagnosis. These points were:

1. A profound lack of affective contact with other people.
2. An anxiously obsessive desire for the preservation of sameness.

3. A fascination for objects, which are handled with skill in fine motor movements.
4. Mutism, or a kind of language that does not seem to be intended to serve inter-personal communication.
5. The retention of an intelligent and pensive physiognomy and good cognitive potential, manifested, in those who can speak, by feats of memory and, in the mute children, by their skill on performance tests, especially the Seguin form board.

Kanner also emphasised that the behaviour pattern was present from early childhood. At first he thought that the underlying abnormality was invariably present from the beginning of life (Kanner, 1943) but later he described the same problems in children who had had up to 20 months of apparently normal development (Kanner and Eisenberg, 1956). Later writers have extended this to 3 years though in most cases the abnormality begins before 2 years (Kolvin, 1971; Rutter, 1968) and in a large proportion some abnormality appears to be present from early infancy. Kanner and Eisenberg (1956), in their review of 12 years of clinical experience of autistic children, decided that the first two points in the above list should be regarded as the primary features from which the other problems followed, and without which a diagnosis of autism could not be made.

Although Kanner considered that the above points summarised the essential features of the condition, during the course of his writings on the subject he described in great detail and clarity the full range of behaviour seen in autistic children (Kanner, 1973). Many different interpretations of the behaviour pattern have been suggested by later writers and many kinds of laboratory investigations have been carried out but virtually nothing has been added to the original clinical descriptions.

Kanner discussed the significance of the behaviour pattern from the point of view of a psychiatrist who, despite his own criticisms of psycho-analytic theories (Kanner, 1959), was working in an environment where these theories had considerable influence. He emphasised, above all, the abnormality in the children's emotional response to other people. He considered this to be the fundamental impairment which explained all the other characteristic features of the syndrome.

Problems in applying Kanner's criteria

Kanner's own criteria, if applied with care, limit the diagnosis to a small group of children. Rimland (1971a) suggested that only 10 per cent of children who are classified under the general heading of childhood psychosis (presumably in the U.S.A.) have the genuine Kanner's syndrome. Some people have misunderstood Kanner's summary of the syndrome and have refused to accept as autistic any child who shows any sign of awareness of the existence of other people, thus excluding virtually every eligible child. The general tendency however has been for the label to be applied more widely than Kanner intended (Kanner, 1969).

Much of the difficulty has arisen from the fact that both clinicians and research workers have tended to use Kanner's abstractions from the clinical data (his "5 points" or his "2 points") instead of returning to his detailed descriptions. The trouble with abstractions is that they can so easily be misinterpreted. Thus a child who appears indifferent to the usual forms of social approach but who responds enthusiastically to active, boisterous tickling and romping (a common finding in young, "classically" autistic children) may be rated as "lacking affective contact" by an observer who offers only verbal approaches but not by another who tends to interact with children in direct physical ways. If, instead, the child's behaviour in different situations is described, such discrepancies in interpretation can be avoided. Similarly, someone who sees an autistic child for an hour or so only may be unable to detect any meaning in his utterances, whereas another person who knows the child well may have learnt to interpret his idiosyncratic use of noises and words, and therefore refuse to accept that the child's language "is not intended to serve inter-personal communication".

Kanner's belief that autistic children must have "good cognitive potential" has perhaps given rise to more difficulties than all the other abstractions put together. He based this on the presence of isolated skills which depended either upon memory or upon ability to manipulate objects. Since Kanner first published in this field, work with children and adults with specific learning impairments has shown that skills in some areas can co-exist with gross impairments in others and that a general level of intelligence cannot be predicted from one special ability. It is now clear that the autistic pattern of behaviour can be and often is found in association with mental retardation of varying degrees of severity. Furthermore, the syndrome can occur together with diagnosable abnormalities of the central nervous system although these are sometimes not clinically manifested until adolescence or early adult life (Rutter, 1970a).

Can the syndrome of early childhood autism be considered as a separate entity?

There is no doubt that it is possible to recognise children who have the classic syndrome described by Kanner. It is easiest to do so when the child has good non-language-dependent skills and enough speech to show the characteristic language abnormalities. The problem is that the borderlines of the condition are not at all clear. The central "nuclear" syndrome shades into a personality that is untalkative, unsociable and pedantic, but within the normal range and, at the other extreme, into certain forms of severe mental retardation (Wing, 1975). The classic syndrome is easy to differentiate from an equally classic developmental receptive speech disorder, but between these two lies a range of children with some of the elements of both syndromes. If children with these problems could be arranged in an orderly series, starting from the most autistic child at one end and extending to the child who most clearly had nothing but a developmental receptive speech disorder at the other, to say where the dividing line should be drawn would need the judgement of Solomon. Other problems involving language, perception or motor control could be treated in the same way, with the same result.

It is tempting to make a case for including only those children who have Kanner's 5 diagnostic criteria in their classic form and excluding those with the problems most often associated with severe general retardation, such as self injury or stereotypies of movement.

The problem is that these latter abnormalities are also found to some degree in many classically autistic children, especially when they are under 5 years old (Kanner, 1973; Rutter, 1970a; Rutter and Lockyer, 1967; Rutter *et al.*, 1967; Wing, 1969).

Although Kanner insists, in theory, that precision is possible, in practice he has evidently experienced the same problems as everyone else, as he demonstrated in his paper, "The evaluation and follow-up of 34 psychotic children" (Kanner, 1973). In this he diagnosed one child (case 2) as autistic "even though there is not much of a desire for the preservation of sameness". Case 14, a child with apparently no skills at all apart from the ability to spin things, tapped objects against his mouth, beat the backs of his hands against each other and performed dance-like movements, all of which were said to be ritualistic behaviour fitting in with a diagnosis of autism. Case 18, a child performing at the $2\frac{1}{2}$- to 3-year old level, was diagnosed as schizophrenic by Kanner at the age of $5\frac{1}{2}$, but was tentatively re-classified as autistic at $19\frac{1}{2}$ because stereotypies and preoccupations had been observed since the first examination.

Kanner discussed the difficulties with honesty and humour in another paper, agreeably entitled, "The children haven't read those books" (Kanner, 1969). In this paper, he pointed out that the problems of differentiating between psychiatric syndromes should not be used as an excuse to "relinquish all diagnostic differentiations" or to "shove different conditions under a common etiologic umbrella". He emphasised that clinicians are under the obligation to study each child as an individual, but also to take every opportunity to classify and to refine classification in the light of new knowledge. This is the way that other branches of medicine have progressed and there is no reason to believe that psychiatry will prove the exception. It is, of course, important to try to explain why there are similarities between different syndromes, while still recognising that similarities do not necessarily mean that the syndromes are identical. To take an example from general medicine, there are similarities between acute pulmonary tuberculosis and pneumococcal pneumonia, but they are different diseases with different causes, and they require different treatments.

Where does all this leave the syndrome of early childhood autism?

There is as yet no proof that there is a unitary syndrome with one single cause, but there is equally no doubt at all that children with some or all of the elements of the syndrome do exist and that they and their families are in need of specialised help.

The only rational way of dealing with problems of this kind, which abound in psychiatry, is to adopt operational definitions pending the discovery of the aetiology and pathology. In the field of research into diagnosis, classification, aetiology, prognosis and evaluation of treatment, it is extremely important that the subjects to be studied are selected with care according to precisely defined criteria. Incompatible findings from different research groups may well be due to different methods of case selection. To enable comparisons to be made between results of studies it is necessary to give detailed clinical descriptions of the children who took part, couched in terms of observed behaviour and not in terms of inferences from that behaviour.

If the research is concerned with Kanner's "nuclear" syndrome then Kanner's criteria should be rigorously applied in the light of his detailed clinical descriptions, not his 5 point or 2 point summaries. If the investigators find difficulty in applying these criteria in some cases, as well they might, these difficulties and the steps taken to resolve them should be described. If a wider or a different definition is to be adopted this should be made clear and the label of childhood autism should not be used without careful explanation. It may seem unnecessarily pedantic to refer back to Kanner's work in every investigation involving childhood autism, but he after all originally introduced the term for a condition which he delineated with much detail. Care in the way the term is used by other workers would diminish the confusion surrounding the subject even if it would not remove it completely.

Terminology

The confusion in terminology in which labels such as childhood psychosis, schizophrenia and autism have sometimes been used as synonymous and sometimes as separate entities has not helped to clarify the situation (Laufer and Gair, 1969). For example the British

Working Party which, under the chairmanship of Creak (1961), drew up the Nine Diagnostic Points, used the term "childhood schizophrenia" although the description given had very many similarities to the autistic pattern. Clancy *et al.* (1969a) refined the Nine Diagnostic Points, giving concrete examples of behaviour under each heading. These authors used the term "infantile autism" but it is clear that the children they included under this heading constituted a much wider group than that defined by Kanner.

The most unequivocal name is "Kanner's syndrome" and the pure or nuclear group, comprising the brighter children with the characteristic features described by Kanner, is probably best specified in this way.

Kanner's own preferred name "early infantile autism" is not entirely appropriate since, in some cases, an otherwise typical syndrome has developed during the second or third year of life. "Early *childhood* autism" is probably the most satisfactory term, since it does not carry the implication of an inevitable onset from birth and it does suggest that the "autism" is maximal in early life and may improve later. This label will be used by the present author to refer to children with all the features of the autistic behaviour pattern, but will include those who are mildly or severely retarded or who have known organic conditions, as well as the group with the nuclear Kanner's syndrome.

There is also a group of less typical conditions, in which many, but not all, of the elements of early childhood autism are present. Even if such cases should not, for purposes of research into that condition, be classified as early childhood autism, there seems little point in excluding them when considering service needs, since the social, educational and administrative problems are so similar. The best compromise seems to be to refer to them as "children with autistic features".

The label "childhood psychosis" is a very general term which includes childhood autism but is also applied to many other quite unrelated conditions. Reasons for rejecting the term "schizophrenia" are given in the section on differential diagnosis.

Ideally, a new name is needed to replace the label "autism" which, for reasons discussed in Chapter 1, is inappropriate and confusing.

A really suitable name would be derived from the underlying neurophysiological impairments, so its coining must be deferred until the aetiology and pathology of the condition is known.

Clinical Description

The clinical description to be given here covers the main items of behaviour found in early childhood autism. All the features mentioned can be found in Kanner's publications on the subject (Kanner, 1973) but, unlike Kanner's accounts of the syndrome, the items have been grouped according to a logical scheme.

Kanner thought that the autistic pattern of behaviour could be entirely explained by the children's lack of affective contact and desire for the preservation of sameness. This is an unsatisfactory formulation since, as will be discussed below, the decision that a child lacks affective contact is based upon the observation of a series of different abnormalities. Observers differ in the weight they give to the different elements contributing to the impression of social aloofness and may well disagree in their final decision as to whether or not the child shows the problem. In any case, an autistic child's social responses differ in different situations and with different people. Sociability tends to improve with increasing age. For all these reasons, the problem of affective contact appears to be a rather unlikely candidate for the primary impairment underlying autistic behaviour.

In recent years there has been a considerable increase in experimental work involving autistic children and, at the same time, a growing interest in the development of language in normal and handicapped children. As a result, ideas concerning the impairments basic to childhood autism have developed and changed. The new formulations link the children's behaviour to underlying organic impairments, the most important of which are cognitive problems affecting the comprehension and use of linguistic symbols and the interpretation of all kinds of sensory experience (see Chapters 4, 5 and 6). Looked at in this way, the elements making up the complete syndrome form a logical pattern and the similarities between autism and other kinds of childhood handicaps such as blindness, deafness and the developmental speech disorders become easier to understand.

In the following description, the items have been classified into basic impairments, special skills and, finally, the behavioural abnormalities that are secondary to the underlying impairments. Examples from actual children are given as illustrations.

This method of grouping the features of the syndrome has been used as the basis of a standardised scheme, given in Appendix I of this chapter, for listing the abnormalities observed in children suspected of being autistic, as an aid to diagnosis and as a framework for describing subjects taking part in clinical and experimental studies of autism and related conditions. The scheme can be adopted without any necessary agreement with the hypotheses underlying it.

Severity of the disorder

It is most important to remember that the severity of the condition is not uniform in all children (Wolff and Chess, 1964). The many reasons for this variability are often confused although it is difficult to make recommendations about education and management unless an attempt is made to examine each component separately. In the first place, the various underlying impairments may be more or less severe and frequently some disabilities are more prominent than others. Each child has his own pattern of affected and unaffected functions. The second component in severity is due to the interaction between the primary disabilities and the environment. Even normal children brought up in some environments will be disturbed in behaviour or educationally backward (Rutter, 1972a). Handicapped children are particularly vulnerable to such harmful social milieux and need, in addition, very skilled management if an otherwise normal environment is to be of maximum value. Thus social withdrawal, disturbance in behaviour and educational backwardness may vary markedly depending both on the severity of the impairments *and* on the suitability of the environment.

Finally, there is the improvement due to maturation, which is seen in many children with childhood autism as in other disorders affecting specific aspects of cognitive development such as the developmental speech disorders and dyslexia. A child who was mute, withdrawn and extremely difficult in behaviour at the age of 4 may, by the age of 10, be affectionate, competent in self care, able to talk in a simple fashion and reasonably well behaved in familiar situations.

Thus *general* statements about the severity of the syndrome are likely to be wrong and they can be harmful.

Behaviour during the first year of life

Although it is almost impossible to make the diagnosis during the first year of life, some mothers of autistic children feel that there is something wrong with their child almost from his birth, although they cannot explain why. In other cases the realization that the child is developing abnormally comes only slowly, and it may be two or three years before the parents clearly recognise that there is a problem. In perhaps one third of the children, the parents report a period of apparently normal development before a set back occurs and autistic behaviour begins at some time before the age of 3. This may follow an event such as an illness or the birth of a sibling, but it can also occur without any apparent precipitating factors. It is difficult to say exactly what proportion of autistic children really have an early period of normality before becoming autistic, because, in some cases, careful questioning of the parents reveals that there had been some developmental abnormalities even before the noticeable set back (Wing, 1971).

Some autistic babies are extremely placid and rarely cry or demand any attention. Others are at the opposite extreme. They are restless, scream for long periods and cannot be comforted. Disturbed sleep, erratic patterns of sleeping and feeding problems including poor sucking are common in these difficult babies. Later, prolonged rocking and head banging may be reported.

Lack of interest in social contact may be apparent from early on. Autistic babies may show little interest in the human voice. They often do not adopt an anticipatory posture or lift up their arms to be picked up. In contrast to this, they may thoroughly enjoy being tickled and bounced up and down. Smiling and chuckling may develop at the expected times but these responses are elicited most easily by physical stimulation rather than a social approach.

The babies manifest little of the normal curiosity usually seen in the last part of the first year. They do not explore their environment eagerly, they do not point to things that they want, nor do they attract the attention of their parents in order to share an interest in an object or an event. They appear self contained and content to manipulate the same few toys over and over again.

In some cases there is a very early history of intense fascination with certain sensory experiences. An autistic baby may gaze at a lighted lamp for long periods of time, tap and scratch on his chair or pram cover, or be completely absorbed in one section of a pattern on the wallpaper. Occasionally, instead of fascination, certain objects or situations produce intense, inexplicable fear. One autistic baby used to scream at the sight of a silver tea pot and would not stop until it was removed from his sight.

One to five years

During this period the autistic pattern of behaviour becomes clearly manifested. The characteristic features are seen most obviously and most severely from about $2\frac{1}{2}$ to 5 years of age and this is usually the time that the parents find the hardest. Some mothers of the more active autistic children have graphically described the feeling that they have a cuckoo in the nest, or a changeling child who makes incessant demands, has frightening temper tantrums if thwarted in any way, but who gives nothing in return and seems oblivious of the existence of anyone but himself.

All of the items of behaviour mentioned in this section are common in autistic children but it is very rare for one child to show all the features together at one time. The abnormal behaviour typically occurs in children who appear alert, lively, graceful in spontaneous movement and normal or even unusually attractive in physical appearance, although there are many exceptions to these generalisations. Motor milestones may be delayed but are often within the normal range. Speech is almost always delayed, though sometimes it is reported to have developed normally for 1 or 2 years and is then lost. If a detailed history is obtained of this early speech, however, it may be found to consist almost entirely of echolalia.

Underlying impairments

Problems affecting language. The cognitive problems which affect the comprehension and use of language in whatever form it is presented (spoken, written, gestured, etc.) are of major importance in the syndrome of early childhood autism and may eventually be proved to be the primary impairments which explain the whole behaviour pattern. The typical language abnormalities are described and the theoretical implications are discussed in detail in Chapter 4, so only a brief description will be given here.

Autistic children have problems in the comprehension of speech which may vary from a total lack of any understanding to a subtle problem in grasping the associations surrounding words and phrases, leading to a limited, concrete interpretation.

There are also abnormalities in the use of speech. A substantial minority remain mute all their lives. Those who do speak may have immediate or delayed echolalia, which may be the only type of speech heard. Those who have some spontaneous speech usually show confusion over the use of pronouns. Many have immaturity of grammatical structure, abnormalities like those found in the developmental receptive and expressive speech disorders, and a tendency to use words and phrases in a repetitive, stereotyped, inflexible way.

Characteristically the control of vocal pitch, volume and intonation is very poor. There may be problems of pronunciation, sometimes heard in spontaneous but not echoed speech.

Unlike deaf children and those with developmental receptive speech disorders, autistic children do not use gesture to compensate for their speech problems. They have poor comprehension and use of any form of language and of non-verbal methods of communication.

Abnormal responses to sensory experiences. Autistic children appear to have difficulty in making use of incoming information from their senses. Variable response to sound is common. A child may not react to a loud noise behind him but will turn at the rustle of a sweet paper. People may ask if the child is deaf, but the parents usually know that he is not. Oversensitivity to some noises is also often seen, causing the child to cover his ears or become distressed. One autistic girl would cover her ears with one hand before she closed a door or a drawer with the other. She also played a drum in the percussion band at school with her shoulders and upper arms raised to cover her ears. On the other hand, these children may be fascinated by certain sounds such as those made by tapping, the whine of a friction drive toy, or the chiming of bells. One child would say "da" very loudly in any large room or corridor in order to produce an echo, which gave him intense delight.

There are equivalent problems in dealing with visual information. Young autistic children sometimes give the impression that they have difficulty in recognising the things they see. A child may not be able to identify people when seen at a few yards distance and parents may acquire (often without realizing it) a technique of waving, calling and whistling to attract their child's attention. People may ask if the child is short-sighted or even blind. The author has to date seen four autistic children who were actually diagnosed as blind for several years until it was recognised that their visual problems were not due to peripheral loss of sight. The mothers of these children had always doubted the diagnosis of blindness. In one case the child could see to pick up minute pieces of cotton which he liked to collect.

Fascination with lights, shiny objects or special patterns may be seen in autistic children as well as babies. Things that spin round have a special attraction and a child may rock, grimace, and flap his arms in excitement while watching a spinning top. Much less commonly, parents report that bright lights cause distress.

The reactions of indifference, distress and fascination may be seen in relation to other sensory modalities. Young autistic children may ignore knocks and bumps and be indifferent to pain and cold, running out of doors with no clothes in freezing weather. As they grow older, this may be replaced by an exaggerated concern over minor discomforts. Some children continually pick at sore places or prick themselves with pins.

The children may react to being gently touched by moving away or pushing the touching hand. Necessary operations such as washing, dressing and hair brushing may provoke screams of fury. In marked contrast, the same children often react with intense pleasure to rough games of tickling, swinging round and bouncing up and down, giving the appearance of complete normality while the game lasts. Fascination with tactile sensations may take the form of scratching on different kinds of surfaces to feel the texture. Sometimes the sound made is enjoyed as much as the feeling. Smooth surfaces such as plastic, wood or fur are attractive to some autistic children and may lead to problems if a child caresses the fur coats of strangers in the street. Even more social embarrassment was caused by an autistic boy who loved to touch women's stockings.

The same patterns may be seen with taste and smell. Some autistic children are indifferent to many foods which normal children love, actively dislike others, but intensely enjoy yet others, sometimes eating the most bizarre diets because of these preferences—nothing but lettuce leaves, chocolate pudding and bananas for example.

"Paradoxical" responses to sensations are also observed occasionally. Thus a child may cover his eyes in response to a sound that distresses him or his ears in response to a visual stimulus as if he had difficulty in sorting out the different kinds of experiences.

Abnormalities of visual inspection. Before the age of 5, some autistic children appear to use peripheral rather than central vision. Thus a child may ride a tricycle without apparently looking where he is going, look past people rather than at them, but sometimes giving them rapid flashing glances, recognise moving objects more readily than things that are stationary and may even watch television out of the corner of his eye.

Some young autistic children appear actively to avoid looking at certain visual stimuli, especially human faces. They may look down under lowered eyelids, turn their heads away or even close or cover their eyes.

Problems of motor imitation. Young autistic children find it very difficult to learn by watching and imitating, especially when the movements have to be reversed in direction; for example, a child may wave his hand towards himself. It is easier for the children to learn the motions if their limbs are moved for them. Doing up buttons, using a knife and fork, or riding a tricycle can all be taught in this way.

There is also marked difficulty in miming actions, such as pretending to use a hammer or to play a musical instrument, even if the real object can be used appropriately. This will be discussed in detail in Chapter 6.

Left-right, up-down and back-front may be confused as is shown by mistakes with tasks such as laying the table, dressing, turning handles or reading and writing letters such as b and d, or m and w.

Problems of motor control. The children may grimace, rock, flap their arms and legs and jump up and down. These movements are exacerbated by excitement or during absorption in some sensory experience, such as watching flashing lights, or a spinning toy. Some children rock from back foot to front foot, bending at the waist at the same time, while listening to music.

When standing quietly, they tend to have an odd posture with head bowed, arms flexed at the elbow and hands drooping at the wrist. Many of them tend to walk on tip-toe with a springy movement, without any arm-swinging.

Spontaneous large movements, or fine skilled movements, or both may be clumsy in some children, though others appear to be graceful and nimble.

Abnormalities of autonomic function, vestibular control and physical development. Erratic patterns of sleeping, eating and drinking are found in some young autistic children. Quite often they like to consume surprisingly large amounts of fluid and become distressed if this is prevented. They are usually very resistant to sedatives and hypnotics, as many parents hoping to have an occasional restful night by giving their child a sleeping tablet have found to their cost.

Lack of dizziness after spinning round has often been noted, since some autistic children love to spin themselves and will do so for long periods of time. Roundabouts and other delights of the fair are also enjoyed by many of the children, whose resistance to vertigo and nausea is astonishing to their less fortunate parents. Some workers consider this abnormality of vestibular function to be of aetiological significance, as discussed in Chapter 3.

Part of the explanation of the physical attractiveness of many autistic children lies in the immaturity of their appearance and the unusual degree of symmetry of their faces. Some of the children are small for their age while others are of normal or above average size, but whatever their physical stature, they give the impression of being younger than their real age and of having a kind of vulnerable innocence which arouses protective feelings in many people with whom they come into contact.

Special skills

The classically autistic child has some areas in which he performs well, despite all his problems. These are of two kinds; firstly the non-language-dependent skills which may be seen even in mute children; secondly the skills that rely upon exact memory, which are easiest to demonstrate in children who can talk.

Skills that do not involve language. The non-language-dependent skills include dismantling and assembling mechanical or electrical apparatus, fitting together jig-saw puzzles which may be completed picture side down, or building constructional toys. These tasks may be performed at or above the child's age level. However, in most autistic children, while the special skills stand out in contrast to the low level of other attainments, the performance expected of a normal child of the same age is not reached.

Most of the children love music and some can sing well. Sometimes this ability fades or disappears in later childhood, especially with improvement in language development. One child could sing accurately long passages from Stravinsky's "Rite of Spring" at age 3, but had lost this skill by the age of 10. A few of the brighter children learn to play a musical instrument or even compose music. A very small number have become piano tuners in adult life, having the necessary manual dexterity and a perfect ear for pitch.

Skills dependent on memory. The classically autistic child appears to be able to store items in his memory for prolonged periods in the exact form in which they were first experienced. The items selected for storage do not appear, on any criteria used by normal people, to be of any special importance and they are stored without being interpreted or changed.

Some children remember the words of songs, poems, long lists of names, whole passages of conversation they have overheard. Bus, train and underground routes are special favourites and some autistic children are experts on these matters. Some can do lengthy numerical calculations in their heads, or else can give the day of the week on which any date in the last 100 years fell. The items remembered cannot always be applied appropriately. For instance, an autistic girl could write out all the multiplication tables from 2 to 12 but could not answer questions such as "What is 3 times 4?".

Memory for visual patterns also tends to be excellent. A young child who perhaps collects objects such as pebbles and who amasses several hundred of these will typically notice at once if the arrangement of the items is disturbed in any way or if one is missing.

In view of the autistic child's love of music, it is not surprising that there are many stories of accurate memory for long passages of music and ability to identify a piece after hearing a few bars. One child was able to recognise from the first note when any record that she knew was being played at the wrong speed.

It has been suggested that the children who display these feats of memory have been pushed into them by over-ambitious parents. In the clinical experience of the present author there is no evidence for this at all. The children choose their own interests and in doing so are exercising a skill that they possess in the only way that is available to them.

Secondary behaviour problems

The following problems are all classified as "secondary" because they can be predicted as consequences of the pattern of impairments and remaining skills.

Apparent social aloofness and indifference. Although Kanner regarded this as a primary impairment, the autistic child's "social aloofness" is, in reality, an inference made by the observer from a number of different items of behaviour. These include the cognitive, language and non-verbal communication problems which seriously interfere with social interchanges; the tendency to look past and through other people instead of at them; the dislike of gentle touches; the odd gait and posture; and the absorption in simple sensory stimuli to the exclusion of other interests.

These behaviours vary with the social situation, being less marked in familiar settings and with well-known adults who understand the child's handicaps. Physical contact of a boisterous playful kind produces far more responsive behaviour than attempts at conversation. The children often become more sociable as they grow older, especially if there is some increase in the ability to understand and use language. An immature and inappropriate friendliness may replace the aloofness. Lack of response is always especially marked in relation to other children and this usually remains the case even if contact with adults improves.

Intense resistance to change and attachment to objects and routines. This problem, which Kanner referred to as "an intense desire for the preservation of sameness" appears to derive from a combination of the autistic child's inability to make sense of the world and his excellent memory for things as they were first experienced.

The children are disturbed by some changes in the familiar environment, but it is often difficult to predict just which changes will upset them and which they will ignore. One child accepted the move from one house to another but became frantic because he was given a new bed cover. Another child refused to wear any new clothes without a series of temper tantrums.

Familiar routines become important to some children. There may be dramatic scenes if a new route is followed for the daily walk, if someone sits in a different place at table, or if the household chores are done in a different order from usual. It is quite common for these "obsessions" to involve the activities of the whole family.

There may be a fascination with regularly repeated patterns of objects or sounds. Making long lines or patterns of household objects is seen in young autistic children. Some like to play the same record over and over again. Objects may be collected for no discernible purpose. These include dead holly leaves, plastic bottles, ash trays from restaurants, bits of X-ray paper, bicycle chains, battered petrol cans, specially shaped lumps of concrete, segments of old rubber balls found lying around in parks and small pieces of metal from telephone kiosks. However bizarre and rare these collector's items appear to the uninitiated to be, the discerning eye and speed of movement of a really determined autistic child ensure that a large number will be amassed in a surprisingly short space of time.

Older children who have a good vocabulary and some command of grammatical constructions may be absorbed in certain topics, such as electricity, astronomy or species of birds. They ask repeated questions on these subjects and demand standard answers. The interest is not a creative one but is repetitive and stereotyped in form.

Inappropriate emotional reactions. There may be a lack of fear of real danger in young autistic children. Many parents can tell stories of how their child climbed onto the roof, walked up and down a narrow ledge high above the ground or ran fully clothed into deep water. On the other hand, the same child may be terrified of harmless objects or situations such as one special room, but only when the curtains are drawn, getting into the bath, wearing shoes, or of friendly pets.

Autistic children do not have much understanding of other people's feelings. They may laugh if someone falls down or if another child is scolded. Laughing and giggling or crying and screaming may also occur for no obvious reason.

Lack of imagination. One of the major problems with autistic children is their lack of imaginative play. They do not play pretend games, either by themselves or with other children. Sometimes a quiet autistic child will be involved in a game of, for example, mothers and fathers, but he always takes a passive part and is pushed around by the normal children. It is difficult for an autistic child to imitate other people's actions and to build on this imitation in a creative way.

Toys are not used as material for imaginative games. Instead, the children tend to handle, taste, smell and gaze at toys and other objects to obtain simple sensations. Often, minor or trivial aspects of objects or people are selected for attention, rather than the whole. Thus a child may be preoccupied with one ear ring instead of the whole person, a wheel instead of the whole toy train, a switch instead of the complete electrical apparatus. He may react to the needle used for an injection while ignoring the person who is giving it.

Because of their lack of imagination, autistic children do not understand the purpose of any pursuits that do not bring an immediate and obvious reward. They have little interest in, for example, reading fiction, or playing complicated games.

In the absence of normal imaginative pursuits, autistic children tend to occupy themselves in various repetitive, uncreative ways. The brighter children may be able to do jig-saws and other mechanical puzzles. The less able may spend long periods twiddling pieces of string, spinning the most unlikely objects, or else twisting and turning their hands near their eyes. Monotonous, stereotyped movements such as rocking may be the only activity in some severely handicapped children. Most distressing of all are the children who seek stimulation by head banging or other forms of self injury.

Socially immature and difficult behaviour. As in any condition which interferes with maturation and the learning of social skills, difficult behaviour is common in autism. The children may have temper tantrums and long periods of screaming especially if frustrated in any way. They may grab things off the counters in shops, run into other people's houses in search of things to add to the collection of the moment, take off their clothes in the street and sit in inviting puddles regardless of the traffic. Children who can talk may make naive and embarrassing remarks loudly in public, such as "There's a lavatory room" on seeing a window with frosted glass.

Not all young autistic children have such disturbed behaviour. Some are very quiet and worry their parents because of their passivity and the difficulty of persuading them to do anything for themselves.

After 5 years of age

Improvement in behaviour quite often occurs between 5 and 6 years of age. In general the secondary behaviour problems especially the social aloofness, tend to become less severe. The basic impairments may improve but show less marked change than the behaviour problems (Wing, 1971).

The autistic pattern is still recognizable in later childhood but the differences between the mildly handicapped and the severely handicapped children become more marked than is the case before 5 years of age. Also, it becomes clearer with increasing age that within the general category of early childhood autism there are many variations in the pattern depending on which of the features are most obvious and which are present in a less severe form.

Further details of progress in later childhood and early adult life are given in the section on prognosis.

Partial syndromes

The complete syndrome of early childhood autism has been outlined. It should be emphasised that any of the elements making up the complete syndrome can occur alone without the others, or any combinations of items can occur together without the rest. Some of these combinations of items are sufficiently common to be named as syndromes, for example the developmental receptive and expressive speech disorders. Others have not as yet been given such recognition. The exact relationship between the complete and the partial syndromes is ill understood but any theory of the nature of autism must, to be acceptable, attempt to explain why both can occur.

Diagnosis and Differential Diagnosis

Diagnosis

Whatever the theoretical complications of differentiating early childhood autism from other conditions, in clinical practice these problems are of peripheral interest only. Research workers can legitimately concern themselves with defining Kanner's nuclear syndrome and exclude from their studies all children who do not fit the definition. Clinicians, on the other hand, cannot refuse to see those who do not fit neatly into categories.

When prescribing education, management and treatment for children with chronic handicaps which affect learning and behaviour, including early childhood autism, a number of different aspects of functioning have to be taken into account. A diagnostic formulation should not, therefore, consist of a single label but should be multi-dimensional (Rutter *et al.*, 1969; Wing, 1970).

The following points should be covered:

1. The pattern of behaviour.
2. The child's level of ability, including:
   Language development and abnormalities; performance on cognitive (intelligence) tests; perceptual function; any special skills; self care and practical competence.
3. Any associated neurological handicaps.
4. Any other physical handicaps.
5. The underlying aetiology and pathology, if known.
6. The child's social and emotional environment.

The autistic pattern of behaviour is seen most clearly and in its most severe form between the ages of 2 to 5 years. Between 5 and 6 years some children show quite a marked improvement or a change in the details of their pattern of behaviour (Rimland, 1965; Wing, 1971). There is, in any case, some tendency for the behaviour problems and impairments to become less severe with increasing age, particularly the social withdrawal. An adequate formulation must therefore be based upon a detailed history from early infancy as well as the present behaviour.

Such an "operational" diagnosis avoids the problems which arise if a more theoretical approach to the nature of childhood autism is adopted. For example, if it is assumed that true childhood autism is a specific identifiable condition which cannot be associated with any neurological abnormality, then many children in whom both conditions co-exist may fail to receive the appropriate services because of confusion over diagnosis. In any case, underlying neurological abnormalities may become evident in later childhood in classically autistic children who were thought to be free of additional handicaps when first diagnosed (See Chapter 3).

The separation of the behaviour and learning problems from the associated handicaps and from the problems (if any) found in the child's environment should allow each of these factors to be identified and dealt with appropriately.

Differential diagnosis

There are two aspects to differential diagnosis. Firstly, the child's pattern of behaviour has to be studied in detail, using clinical observation and appropriate psychological testing, so that some conclusion can be reached concerning the basic impairments and potential skills. A decision can then be made as to how closely this pattern resembles the classic autistic syndrome. The second part of the exercise is to try to exclude any of the conditions, such as congenital deafness, which may give rise to such a pattern of behaviour. This is especially important since, if the behaviour is secondary to certain types of abnormalities, it may be possible to produce a marked improvement through treatment and remedial teaching.

Childhood schizophrenia

Childhood autism has frequently been called childhood schizophrenia. There are some behavioural analogies with the non-paranoid forms of adult schizophrenia in which social withdrawal is common. In addition, institutionalized adults tend to look alike anyway. Autistic children are probably as vulnerable as people with schizophrenia to an understimulating environment (Wing and Brown, 1970), so, if they grow up in an institution, they may come to show very few differentiating features after several years. These behavioural analogies have no diagnostic implications and, in any case, do not hold for children brought up in their own families and given adequate education.

None of the positive features of schizophrenia such as specific kinds of delusions or hallucinations occurs in autistic children, nor do they develop in adulthood. Adult schizophrenic patients do not have a history of Kanner's syndrome in childhood. Speech disorder of various kinds is common in schizophrenia but it does not resemble the speech of autistic children when the two are compared in detail. The marked excess of males found in autism does not occur in schizophrenia.

None of the well-documented series has demonstrated an increased risk of schizophrenia in the relatives of autistic children, nor of Kanner's syndrome in the relatives of schizophrenic patients. Kallman's series (Kallman and Roth, 1956) did not refer to autistic children. The mean age of onset, for example, lay between 9 and 11, and a feature of the diagnosis was that there had to be a period of normal development before the onset of symptoms.

Kolvin and his colleagues (Kolvin, 1971a,b; Kolvin *et al.*, 1971a–e), in a study of 80 children with psychosis admitted to two hospitals over a period of years, found that they could be classified according to age of onset. The age groups used were those described by Anthony (1958a, b; 1962). Group I had an onset before 3 years of age, Group II between 3 and 5 years and Group III after 5 years old. The authors found so few children in Group II (which appeared to consist of a mixture of syndromes including those with severe organic deterioration such as Heller's disease) that they confined their detailed investigations to Group I, which they termed infantile psychosis (47 children) and Group III, referred to as late onset psychosis (33 children). The infantile psychosis group showed the items of behaviour characteristic of childhood autism, whereas the late onset group showed the symptoms and signs associated with adult schizophrenia, including hallucinations and disorders of thought content and an attitude of perplexity or suffering.

Various other differences were found between these groups. One parent of a child with infantile psychosis had a schizo-affective illness whereas among the parents of the children with late onset, 6 individuals showed evidence of schizophrenia. In the infantile psychosis group, 54 per cent of the children showed evidence of cerebral dysfunction compared with 31 per cent in the other. The former group had an excess of parents in professional occupations, whereas the latter had an excess in unskilled or semi-skilled manual work. Seventy-eight per cent of the children with infantile psychosis had an IQ which was below 70 or else "untestable", whereas only 16·6 per cent of the late onset group were in this category.

It is fair to say, on these findings, that it is possible to differentiate between these types of childhood psychosis on the evidence from history and present behaviour and that there is independent evidence for the validity of this differentiation. In the absence of any evidence connecting the two conditions it is misleading to use the labels interchangeably. Childhood schizophrenia should refer only to a condition in which a recognisable schizophrenic picture, with adult-type symptoms, develops during childhood—usually pre-pubertally.

Asperger's syndrome

Asperger (1944, 1960) described a group of children who had a syndrome he termed "autistic psychopathy". He believed that this was an abnormality of personality rather than a psychosis and should therefore be differentiated from early childhood autism. Van Krevelen (1971) described the main features of autistic psychopathy as a lack of social intuition leading to naive and tactless behaviour and difficulty with social relationships, plus unusual circumscribed interest patterns such as genealogy or astronomy. There might also be difficulty with motor co-ordination and poor performance in active games. Asperger and Van Krevelen thought that there were differences between early childhood autism and autistic psychopathy in age of onset and in other clinical features. However, in the present author's experience, the picture they describe as autistic psychopathy can be seen in some adults who have clearly been classically autistic as children but who have made progress in language and other skills. The relationship between the two conditions is most interesting but it is as yet unsolved. This question is considered further in Chapter 3 in the section on possible genetic causes of autism.

Other childhood psychoses

Many patterns of psychotic behaviour can occur in childhood in addition to autism and schizophrenia. These include conditions resembling those found in adults such as mania, depression and organic confusional states. Other patterns for which there is as yet no agreed system of classification are also found; for example, the syndromes with bizarre thought content and behaviour disorder, such as the two described by Despert (1955) and Bradley's case (1942). Differentiation from early childhood autism rests on the history and on the details of the behavioural syndrome.

Mental retardation

Mental retardation is a blanket term which covers a large number of different syndromes and patterns of behaviour. Wing (1975) interviewed the parents and teachers of all the severely retarded children in one area of London and found that about one-quarter had many of the elements of the autistic syndrome, including lack of affective contact, dislike of change, stereotyped movements and odd responses to sensory input, although few could be called "classically" autistic.

All these children had very severe deficiencies in comprehending and using spoken or gestured language. The retarded children with some ability to understand and communicate did not show items of autistic behaviour. The presence of autistic behaviour was not explained by the IQ score. Some children (especially those with Down's syndrome) who performed badly in IQ tests were sociable, communicated happily in gesture and mime and had none of the elements of the autistic syndrome, while other children with some ability to perform on non-language-dependent tests but very poor communication showed many items of autistic behaviour.

Many autistic children have scores on intelligence tests which indicate that they are mildly, moderately or severely mentally retarded, but a small proportion score in the normal or superior range.

It is clear from these findings that early childhood autism is not synonymous with general mental retardation, and that mental retardation does not explain autism, any more than it explains, for example, cerebral palsy, which can also be associated with any level of intelligence.

"Brain damage"

Evidence of abnormality of the central nervous system occurs in a substantial minority of autistic children, but, on the other hand, most children described as "brain damaged" are not autistic. The problem is dealt with in detail in Chapter 3. It is sufficient to note here that the term "brain damage" is yet another general category, like mental retardation, which covers many different patterns of behaviour. Advances in understanding will come only when specific lesions, or dysfunctions, or specific delays in development can clearly be linked to specific behavioural syndromes.

Disorders of hearing and vision

Children with undiagnosed congenital deafness may show behaviour like that of autism as a consequence of their problems in communication. For example, they may be socially withdrawn, upset by changes in routine and some like to make long lines of objects regardless of their real function in a way which is very reminiscent of a young autistic child. If they are able to discover for themselves, or are taught, alternative methods of communication through lip-reading, gesture and more formal sign language, they rapidly lose their "autism".

Most classically autistic children are not deaf, as is shown by their reactions to soft sounds that have meaning for them and their ability to recognise and sing tunes, though deafness may need to be considered because of the lack of response to some sounds, especially speech. There is a small minority of children with marked autistic behaviour, however, for whom, on the clinical evidence, it is extremely difficult to decide whether or not they can hear (see Chapter 11). The methods available for testing, hearing and recording responses to sound may enable a firm decision to be made but sometimes the results are equivocal and no final conclusion can be reached. It is most important to try to teach such children non-spoken methods of communication by appropriate operant techniques. If they learn them easily and the behaviour pattern becomes more normal, then it can be assumed that deafness was a major cause of the abnormality. More often, such children fail to learn even after long periods of appropriate teaching. It must then be concluded that, whatever the cause of their lack of response to sound, they also have a central impairment affecting the understanding and use of symbols.

Congenital peripheral blindness or partial sightedness may be associated with self-stimulation and stereotyped movements like those seen in autism (Keeler, 1958). Occasionally a child who has the autistic pattern of behaviour has such marked abnormalities in his response to visual stimuli that he is at first thought to be blind. In two autistic children seen by the author, the tendency to self-mutilating behaviour was so marked that actual damage was caused to the eyes and severe restriction of vision occurred as a secondary consequence.

Children born both partially sighted and with partial hearing, especially because of maternal rubella, may have behaviour closely resembling early childhood autism (Chess, 1971; Wing, 1969).

Developmental receptive speech disorders

Children with developmental receptive speech disorders may show some autistic behaviour, especially before the age of 5 (Wing, 1969). Many autistic children show language problems which closely resemble those found in the developmental speech disorders.

A number of workers have compared these two conditions (Churchill, 1972; Pronovost *et al.*, 1966; Rutter *et al.*, 1971; Wing, 1969, 1971). There are some marked similarities, but the main differences are that the children with receptive speech disorders are much more likely to be able to use gestures to compensate for their speech problems. Children in this group have some imaginative play, which is markedly deficient in those who are autistic. A history of echolalia is common in autistic children, but much less so in the receptive speech disorder group.

Rutter *et al.* (1971) studied children from these two diagnostic groups who had IQs of 70 or more. Their findings suggested that the autistic children had the more severe and the more widespread language handicaps. They noted a marked excess of boys among the autistic children but not among those with developmental receptive speech disorders. Some degree of deafness was common in the latter but not the former group.

Churchill (1972) demonstrated close similarities between the language problems of autistic children, and those with a "central" language disorder. He found that children in both groups had their own particular profile of handicaps which differed *between* individuals but was stable *within* individuals. Like Rutter *et al.* he observed that the problems in the autistic children were more severe.

The differential diagnosis therefore depends upon observation of the child's use of symbols apart from spoken speech. If he has a pure developmental receptive speech disorder he should, like a deaf child, be able to learn alternative methods of communication reasonably quickly. His play with dolls and other toys should show evidence of the development of imagination and inner language, in contrast to the autistic child's tendency to manipulate objects regardless of their function.

Problems occur with the children who show features half way between autism and developmental receptive speech disorders. The most important point is to define the child's specific impairments, behaviour problems and skills and then decide upon the best plan of management, education and treatment. As Griffiths (1972) emphasises, the prescription of education should depend upon the level of symbolic function which the child has reached, rather than upon medical categories or his secondary disturbances of behaviour.

The "repetitive speech" syndrome

In the course of an epidemiological survey of retarded children, which is not yet completed, the present author has found a few children who are able to talk freely in sentences but whose utterances are repetitive and contain much material copied from other people. These children have a superficial sociability. They will talk to anyone although their conversation frequently consists of repeated questions, the flow of which cannot be stemmed by giving answers.

These children are able to play by copying activities in which they have taken part, but they do not create new ideas. Their ability to interact with other children is limited, although they sometimes join in because they can imitate the actions of the rest of the group. They may have some isolated skills such as reading, but with little understanding. There is a tendency for parents and teachers to overestimate the learning ability of such children until they show the limitations in their performance.

There may be some items of autistic behaviour, such as resistance to change and various "obsessional" activities, in addition to their repetitive, stereotyped speech. The differentiation can be made only by studying the complete pattern of behaviour. In some cases it may be difficult to decide on which side of the dividing line to place such a child, especially if he has a history of marked autistic behaviour before the age of 5.

Elective mutism

This is a condition in which the child speaks in some situations but not in others. He may talk at home but not at school or he may talk to certain other children but not to adults (Reed, 1963). This behaviour is sometimes seen in toddlers who are just beginning to speak but if it lasts into school age it can be classified as abnormal. The children may have odd personalities and they may also have some speech difficulties, but the diagnosis depends upon obtaining evidence that they can and do converse normally at times. Autistic children retain their characteristic language abnormalities in all situations. In any case the whole pattern of behaviour is different in the two conditions.

Delayed echolalia in autistic children may be a source of confusion to those who are not familiar with it. Some autistic children are able to repeat long passages from songs, nursery rhymes, lists of words, or even from conversations they have heard. This is easily identified as echolalia by those who know the source of the original words. It is essentially a monologue and not part of a conversation and it is usually repeated without alteration.

Psycho-social deprivation

Rutter (1972b) and Rutter and Mittler (1972) discussed this problem. They pointed out that there is much evidence to show that groups of children reared in environments in which they are deprived of language stimulation tend to be immature in their use of *spoken* language. On the other hand there are very few studies of severe language delay involving comprehension produced by social deprivation, though it is commonly mentioned as a possible cause of such delay. Its prevalence is unknown. Published descriptions of individual cases of gross physical and mental deprivation over several years resulting in severe retardation of all aspects of development are mentioned in Chapter 3. Some of the children who had been deprived in this way made rapid strides in development when they were rescued and put in a caring and stimulating environment. They showed no evidence of early childhood autism.

Young children, whose parents work long hours and are too tired to talk and play when at home, or who are looked after by child minders who pay no attention to their charges beyond feeding and changing them, may show delay in talking. Rutter (1970b) noted that children with this type of problem usually do not show impairment of language comprehension or inner language. Careful history taking, observation of the nature of the language disability as well as other aspects of behaviour and the rapid response to improvement in the environment should differentiate this condition from early childhood autism.

The differential diagnosis may be complicated when a child with congenital cognitive disabilities also has a home background which does not provide experience in language. The factors contributing to the child's handicaps can be disentangled only by a combination of careful assessment and the provision of a better environment, as for example in a special unit in a day nursery.

Difficult phases in the development of young normal children

All the problems seen in autistic children can occur in young normal children, perhaps in response to the unhappiness caused by admission to hospital, an illness or the birth of a sibling. Some of the elements of the syndrome may occur as part of a "phase" without any obvious precipitating factor. The difference is that in normal children these phases are mild and comparatively short-lived whereas the problems are severe and last for many years or for a lifetime in those who are autistic. Normal children show a wide repertoire of other behaviour, especially in their play and social relationships, in marked contrast to the limited range of behaviour (most of it abnormal) characteristic of autism.

Prognosis

Kanner and Eisenberg have published follow-up studies on Kanner's own cases (Eisenberg, 1956, 1957a; Kanner and Eisenberg, 1955, 1956; Kanner and Lesser, 1958; Kanner, 1973). Creak (1963) followed up 100 children with early childhood psychosis. Both series indicated that the prognosis was poor except for a small minority.

Two follow-up studies have systematically investigated a series of variables in an attempt to find factors which can be related to prognosis in the childhood psychoses of early onset. Rutter and his colleagues (Rutter and Lockyer, 1967; Rutter *et al.*, 1967; Rutter, 1970a) studied 64 children with a prepubescent onset of psychosis seen at the Maudsley Hospital during the years 1950 to 1958. Four children had an onset after 30 months and three did not have any ritualistic phenomena. The remaining children had the autistic pattern of onset and behaviour. The whole group was seen and examined during 1963 and 1964 and followed up again in 1970 by means of a postal questionnaire to parents and inspection of medical reports. At the latter time the children's ages ranged from 15 to 29 years.

About half were in full-time residential care. Only 5 per cent of those aged 16 and over were in regular paid employment, compared with 33 per cent of a control group consisting of non-psychotic children who first attended the Maudsley hospital during the same period of time as the psychotic children.

In the final follow-up, 17 per cent had a "good" adjustment although only 1 could be described as completely normal. The others had some difficulties in relationships or minor oddities of behaviour. Another 19 per cent had a fair adjustment, with some degree of independence but still needed supervision. The remaining 64 per cent remained severely handicapped and unable to lead an independent life.

Difficulties in social relationships remained in almost all the children, though some had improved in this respect. Some wanted to have friends but lacked the necessary skills to make inter-personal relationships. Just under half remained unable to speak. Resistance to change and rituals tended to persist, though on the whole the children became more adaptable with increasing age.

In general, adolescence did not produce any major changes, but 6 children became more difficult at this time and had to be admitted to institutions. Seven children showed progressive intellectual deterioration in adolescence and in 4 of these signs of neurological abnormality developed.

Three children had a history of epilepsy when first seen, but by the time of the second follow-up one-third had at some time had fits. Two had died in fits.

The study showed that the most useful predictor of outcome in autistic children is an IQ measured in early childhood, providing always that it is administered by someone experienced with testing autistic children. Even if a score could be obtained on a few sub-tests only it still correlated with outcome (see Chapters 6 and 10).

Lack of speech by age 5 and a very marked lack of response to sound in early childhood were both correlated with a poor outcome. Although none of the other items of behaviour found in the syndrome were individually significantly correlated with outcome, there was a tendency for the children who showed the total picture in a less severe degree when young to have the better prognosis.

The amount of schooling received by the children also seemed to help in social adjustment as an adult, as well as the teaching of specific skills.

Another recent systematic study has been carried out by DeMyer *et al.* (1973). This involved a group of 120 children whose mean age when first seen was $5\frac{1}{2}$ years and who were followed up for an average of just over 6 years. The children were diagnosed as autistic and all had serious emotional withdrawal, non-communicative speech or muteness and non-functional object use. About two-thirds were interviewed and tested at follow-up and, for the rest, the parents were interviewed by telephone and were sent postal ques-tionnaires because of difficulties in arranging visits. Reports from professional workers who had seen the children were obtained where possible.

In general, the findings were very similar indeed to those of Rutter, the outcome being slightly worse in DeMyer's sample. The incidence of epilepsy was only 14 per cent compared with Rutter's total of 33 per cent but this may have been due to age differences in the samples.

DeMyer *et al.* agreed with Rutter's findings that IQ, attainment of useful speech by age 5, amount of schooling and the severity with which autistic behaviour was manifested were all correlated with outcome. In addition they found that the best predictor of how the child functioned educationally at follow-up was how well he functioned in this respect when first seen.

They used an index of brain dysfunction which also had predictive value though it was not as useful as the other variables mentioned.

The authors measured the parents' emotional warmth, consistency and adequacy of communication and found that these were not related to outcome.

They concluded from their findings that autism is due to biological factors. In a few cases the cause may be a progressive degenerative disease, but in most the lesion is likely to be a static one occurring during gestation or infancy.

These studies underline the fact, which has to be faced by parents sooner or later, that most autistic children will remain dependent all their lives. Appropriate services are of vital importance in any chronically handicapping condition and the types of provision needed by autistic children, adolescents and adults will be discussed in Chapter 12.

A SCHEME FOR CLINICAL DESCRIPTION
AND DIAGNOSIS

It is important to note that most of the relevant details of the children's behaviour cannot be observed in the clinician's office. They must be elicited by questioning the parents or parent substitutes concerning the history and present state. The interview must of necessity be a lengthy one. The parents should be asked to describe how their child behaves in everyday situations and the questioning continued until the clinician is satisfied that he has enough information to make a judgement concerning the presence or absence of each of the items listed. For example, there is no point in asking "Does your child understand what you say to him?". Many parents who have no knowledge of the steps in language development will reply, "Yes, he understands everything", even if their child has a severe problem of comprehension. The most useful approach is to ask a series of questions as to how the child actually behaves; for example, "What does he do when you call his name?"; "Does he point to any objects when you ask him to in words?"; "Does he give you any objects when you ask in words, without gestures?"; "Does he bring you things from another room when you ask him?"; and so on. It is not surprising to find that the same parents, who, in reply to the general question, say that their child understands everything, are able to give precise answers when asked specific, limited questions about concrete items of behaviour. All the other points in the following scheme can be dealt with on the same principle.

A. *Basic impairments*
1. Problems affecting language and communication.
(a) Spoken language.

    * (i) Problems in comprehension of speech.
    * (ii) Abnormalities in the use of speech.
       *Complete absence of speech (mutism) *or*, in those children who do speak:
       *Immediate echolalia.
       *Delayed echolalia.
       *Repetitive, stereotyped, inflexible use of words and phrases.
       *Confusion over the use of pronouns.
       Immaturity of grammatical structure in spontaneous (not echoed) speech.
       Abnormalities like those found in developmental receptive speech disorders in spontaneous (not echoed) speech.
    *(iii) Poor control of pitch, volume and intonation of the voice.
    (iv) Problems of pronunciation.
  (b) Non-spoken language and non-verbal communication.
    * (i) Poor comprehension of the information conveyed by gesture, miming, facial expression, bodily posture, vocal intonation, etc.
    *(ii) Lack of use of gesture, miming, facial expression, bodily posture and vocal intonation to convey information.
2. Abnormal responses to sensory experiences (indifference, distress, fascination).
    (i) Abnormal responses to sounds.
    (ii) Abnormal responses to visual stimuli.
    (iii) Abnormal responses to pain and cold.
    (iv) Abnormal responses to being touched.
    (v) "Paradoxical" responses to sensations.
3. Abnormalities of visual inspection.
    (i) The use of the peripheral rather than central visual fields.
    (ii) Looking at people and things with brief flashing glances rather than a steady gaze.
4. Problems of motor imitation.
    (i) Difficulty in copying movements.
    (ii) Muddling right-left, up-down and back-front.

---

*Items essential for a diagnosis of autism as described by Kanner (1943).

5. Problems of motor control.
  (i) Jumping, flapping limbs, rocking and grimacing.
  (ii) A springy tip-toe walk without appropriate swinging of the arms.
  (iii) An odd posture when standing, with head bowed, arms flexed at the elbow and hands drooping at the wrist.
  (iv) Spontaneous large movements, or fine skilled movements, or both may be clumsy in some children though others appear to be graceful and nimble.
6. Abnormalities of autonomic function, vestibular control and physical development.
  (i) Erratic patterns of sleeping and resistance to the effects of sedatives and hypnotics.
  (ii) Erratic patterns of eating and drinking, including consumption of large quantities of fluid.
  (iii) Lack of dizziness after spinning round.
  (iv) Immaturity of general appearance and unusual symmetry of face.

B. *Special skills*

*1. Skills that do not involve language.

These include music, arithmetic, dismantling and assembling mechanical or electrical objects, fitting together jig-saws or constructional toys.

*2. An unusual form of memory.

The ability to store items for prolonged periods in the exact form in which they were first experienced.

C. *Secondary behaviour problems*

*1. Apparent aloofness and indifference to other people, especially other children.

*2. Intense resistance to change, attachment to objects and routines or a repetitive, uncreative interest in certain subjects.

*3. Inappropriate emotional reactions.

*4. Lack of imagination.

(a) Lack of imaginative play or creative activities.

(b) Attending to minor or trivial aspects of people or objects instead of attending to the whole.

(c) Absorption in repetitive activities, stereotyped movements, self-injury, etc.

5. Socially immature and difficult behaviour.

CASE HISTORIES OF THREE YOUNG AUTISTIC ADULTS

The three case histories to be given here originally appeared in the first edition of this book and have been brought up to date. The stories of Sally, Paul and Clifford are given in order to illustrate the diversity of the syndromes which are labelled "childhood autism". Sally has had practically all the features described in Chapter 2 and the diagnosis of autism was never in doubt. Paul had rather fewer of the characteristic features. In the past he was seen by a neurologist who diagnosed congenital auditory imperception, by a psychiatrist who diagnosed gross mental deficiency and possible aphasia and a paediatrician who diagnosed juvenile schizophrenia. Eventually he was classified as autistic when he was found a place at a special school. Clifford was diagnosed as autistic, but, in fact, shows fewer of the features than Paul and cannot be said to have Kanner's syndrome, although he presents problems of education and management which are very similar to those who have classic childhood autism.

Sally and Clifford function in the low ESN range of intellectual ability, while Paul has normal intelligence on non-language-dependent tests. As the case histories show, their specific handicaps make it difficult for even the brightest autistic children and adults to use their potential to the full. The stories illustrate the necessity for the provision of appropriate services to help both the children and their families.

As children, all three were supported at school by their respective local authorities which deserve praise for this enlightened recognition of the value of special education.

1. Sally (born 22.11.56)

Both parents are professional workers. Mother was 28 at the child's birth: there were no complications except for mild hypertension during the later stages of pregnancy. Mother is right-handed and had normal speech development. Father is right-handed and footed but left-eyed. Details of his early speech development are unknown. Sally is an only child. For many years she was ambidextrous but is now mainly right-handed. She is left-footed. She has a cousin whose speech was markedly late in developing but who is now normal. Two other cousins are left-handed and one had mild dyslexia.

At birth, Sally appeared to be a normal healthy baby with no signs of prematurity, but from the outset she sucked very poorly. Feeding difficulties continued until about 3 months and then gradually improved and by 6 months she was feeding well. However, routines of feeding, sleeping and excretion were never established during the first year of life. Some nights Sally would sleep 15 hours and others for only 2 or 3 hours. She regularly screamed for long periods, which produced occasional nose bleeds in early infancy. The most distressing feature was that she could not be soothed even if cuddled and rocked. When awake she was very active with many movements of her limbs.

The screaming gradually lessened, although, until she gave up her day-time nap at 2 years of age, she would cry loudly for $\frac{1}{2}$ hour or so immediately on waking and could not be consoled.

She began to smile at 8 weeks and by 16 weeks she chuckled happily if tickled and bounced on her mother's knee, but she did not show any anticipation or readiness to be picked up when approached, even by her mother. She was given a toy panda at birth and from 4 months to 7 years this was her inseparable companion. If the toy was mislaid, Sally would scream until it was found again.

Apart from this, Sally had little interest in toys. She spent much time scratching on her pram cover or tapping on different kinds of surfaces. She was also fascinated by bright lights.

She was always responsive to physical contact and tickling games, but she never pointed things out to her parents or showed any interest in the immediate environment.

Motor milestones, teething and self-feeding were quite normal. Toilet training was not achieved till 5 years of age because she screamed if sat on a pot, but her parents did not make an issue of the matter. She seemed to lose her fear quite suddenly one day and was reasonably reliable from then on.

The years from 2 to 5 were the most difficult. Sally did not speak until over 3 when she acquired a very few words. She had no understanding of speech, did not respond to her name, tended to cover her ears when she heard loud noises and had difficulty in locating the direction of sounds. People often asked if she was deaf, but she could hear and respond to the rustle of a sweet paper. Her only means of communication was to take people by the hand and lead them to things she wanted.

She looked through and past people, not at them. She seemed unable to see objects that were stationary, even if she wanted them, but would find them rapidly if they were moving. She would walk downstairs and even ride her tricycle without appearing to look where she was going, but would not fall or bump into things. She would examine objects by holding them near her eyes and then far away and would twist and turn them at the edge of her visual fields. She also examined objects by touching, tasting and smelling them and seemed to find enjoyment in the feel of smooth surfaces. At this stage, Sally appeared to be oblivious of pain, heat and cold. She would run outside with few clothes on and appear to feel no discomfort. She never cried when she bumped herself but merely seemed puzzled. She had no fear of real dangers.

She collected objects such as stones, leaves and plastic bottles and would scream if they were lost or taken away. She often arranged them in long straight lines and sometimes in special patterns. She insisted on wearing the same clothes each day and, when walking, screamed if a corner was turned.

Sally was mildly hyperactive, but the most noticeable motor abnormality was her odd movements—jumping, flapping arms and legs and making facial grimaces especially when excited. She tended to walk on tip-toe and appeared graceful in movement, although she was clumsy with her fingers.

She was active and immersed in her own pursuits, which were

often destructive. She completely ignored other children and seemed oblivious of her parents as well, although the fact that her behaviour became worse if they went away showed she had some awareness of them. She was a sad child and sometimes she would stand dejectedly with tears streaming down her face as if everything was too much for her. Her only real pleasure was music. She loved to listen to records and could sing well. She enjoyed special sounds such as echoes or noises made by mechanical toys.

After the age of 5, the first signs of improvement were seen. Her parents had realized that her inability to understand language was the basic problem and they carefully adapted their behaviour to help her understand as much as possible. Her vocabulary of nouns and verbs was growing and improved with careful teaching. Most of her speech was echolalic, but she learnt some useful sentences this way, even though the pronouns were reversed ("you want dinner" etc.). She soon learnt to say "No" but by 9 years was just beginning to say "Yes". Confirmation was expressed by repeating the phrase (Q: "Would you like a drink?" A: "You like drink"). Screaming decreased markedly from the age of 5 although Sally became upset if she could not understand what was expected of her. Her ability to use her eyes improved dramatically at 6 years of age and after this she enjoyed looking at pictures in books, which before had held no interest for her.

Sally had always "chattered" to herself, making noises even before speech began and when she could speak she echoed phrases first spoken by other people long after she had heard them. She used the precise accents of the speakers very fluently. Her own sentences, when she tried to express herself spontaneously, were quite different from the echoed speech, being halting, spoken in a monotone, missing out all but the main words, and seemingly forced out with great effort. She frequently confused the names for objects which go together, such as "knife and fork" and "brush and comb", although she did not confuse the objects themselves. She would try to find names for things she did not know or could not remember, such as "doggie-bunnie" for kangaroo and "candle" for a mushroom with its stalk.

With the development of speech, Sally changed from a sad and aloof child to an affectionate and happy little girl. Her social behaviour improved and she seemed to enjoy life. She still liked to collect useless objects such as tins and pieces of wood, but she would relinquish them without protest if her parents thought she should not have them. She started school at 7 and was soon used to the presence of other children, although she still did not play with them. At first she furiously resisted attempts to teach her, but she became more amenable as time went on. She learnt to identify letters and numbers, to read simple words phonetically and to do simple arithmetic. She had a marked tendency to reverse letters, which interfered with reading and she had considerable difficulty in imitating other people's movements and gestures.

Sally continued to attend her special school until she was $17\frac{1}{2}$ years old. Her academic progress was very limited because, although she learnt the rudiments of the mechanical skills of reading and number work, she had severe problems in comprehending the *meaning* of the work she was doing. Much more useful to her were the lessons in practical and domestic skills, which she enjoyed far more and at which she achieved a fair level of competence. While at school she also improved in general social behaviour and, in adolescence, was able to go with her family to musical shows at the cinema and theatre, which gave her a great deal of pleasure.

After leaving school Sally attended the local Adult Training Centre for mentally retarded people. She was very disturbed in behaviour at first. She had the manual skills necessary for the work at the centre, but found the noise, the sociable chatter and the informal atmosphere confusing and frightening. After a week or so she was placed with the special care group of very retarded and disturbed adults. This group had only a few people in it with several staff, away from the noise and bustle of the main centre. Sally had a higher level of skill than the rest of the group but was much happier and more settled in behaviour with them because of the greater degree of supervision and organisation.

Perhaps the ideal solution for Sally would be a special unit in or near an adult day centre which could provide the necessary structure but also allow her to use the skills she does possess to the greatest advantage.

Sally's physical health is excellent. The only illnesses of note were a high fever due to vaccination at 6 months and severe haemorrhagic measles at 4 years of age. She is still cheerful and socially responsive in familiar environments and with people she knows well. Outside the situations in which she feels confident, her behaviour is inclined to become difficult, with screaming and temper tantrums, but, on the whole, she is very much happier and easier to live with than would have been predicted in her early childhood.

2. Paul (born 15.3.52)

Father has higher technical qualifications and runs his own business and mother has an administrative post. She was 28 when Paul was born, and there were no complications during pregnancy. Mother is right-handed and footed but left-eyed. Her speech development was normal. Father is right-handed, right-footed and right-eyed. His speech development is unknown, but he had difficulty with spelling. Paul has one brother, 19 months younger, who is left-handed, left-footed and right-eyed. He suffers from severe dyslexia. Paul's uncle (his father's brother) has a childhood history suggestive of mild autism and is still a quiet, unsociable person. An aunt (his mother's sister) is left-handed and had delayed speech, difficulty with pronunciation and dyslexia as a child.

The delivery was normal, but Paul did not cry when he was born and he had two episodes of cyanosis in the first 6 weeks. He was a sleepy baby and sucked poorly for the first 3 months. After this he became lively and affectionate. He enjoyed the usual baby games and always showed eagerness to be picked up. He imitated sound at 8 months.

When he was about 10 months old it was noticed that he spent a lot of time scratching on the cover of his pram, and tapping on surfaces. At 1 year he suddenly began to scream if he saw an electric light bulb, whether switched on or off, if it was not covered by a shade. At about 14 to 15 months, Paul seemed gradually to become less and less responsive to other people and stopped looking at them at all. During this period he wanted his mother to hold his hand all the time she was pushing him in the pram. She knew that something was wrong and tried desperately to help him, but received no useful advice from those to whom she turned for assistance.

Paul started to rock and bounce in his pram and cot. He would wake from his daytime sleep screaming loudly and could not be soothed. Although previously he had known and responded to his own name, he now seemed oblivious when called. He had been babbling "Mum-mum" and "Dad-dad" but this ceased. He showed his wants by taking people by the hand and leading them to the object in question. He was fascinated by some mechanical noises but covered his ears to exclude others. He ignored speech but would respond to the rustle of a sweet paper. Many people asked if he was deaf. He always enjoyed physical contact, romping and tickling and would seem normal when played with in this way, but would become silent, aloof and remote immediately afterwards.

At 19 months his brother was born and Paul showed no interest in him. He began to be fascinated by objects made of metal, which even now he still likes to collect. He liked to bend tins and tin-lids into a crescent shape, showing considerable skill at this. He played with lettered bricks and sorted them out; the A's in one pile, the B's in another and so on. He did not look at illustrations in books but gazed at the print, and was interested in the credit titles, but not the pictures, on television.

He was able to see tiny details of things in the environment, but his mother felt that he had difficulty in recognizing large objects, such as a horse, if pointed out to him in the street.

He examined things by touching, tasting and smelling and loved the feel of smooth surfaces.

He would jump up and down, grimace and flap his arms and hands when excited. He did not twist his hands in front of his face.

There was never any particular insistence on routine. Special fears were marked, beginning with the light bulb and including fear of a sugar basin at the age of 10.

He enjoyed music, and could sing nursery rhymes with perfect pitch at the age of 3. He liked his mother to tell him about things in song—seeming to understand them better that way.

In his early years, Paul did not show resistance to learning new skills. He enjoyed being taught by visual though not by auditory methods, and this made it possible for him to go to a small, private and very understanding nursery school at $3\frac{1}{2}$. On his first day he showed he could make good use of the Montessori equipment.

Paul's parents noticed that if they told him to "shut the door" he took no notice, but if they pointed and mimed the action of shutting, he obeyed. They realized that he had no understanding of speech and resolved to help him comprehend in other ways. By 4 he was beginning to try to say words, but he had severe dysarthria. His mother pointed to objects and said the name and Paul copied as best he could. She also acted verbs and his vocabulary improved rapidly, but lacked words such as "the", "but", "to" and abstract ideas which could not be demonstrated. He tended to repeat sentences or phrases immediately, but he did not have delayed echolalia. He learnt to say "no", but rarely used "yes", repeating the appropriate words instead. He sometimes reversed pronouns, but usually referred to himself as "Paul". Nowadays he usually says "I". He would sometimes speak in a gruff voice, for amusement, or else in a small whisper.

At school he learnt the names of capital and small letters in a week and later on he learnt 3-letter words. He started to read before he was 5 and read fluently by 6. After this he would ask his mother to write down any new words he heard because he learnt them much more easily when he saw them than when he heard them. He could subtract, multiply and divide by 7. His behaviour at school, which had been restless and difficult at first, became almost normal. At 8, he should have progressed to a higher class but was kept back because, although his arithmetic was excellent, his language comprehension, despite his reading ability, was very poor. He began to be most unhappy, realizing that he was handicapped and, for the first time, showed resistance to learning.

He was sent to a special school for children with problems of this kind, but the staff had theoretical objections to a directive, remedial teaching approach. Lacking stimulation, Paul became more and more withdrawn and seemed to be losing the skills he had acquired.

He left this school and went to another where remedial education was considered to be important and made good progress there. He obtained CSE grade 2 certificates in arithmetic and art before he left school at 18.

After school, Paul went to an Industrial Rehabilitation Unit for a 6-week course which it was hoped would enable him to obtain employment. He had to travel to the Unit by public transport and to do this his mother had to teach him how to use the tubes and buses. He eventually became quite proficient in this.

He had to get up at 6 a.m. to be at the unit at 8 a.m. On three occasions, because of a misunderstanding and because he could not explain that he was being helped on to the wrong bus, he was over an hour late in arriving home. After somewhat laborious questioning, (necessary because Paul could not give a narrative account of what had happened) it was discovered that the bus, on to which a kindly person at the unit had put him, had taken him to an unfamiliar destination. Despite this, however, Paul had found his own way home which involved him in changing from one tube train to another at Piccadilly Circus in the rush hour.

He was recommended for work at a Remploy factory, but the hoped-for vacancy never occurred. Eventually he went to the local Adult Training Centre. He was happy there, although his skill in wood and metal work and other practical tasks was never exploited to the full.

After about a year at the centre, Paul's family moved away from London and Paul is now having difficulty in adjusting to his new environment. He was extremely anxious and worried at the prospect of the change some weeks before the move was made. Although he is now happy enough while at home, helping with painting, decorating, gardening and housework, he has a marked fear of going out, making it impossible for him to find outside employment or to attend the Adult Training Centre. The fears are very slowly improving with time and it is to be hoped that they will eventually settle sufficiently for Paul to be able to find some work outside his own home.

Paul tends to suffer from travel sickness in cars but otherwise has good physical health. He is very quiet and always rather sad because he is aware that he is handicapped. His vocabulary is good, but his sentence construction and grammar are poor and he has no skill in the use of spoken language. His dysarthria has improved and his diction is now fairly good. He can understand a conversation if it is carefully tailored for him and includes only those words he has been taught. On the other hand, he is excellent at arithmetic, and wood and metal work, and had attended classes in the latter subjects at a technical school. He behaves well. The major problems are his distress when he is faced with words and situations that he cannot understand, and his high level of anxiety.

3. Clifford (born 21.8.47)

Father is a senior Army Officer and mother has a responsible administrative job. Both are right-handed and had no speech delay themselves, though father had some trouble with reading and writing and only just managed to get into grammar school, aged 13, but then developed rapidly. Mother was 20 when Clifford was born after a normal pregnancy and labour, the eldest of four children. All the siblings are right-handed and right-footed, but Clifford is ambidextrous. The second boy, Richard, has mild difficulty with spelling (transposing syllables and mixing letters such as "b" and "d") and has a rather hesitant, jerky manner of speech which, when he is embarrassed, sounds very much like Clifford's. Richard is otherwise normal.

From birth, Clifford did not suck properly and required a teat with a very large hole. He cried a great deal during the first 2 months and seemed to be more alive at night-time than during the day. He seemed unresponsive to his parents and did not lift up his arms in anticipation of being picked up; nor did he point things out and gurgle at passers-by. He was a quiet baby who slept well and was cuddly to hold. He sat up at 10 months, stood at 2 years and walked at $2\frac{1}{2}$ but very shakily. His first words were at 2 years, very clearly enunciated, but speech never developed properly. He showed marked echolalia and repetitive speech and had great difficulty in naming things. His pronunciation was poor ("bathroom" was pronounced "boferam", though he knew what the word meant). He never showed pronominal reversal and had no difficulty with the use of "yes". His parents were sure that he could understand far more than he could express and he preferred to remain silent for this reason. For example, there was often a long pause before replying to questions.

At first he used to look past people and objects and seemed not to recognise things, but he was never thought to be deaf and never showed special interest in particular sounds or visual patterns, or found special pleasure in the touch, taste or smell of things. He flapped his arms and twisted his wrists when excited, but had no other characteristic motor movements. His musculature has always seemed very limp. He did not make collections or insist on special routines, but he developed very early a passionate interest in cars and could recognise from a wing, almost from a hub-cap, the make and year of any model. He never lost this interest. He also greatly enjoys every form of music.

His behaviour was never noisy, destructive or excited, in fact he was very gentle. He could not play with other children, but stood vaguely on the periphery of the group looking puzzled. He was affectionate, with a strong sense of humour, and very close to his brother Richard (2 years younger). He never showed social aloofness or indifference. He was not conscious of dangers. He did not, when crying, produce tears, though his facial and vocal expressions were normal.

He learnt to read by $5\frac{1}{2}$ and was always fairly advanced at this. In most other ways he was backward. To his parents his most marked characteristic was "lack of initiative". He always had to be told to do everything. He was diagnosed as mentally retarded, autistic and psychotic at various times, and was sent to two residential schools until he was 17, supported financially by the local authority. Intelligence tests usually gave an IQ of just above 50.

When he was seen at the age of 17 he had recently been graded "unsuitable for education" because of "lack of initiative". He looked like a child of 12, had cryptorchidism, hypotonic muscles and hyperextensibility of joints. He was cheerful and anxious to please, but clumsy and slow. He could describe how to get to the hospital by bus and use very simple sentences, but there was a marked dysarthria. He would move his lips in an appropriate manner before getting out the words, which tended to be formed explosively. He showed a marked scatter on psychological tests. The W.A.I.S. gave a verbal IQ of 57 and performance IQ of 53. His reading age was 13.7 but he failed many words such as "furniture" while passing difficult ones such as "nautical" and "dinosaur". The Paired Associate learning test for children gave average or above-average scores. He was very slow on manual dexterity tests. It was impossible to arrange further education or remedial teaching through the local authority and, because of his childish size, appearance and emotional development, it was felt that he could not yet be placed in any sheltered workshop or factory. He was admitted to a psychiatric day hospital, although it was recognised that this was not an ideal setting for assessment and remedial work.

After leaving the day hospital, it was decided to try Clifford at the local Adult Training Centre where he settled down very well. When his parents moved house he had to go to a new Centre but, unlike Paul, Clifford accepted this change without difficulty. He is happy to go to the Centre and is able to do the various types of assembly and other work available there. He travels to and from the Centre on two buses, by himself, and can manage this competently.

He attends a special social club run by students in collaboration with the Adult Training Centre and enjoys the activities, which include outings and holidays. He goes to the cinema with his brother every week, still loves listening to music, and has developed an intense interest in bus routes, which he knows in great detail.

Clifford has always had good health. He is sociable and responsive to people and has no behaviour problems at all.

CHAPTER 3

EPIDEMIOLOGY AND THEORIES OF AETIOLOGY

LORNA WING

The fact that the basic pathology underlying autistic behaviour is still unknown has led to the proliferation of theories ranging from the banal to the bizarre. The number which need to be given serious consideration can be reduced by excluding those that are, in our present state of knowledge, implausible. Among these must, sadly, be counted the hypothesis that autistic children are beings from outer space.

There is, as yet, no conclusive proof for any of the available theories, but some are more compatible than others with the facts which have been established by epidemiological studies. In this chapter, the results of the few such studies which have been done will be discussed first, so that the various aetiological theories can be evaluated critically.

Epidemiology

The Middlesex Survey

The first detailed epidemiological study of the autistic syndrome was conducted by Lotter, who investigated all the 78,000 children aged 8, 9 or 10 who had home addresses in the former county of Middlesex on 1 January 1964 (Lotter, 1966, 1967a,b; Wing et al., 1967). Preliminary screening yielded 135 possible cases of early childhood autism. These 135 children were intensively investigated by means of cognitive testing, interviews concerning the children's behaviour with teachers, supervisors or nurses, interviews with the mothers to elicit the history and present behaviour at home and examination of all available medical records.

All the information collected was combined and the children were given ratings on 24 items covering the following aspects of behaviour: abnormalities of speech; social aloofness; stereotyped movements; abnormal responses to sounds; repetitive, ritualistic behaviour including resistance to change.

Fifty-four children out of the 135 showed some abnormalities on this scale. They were divided into three groups on the basis of their scores.

Group A, the nuclear autistic group, contained 15 children who showed in marked degree the two items that Kanner considered essential for the diagnosis of his syndrome—namely, lack of social responsiveness and repetitive, ritualistic behaviour.

Group B, referred to as the "non-nuclear" group, consisted of 17 children who did not show the marked combination of the above two items, but who did have many autistic features.

It should be noted that Lotter's diagnosis of nuclear and non-nuclear autism was based on the behaviour pattern alone. Children with gross organic features and with severe mental retardation were included if they showed autistic behaviour.

He also included 3 children with onset betwen 3 and $4\frac{1}{2}$ years of age, who regressed severely and rather rapidly and were left with autistic behaviour by the time they were 8 to 10 years old. The definition is, therefore, in certain respects, wider than that which was used by Kanner.

The remaining 22 children, Group C, were not autistic but nevertheless had some behaviour similar to the autistic children.

In addition to the children for whom full information was available, there were 11 on whom the data were incomplete. From what was known about them, 3 would have been in Group B and 4 in Group C. Taking these extra children into account, the age specific prevalences were 2·0 per 10,000 children aged 8 to 10 in Group A, 2·5 per 10,000 in Group B and 3·3 per 10,000 in Group C.

Nearly one-third of the children in Groups A and B had recorded evidence suggestive of neurological abnormalities. Non-verbal intelligence tests suggested that 19 per cent had performance IQ's of 70 and above, 25 per cent between 50 and 69, and 56 per cent below 50, that is in the severely retarded range. (These percentages were calculated by the present author from the information given in Lotter's thesis, 1967b.)

Approximately two-thirds of the children were abnormal from birth or early infancy and the rest had a setback after a period of apparently normal development.

There was an excess of boys in all the groups. In the nuclear group the ratio of males to females was 2·75 to 1, and in the non-nuclear group it was 2·4 to 1. The 10 children with IQ's above 55 were all boys.

Just under one-third of the children were mute and another one-third had only very limited use of speech. All of these were functioning at a low level of intelligence. (In this connection, it should be noted that there is a small number of autistic children who cannot speak at all but who have good non-language-dependent skills (Wing, 1969) though none were found in Lotter's study.)

No evidence was found that autistic children were likely to be first born or to have any other special birth rank. There were no significant findings regarding maternal age. There was no excess of prematurity. There was a slight excess of other complications of pregnancy and delivery in the autistic children as compared with their siblings but the numbers were not high (6 out of 28 for autistic children for whom records were available compared with 3 out of 44 siblings).

The parents of Group A children were most likely to be in the Registrar General's social class I or II (occupational classification), to have had professional training and to be superior to the general population on tests of intelligence (Mill Hill vocabulary and Raven's progressive matrices). The group B parents were less likely and the Group C parents least likely to have these characteristics.

Lotter pointed out that although many observers have noted the unexpectedly high socio-economic status of the parents of autistic children (Allen *et al.*, 1971; Creak, 1963; Gillies *et al.*, 1963; Kolvin *et al.*, 1971b; Rimland, 1965; Rutter, 1966), none have found the frequency as high as that of Kanner. In a paper written by Kanner and Lesser (1958), 90 per cent of the occupations listed could be classified in social class I or II. Lotter found 60 per cent of Group A parents were in social class I or II, compared with 31 per cent of Group B. Among his Group B children those who were severely retarded in development from birth did not have parents in social class I or II. Including children of this kind may therefore affect the findings concerning social class. Ritvo *et al.* (1971), for example, compared 74 hospitalised "autistic" children with 74 children hospitalised for other neuropsychiatric disorders and failed to find any social class bias in the parents of the former. The criteria used by Ritvo *et al.* are described in another paper (Ornitz and Ritvo, 1968a). There is considerable emphasis on the children's stereotyped movements and abnormal responses to sensory stimuli as well as their poverty of social relationships and disturbance of language development. Repetitive manipulation of objects is described but the more complex routines and preoccupations, often involving prodigious feats of memory, which tend to occur in the more classically autistic children (Prior and MacMillan, 1973) with higher levels of non-language-dependent skills (Wolff and Chess, 1964; Rutter, 1966) are not mentioned. Although details of the non-language-dependent skills of children diagnosed as autistic by Ritvo *et al.* are not given, it seems likely that they have widened the definition to include many severely retarded children with some elements of the autistic behaviour pattern and this, as Lotter observed, may be the explanation of the difference between these workers' findings and those of other authors.

The parents of the autistic children in Lotter's study did not have a raised prevalence of schizophrenia or other psychotic illness although other forms of mental illness were more common in the parents of Groups A and B as compared with C.

Three (4·8 per cent) of the siblings of children in groups A and B were retarded or disturbed before reaching school age. They had all been described as "psychotic" at one time or another. Two other siblings had had relatively minor behavioural or learning problems and the rest of the total of 86 siblings were not, at the time of the survey, known to have any psychiatric problems.

The Aarhus Survey

Brask (1970) carried out an epidemiological study of children, aged 2 to 14, in the county of Aarhus in Denmark. She screened children in psychiatric, paediatric and retardation services but not those in normal schools. (Lotter found only one autistic child in such a school). The final prevalence rate found by Brask was almost the same as Lotter's. The distribution of intelligence level, severe speech problems and age of onset was closely similar in the two areas. The boy–girl ratio was lower in Aarhus (1·4 to 1), the difference being mainly in the severely retarded group. In both surveys the excess of boys occurred mostly among children of higher intelligence.

In the Aarhus group, there were 24 per cent with epilepsy as against 12 per cent in Middlesex. Brask suggests this is due to the inclusion of older children in Aarhus which is almost certainly true in the light of Rutter's findings of increasing prevalence of fits with increasing age, until one-third have a history of epileptic fits by the time of early adult life (Rutter *et al.*, 1971). More of the Aarhus children had other neurological abnormalities than those in Middlesex. Brask also noted the high prevalence of items of autistic behaviour in the total population of severely retarded children that she screened as part of her study. About 20 per cent of moderately or profoundly retarded children showed either the full or partial picture of autistic behaviour. This is similar to the findings in a study by Wing (1975).

Brask writes in her discussion that she is sceptical of Lotter's finding concerning the higher social class of parents of the autistic children. She remarks on the small size of both samples. In the parents of the Aarhus group she says she found "a small bunch of teachers". Unfortunately she does not give any figures, nor does she say how this compares with the general population of Aarhus County.

The Wisconsin Survey

Treffert (1970) examined details from the case records of all children, aged 12 and under, seen for evaluation and treatment during 1962 to 1967 in 30 centres in Wisconsin (including out-patient and in-patient facilities, special schools and colonies) and given a diagnosis of childhood schizophrenia (which included childhood autism). He found 280 children, which is an age specific prevalence of 3·1 per 10,000. His definitions differed somewhat from those of Lotter and he counted only those children actually diagnosed by the agencies. He did not screen a total population like Lotter or a population of children known to be handicapped as did Brask. Approximately half of the cases identified by Lotter had not been diagnosed as autistic or psychotic before the survey, so that Treffert's method of case finding may be the explanation of the lower rate he found (Lotter, 1967b).

Treffert picked out a sub-group of children he considered to have classic early childhood autism. He defined these strictly on Kanner's criteria but included those with evidence of organic conditions. The age specific prevalence rate for this group was only 0·7 per 10,000 children. There was an excess of college graduates among the fathers of this group (47 per cent as compared with 19 per cent of the parents of the children who did not have the classic syndrome). In the whole group, boys outnumbered girls by 3·4 to 1. The classically autistic group did not differ from the others in this respect. Complications of pregnancy were relatively uncommon both in the group as a whole and among the classically autistic children.

Both Lotter's and Treffert's findings on peri-natal abnormalities differ from those of some other writers who have reported a significantly raised prevalence of pre- and peri-natal complications in autistic or "schizophrenic" children (Gittelman and Birch, 1967; Knobloch and Pasamanick, 1962; Lobascher *et al.*, 1970; Pollack and Woerner, 1966; Rutt and Offord, 1971; Whittam *et al.*, 1966). None of these authors gives detailed descriptions of the types of children included in the studies.

It seems likely that the more widely the term childhood autism is defined the higher will be the prevalence of problems during pregnancy, birth and early infancy.

Treffert did not find any excess of first-born children. In fact, in the classically autistic group, he found an unusually low incidence of first-born males. It is interesting to note that two epidemiological studies (Lotter's and Treffert's) failed to confirm Kanner's finding of a very high prevalence of first-born males (Kanner, 1954). Brask gave no figures on this in her study. Analysis of figures obtained from Lotter, another series of children studied by Pitfield and Oppenheim (1964) and from the early membership of the National Society for Autistic Children (372 children altogether) were in close agreement with each other (Wing, 1966). In the three series, in families of 2 siblings, the first was most likely to be affected, but in families with a large sibship the affected child was more likely to occur in the second half of the sibship. There was no significant overall association with birth rank. It would be interesting to know if Brask's and Treffert's samples showed the same picture.

General conclusions

Taking into account differences in definition and methodology it seems fairly certain that the age specific prevalence of the partial or complete autistic syndrome is between 4 and 5 per 10,000 children. This total group can be divided into a small number of children who function in the normal or mildly retarded range of non-verbal skills and a much larger group who are severely retarded. The former are closest to Kanner's description of his syndrome and comprise the group most likely to show a high boy : girl ratio and, probably, to have parents of a high socio-economic status. Overt neurological abnormality is least common in this group, though a few develop fits by the time of adult life. The precise prevalence of the nuclear, classic Kanner's syndrome is still arguable because it depends upon where the line is drawn. This is a much harder exercise than making a decision, on operational criteria, as to which children show some or all of the elements of the autistic syndrome.

Theories of Aetiology

The current theories can be divided into two main groups: firstly, those concerned with the basic causes of the abnormality and, secondly, those that postulate disturbances in specific psychological or psychophysiological functions whatever the underlying pathology. The different theories are not necessarily mutually exclusive. Thus a genetic mechanism could be responsible for a structural or biochemical abnormality which might interfere with a specific brain function. None of the formulations so far put forward has been worked out in enough detail to show how it could be related to any of the others.

The ideas on aetiology which have received the most attention from workers in the field and those which seem to have some relationship to the known facts will be summarised and discussed.

Theories concerning basic causes

Abnormalities of the psychological environment

These theories pre-suppose that autistic children are potentially normal at birth, but became abnormal because of adverse factors in the psychological climate in which they are reared.

Abnormalities in the parents. Kanner (1943, 1949) described the parents of autistic children as highly intelligent, usually professionally qualified, but unsociable, undemonstrative, formal even in their closest relationships, detached, obsessional and lacking in warmth. Later, Eisenberg (1957b) suggested that these qualities occurred in the fathers rather than in the mothers of autistic children. Kanner discussed parental behaviour in a number of papers, tending to favour the view that the children's problems were inherited from, though perhaps exacerbated by, the parents, rather than caused by the environment they created (Kanner, 1973). In a paper written in 1968, Kanner states "at no time have I pointed to the parents as the primary, post natal sources of pathogenicity".

Subsequent authors have also given descriptions of abnormal

personalities of many different kinds in parents of autistic children, but these accounts tend to be anecdotal rather than experimental or epidemiological (Bettelheim, 1967; Despert, 1951; Goldfarb, 1961; Rank, 1959; Zaslow, 1967).

Creak and Ini (1960) investigated the families of 100 autistic children and did not think that the personalities or attitudes of the parents were particularly abnormal.

Rutter *et al.* (1971) compared classically autistic children whose intelligence, measured on non-language-dependent tests, was in the normal range, with children of the same intelligence level who had developmental receptive "aphasia". The parents of these two groups were investigated, using structured interviews and question-naires. Apart from social class, which was higher in the parents of the autistic children, there were no differences between the parents on measures which included psychiatric illness, obsessionality, emotional warmth towards the child, enthusiasm and empathy. The parents scored above the general population norm for obsessional traits, but there was no difference on this measure between the two groups.

Neurotic or depressive disorders had occurred in about half of the mothers in each group but this was probably a reaction to caring for a young handicapped child.

Kanner's observation that the parents of classically autistic children seen by him were of markedly higher intelligence and occupational level than the average was discussed above. It was pointed out that the disagreements between authors who have in-vestigated this problem, some of whom support Kanner and some of whom do not, may be due to case selection. The more typically autistic children with higher intelligence levels seem to have parents who fit Kanner's description, at least as far as their attainments are concerned, while the parents of the more handicapped, less typical children do not. The findings on higher parental intelligence should be separated from those of abnormal parental personality. There is some acceptable evidence in favour of the former, but, so far, little has been found to support the latter (e.g. see Rutter *et al.*, 1971).

The significance of these findings for theories of aetiology is hard to assess. Intelligence and higher social class are usually considered to be an advantage in coping with life rather than the reverse, and, as shown in the findings of DeMyer *et al.* (1972c) reported below, these attributes are not usually correlated with poor child-rearing practices.

The evidence for theories which consider parental abnormalities to be the primary cause of childhood autism is unconvincing. But the problem remains that Kanner, who observed the children so accurately, was so sure that there were specific characteristics of personality which could be found in many, though certainly not all, of the parents of children whom he diagnosed as autistic. The views of someone with such clinical acumen cannot be dismissed without explanation.

It may be that some parents (especially fathers) of the small group of autistic children who fit Kanner's criteria exactly, do themselves have a partial form of autism. People with the characteristics listed by Kanner do exist, but, in the present author's experience, they are not so much detached from life as puzzled by it and, like autistic children, tend to deal with problems by following the rules with pedantic accuracy. Some of these people closely resemble the description given by Asperger of the condition he called "autistic psychopathy" (Asperger, 1944, 1960) which was mentioned in Chapter 2. Van Krevelen (1971) discussed the possibility that this type of personality could be transmitted genetically. He postulated that the child with early childhood autism might have developed into an "autistic psychopath" but instead has the more severe Kanner's syndrome because of additional organic damage received pre-, peri- or post-natally. It is true that a number of people who appear to fit Asperger's description have autistic children, but often they do not.

I have never met any parents who have brought up their autistic child on a rigid schedule of feeding and with the minimum of handling as described by Kanner, but this may be because no one prescribes these rules for child-rearing any more. When Kanner was originally collecting his cases in the 1930's, rigid time-tabling in the Truby King manner was the fashion and some pedantic, partially autistic parents may have done their best to apply this regime because it was the only guide-line they had.

These are only speculations. In order to investigate the problem, an objective way of identifying this type of personality must be devised and then the epidemiology among parents of autistic children as compared with parents of other handicapped and normal children needs to be studied. Anecdotal evidence is no longer acceptable in this field. What is clear, from the best evidence available, is that the majority of parents of children with autistic behaviour do not conform to the Asperger's personality type.

Even if a specific abnormality can be identified among the parents of a special group of autistic children, a genetic rather than an environmental hypothesis is, on balance, the most likely. It is hard to conceive how the characteristic impairments of language and of other cognitive functions could be caused by environmental factors. It would be difficult to uphold a theory of an environmental cause for one small group of autistic children only, when it is clear that identifiable organic impairments are so frequently associated with the same pattern of behaviour in children outside the nuclear group (see below and Chapter 2) and when even some of the most typical children develop signs of organic involvement with increasing age (Creak, 1963; DeMyer *et al.*, 1973; Kanner, 1973; Rutter, 1970a).

Abnormal child-rearing practices. Kanner (1954) suggested that parents of autistic children had a rigid mechanical approach to child-rearing, but carried out no epidemiological studies to examine this. There have been few studies in this field which have used control groups and objective measures. Pitfield and Oppenheim (1964) used questionnaires to measure attitudes towards child-rearing, such as over-protectiveness, rejection, objectivity and strictness, in the mothers of 100 autistic, 100 normal and 100 Down's syndrome children. Not many differences were found, but the mothers of the Down's syndrome children tended to respond to them "with a little less love and little more detachment and with a firm regime". The mothers of psychotic children "love their children no less than mothers of normal children, but they are in many respects more indulgent. They are also more uncertain in their attitude". The authors felt it was likely that these differences arose primarily from variations in the children rather than from characteristics of the mothers. Gillies *et al.* (1963), using the same questionnaire on the parents of a group of psychotic children, also concluded that the parents did not conform to the statements concerning parental personality made by Kanner (1954) and Goldfarb (1961). These studies can, however, be criticised on the grounds that the use of a questionnaire concerning attitudes is much less informative and reliable than direct measures of child-rearing practices (Rutter, 1967).

DeMyer *et al.* (1972c) studied child-rearing practices retrospectively in parents of autistic children, normal children and children who were brain-damaged and emotionally immature but not autistic. They used lengthy semi-structured interviews with both mothers and fathers to obtain information on various aspects of child-rearing and on the children's behaviour in infancy. They found that the parental theories of the causation of autism were not supported by the results. The parents of the brain-damaged, emotionally immature children were the least stimulating, least warm and had fewest outside social contacts. This may have been explained by the fact that the parents in this group were of lower socio-economic status than those in the other two, owing to problems of matching.

It is relevant to this discussion that children brought up from birth in, for example, an institution run on really mechanical lines with no opportunity to develop a stable relationship with any adult do not seem to run any special risk of developing childhood autism, although there may be personality disorders or, possibly, mental retardation (Rutter, 1972a). There is now a large literature on the subject of deprivation during infancy, with many clinical descriptions (Ainsworth, 1962; Bowlby, 1952; O'Connor, 1956; Pinneau, 1955; Rutter, 1972a; Stein and Susser, 1960; Yarrow, 1961). If there were a causal connection with autism it would have been amply demonstrated. There are some striking clinical histories of children kept in conditions of extreme physical and mental deprivation for long periods. It seems likely, from such evidence as there is, that children who are potentially normal recover remarkably quickly even after years of such treatment. A recent example (Koluchova, 1972) is that of the Czechoslovakian twins who, from the age of $1\frac{1}{2}$ to 7 years, were cruelly ill-treated by their stepmother, kept in a small unheated closet or locked in a cellar and forbidden to talk or play with the other children in the family. They also suffered from lack of adequate food, sunshine, fresh air and exercise.

When they were rescued at 7 years old they had rickets and they could barely walk. They had only a few words and communicated with each other by means of gestures usually used by much younger children. Their play was mainly the manipulation of objects. It was difficult to measure their mental ages but at this stage they appeared to function as severely mentally retarded, with IQ's below 50. They made rapid progress once removed from their grossly abnormal environment, placed with good foster parents and given education. At 8 years 4 months their WISC full scale IQ scores were 80 and 72 respectively and by 11 years they scored 95 and 93. At first the verbal scores were lower than the performance scores but by 11 years this was no longer the case. From the description of their behaviour after they were rescued it is clear that they did not show the pattern found in early childhood autism.

The excellent progress made by the twins should be contrasted with the more limited gains and the lack of generalisation to other environments found in autistic children given concentrated operant conditioning or a structured educational programme over a period of years (Bartak and Rutter, 1973; Lovaas *et al.*, 1973; Rutter and Bartak, 1973). The implications of this story and of some other relevant cases are discussed by Clarke (1972).

Findings of this kind suggest that Victor, the wild boy of Aveyron (see Chapter 1) was abnormal before he was abandoned. The experiments of Harlow (1960, 1961) who deprived infant rhesus monkeys of certain elements of mother care and demonstrated long-term effects on personality do not allow any parallel with autism, even by analogy. The behaviour of the young monkeys did not in any way resemble that of human children with autism as described by Kanner.

Some leading theorists have suggested that autistic behaviour is the result of faulty conditioning from birth (Ferster, 1961; Phillips, 1957). It is extremely difficult to see how faulty conditioning could have given rise to the complex series of specific impairments in cognitive, perceptual, motor, autonomic and vestibular functions found in autistic children. For so many different families from different cultures all over the world to have conditioned into their children the same basic pattern of gross disturbance seems unlikely.

Those who put forward this view do not deal satisfactorily with this point and have produced no concrete evidence for their theories. Ferster (1961) attempted to specify the types of parental responses that would reinforce autistic patterns and diminish the likelihood of the occurrence of normal behaviour. His suggestions were entirely theoretical and have never been substantiated by any experimental studies. He was concerned mostly with the secondary problems such as temper tantrums and self-destructive behaviour and did not even mention the specific language and cognitive problems nor the special skills shown by the children. The most unconvincing part of Ferster's argument is his suggestion that useful speech, including making requests for objects, begins in autistic children and is not reinforced because of parental inattentiveness. This argument ignores the accumulating evidence that autistic children have profound abnormalities of pre-linguistic behaviour (Ricks, 1972; Rutter *et al.*, 1971; Wing, 1971).

One reason for considering that autism is due to faulty conditioning is the fact that autistic children respond to teaching and management based on operant conditioning methods. This argument does not stand up to close examination. The programmes needed for diminishing difficult behaviour and for stimulating the development of language and other skills in autistic children are very different from the way in which most normal children are brought up. To take one small example, it is certainly not necessary to teach motor skills to normal children by guiding their limbs through the movements, whereas this is the only method that works with many autistic children. Furthermore, operant techniques alleviate the problems only while they are being applied and do not cure the basic cognitive impairments (Lovaas *et al.*, 1973).

Abnormalities in the children exacerbated by parental pathology. Theories of this kind are an attempt to deal with the fact that most parents of autistic children have other children who are normal. There is a raised prevalence of autism and other handicaps among the siblings of autistic children (Rutter, 1968) but not enough to give credence to the theory that everything is due to parental abnormality.

The "vulnerable child in an abnormal environment" hypothesis has been put forward by Kanner (1949), Goldfarb (1961, 1964) and O'Gorman (1970). The same arguments that have been advanced against the hypothesis that parental abnormality alone is the cause of autism are also relevant in considering hypotheses of interaction.

Tinbergen and Tinbergen (1972), on the basis of their ethological work, suggested that, in encounters with adults, every infant is initially in a state of conflict between social tendencies and timidity or fear. In normal children, this is solved by the waning of the fear and the eliciting of socially positive responses. An extremely oversensitive, fearful child in a world crowded with strangers would fail to solve the conflict and become more and more fearful. If his parents were insensitive to their child's problems and therefore failed to protect him against too much exposure to strangers, the fear could spread even to social stimuli such as people's faces and smiles. The Tinbergens suggest that the over-arousal resulting from chronic fear could produce the phenomena of autism.

The authors argue by process of analogy from animal to human behaviour, but give no experimental evidence for their hypothesis. They make it clear that they adopt an extremely wide definition of childhood autism, including a state of "temporary autism" which they describe as occurring in some normal children. The main problem in accepting their view, apart from the absence of any evidence, is that, as with so many general theories, it is impossible to see why the particular and very specific collection of abnormalities found in early childhood autism should result from this cause. The authors do not attempt to explain why some children with all the other elements of the syndrome lose their "social withdrawal" quite early in life but still retain the other items of behaviour; nor do they deal with any of the well-substantiated epidemiological findings listed at the beginning of this chapter which have to be taken into account when formulating aetiological hypotheses.

Autistic children are, indeed, very vulnerable to environmental pressures. The problems arise because they need very special and, in effect, abnormal methods of child-rearing to help them compensate for their specific impairments. The usual story is that the parents of an autistic child assume that they have a normal baby whom they try to bring up in the normal way. The autistic child develops a series of secondary behaviour problems because he is not normal and is confused by the talk, social interaction and general give-and-take of normal family life. The parents, in their turn, also react with confusion because of the strange behaviour of their child. They veer between over-permissiveness and inappropriate attempts to impose control. It is only when and if the parents learn, through professional help, or more often, through trial and error, the special techniques that are necessary, that the problems can be alleviated (Copeland and Hodges, 1973; Lovaas *et al.*, 1973; Park, 1968; Rowland, 1972; Schopler and Reichler 1971a).

There are of course some parents who have abnormal personalities and there are some who, though not noticeably abnormal, find that they cannot come to terms with a difficult child. It is also worth pointing out that some people who could be considered to have personalities which deviate markedly from the norm make an excellent job of managing an autistic child although they may not be so successful with their normal offspring. The point is that all these variations can be found among parents of other handicapped children and of normal children too. There is as yet no good evidence that, as a group, the parents of autistic children are more likely to be abnormal in their personalities or behaviour than the parents of other kinds of handicapped children, except in so far as they are affected by the problems presented by their child.

Schopler and Loftin (1969) examined the effect on parents of abnormalities in their child. They found that parents of psychotic children, who were given an object sorting test in the same clinic in which they were being seen for conjoint psychotherapy with their child, had impaired performances as compared with parents of normal children. Other parents of psychotic children, not taking part in conjoint therapy, who were tested after an interview concerning one of their normal children, showed less impairment on the test. The authors felt that poor performance in object sorting did not demonstrate formal thought disorder, but was a function of test anxiety produced by the feeling of being "on trial" as the parent of a disturbed child.

Theories suggesting organic aetiologies

Genetic abnormalities. The possibility of a genetic abnormality was suggested by Kanner (1949). The somewhat raised prevalence of autism in the siblings of autistic children, which is of the order of 2 per cent instead of the 4·5 per 10,000 age specific rate found in the general population (Rutter, 1968) is not sufficient to suggest any obvious, straightforward genetic mechanism.

Rimland (1965) suggested a genetically determined over-sensitivity to oxygen given at birth, but no evidence to support this is available.

The theory linking early childhood autism with an inherited personality type called by Asperger "autistic psychopathy" has already been mentioned in the discussion on parental personality traits. Böök *et al.*, (1963) did not find any specific chromosomal abnormalities in their study of 11 children, some of whom were autistic. At present one can say only that there is no convincing evidence for or against a genetic abnormality.

Relationship of autism to "brain damage". A number of conditions which damage the central nervous system may precede the development of the autistic pattern of behaviour. The evidence concerning perinatal complications is conflicting (see above). Chess (1971) found that the prevalence of autistic behaviour following maternal rubella was 10 times that of the expected rate in the general population. A history of infantile spasms may be followed by autistic behaviour (Kolvin *et al.*, 1971d; Taft and Cohen, 1971; Wing, 1975). An early history of encephalitis or meningitis and conditions such as tuberose sclerosis and phenylketonuria may also be associated with the autistic pattern of behaviour in complete or partial form (Wing, 1975). Rutter (1970 a) reported that, by the time of adult life, one-third of a group of autistic children who were followed up from early childhood to adolescence and early adult life had at some time had epileptic fits. A very small number of children in Rutter's group showed marked cognitive and physical deterioration in adolescence. In general, follow-up studies have shown that EEG abnormalities, fits and other signs of neurological dysfunction increase as the children grow older even in those who appeared to have no additional handicaps when first diagnosed (Creak, 1963; Rutter, 1970a). Lotter (1966, 1967), in his epidemiological study, found that nearly one-third of the children he identified as autistic had recorded evidence suggestive of neurological abnormality.

There is therefore good evidence for the presence of detectable neurological abnormalities in a sizeable minority of children with autistic behaviour. These tend to be the ones who have more severe handicaps and who function as severely retarded. The children with most skills and with the most classic nuclear syndromes are less likely to have clear evidence of gross pathology. Thus, of Kanner's original 11 children (Kanner, 1973), 2 developed epileptic fits by the time of adult life, that is 18 per cent as compared with Rutter's 33 per cent. It seems not unreasonable to suggest that even the classically autistic children may have some abnormality of brain function too limited to be detectable on currently available tests (which in any case are extremely crude and unreliable) but which underlies their behaviour problems.

The fact that most "brain damaged" children are not autistic suggests that, if there is an abnormality of brain structure or function in autism, it must be very localised and specific in nature. There is no firm evidence as to the possible site or nature of this hypothesised abnormality, although some suggestions have been made, including a lesion in or lack of development of the association areas (Crawley, 1971), the dominant hemisphere (Hermelin, 1966; Ricks, 1972) or the parts of the brain concerned with language (Wing, 1969).

Sub-cortical lesions. Lesions in sub-cortical areas have also been suggested by some workers. Gellner (1959) worked out a theory to account for a variety of impairments found in children with severe learning problems including those with early childhood autism. She postulated that the lesions (complete or partial) accounting for visual and auditory perceptual problems occurred in the corpora quadrigemina, the medial and lateral geniculate bodies, and tracts carrying exteroceptive, proprioceptive and interoceptive impulses to and from these ganglia. These tracts and ganglia are situated in close proximity to the great cerebral vein and its small tributaries and may be injured by rupture of the latter, which can occur as a result of trauma during birth. Gellner believed that specific lesions in these areas could be linked to specific patterns of impairments. In particular she felt that incoming sensory stimuli were given meaning only when they were integrated with interoceptive impulses from the autonomic system. If a lesion completely or partially interrupted this integration, then severe problems of comprehension would be the result. She worked out the possible patterns of pathology and the resulting impairments in great detail. Her hypotheses are highly speculative and unproven, but at least they have the virtue, in contrast to many other theories, of attempting to explain the important items in the clinical picture of autism and related syndromes, and could be tested if there were adequate means of assessing damage in the relevant areas.

MacCulloch and Sambrooks (1972) also considered the possibility of sub-cortical brain damage and suggested a lesion in and around the head of the nucleus of the tractus solitarius in the posterior brain stem, which, according to Bonvallet and Allen (1963), who studied the results of damaging this area in the cat, is a bulbar inhibitory centre. MacCulloch and Sambrooks postulate that such a lesion, caused by birth trauma, could release from damping much of the ascending reticular formation's activity. This would lead to disturbance of perceptual processes and to cortical arousal which would produce many behavioural abnormalities. The authors suggest neurophysiological studies to test this hypothesis. The main problem is, as usual, the difficulty in linking the lesion and its consequences with the specific pattern of impairments and special skills found in classically autistic children. MacCulloch and Williams (1971) found a significantly greater heart rate variability under conditions of free exploration in autistic as compared with subnormal and normal children. This was felt to be evidence in favour of the aetiological theory described above, but the criteria for diagnosing and selecting the autistic children were not made clear.

Dysfunction of the vestibular system. MacCulloch and Sambrooks postulated that the brain stem lesion could affect the vestibular system, thus linking their hypothesis with that of Ornitz and Ritvo (1968b). These workers have examined vestibular function and REM sleep in children with autism and other childhood psychoses. They suggest that the mechanisms, which, in normal people, regulate the episodes of phasic excitation and inhibition in REM sleep, are disrupted in autistic children and that this disruption breaks into the waking life of the children, in the form of behavioural hyperexcitation alternating with inhibition. The authors postulate that the vestibular system is involved in this abnormality. This work is difficult to evaluate because of the authors' all-inclusive attitude towards diagnosis (see Ornitz and Ritvo, 1968a) and the recurring problem of relating a theory postulating a non-specific behavioural abnormality to a syndrome with a specific pattern of impairments and skills.

Abnormalities of the reticular system. Deslauriers and Carlson (1969) have put forward another model also involving the interaction between two systems. They believe that there is an imbalance between the classical arousal system and the limbic, mid-brain arousal system which is concerned with reward and motivation, so that the child is, functionally, in a state of sensory deprivation.

A number of other writers have outlined theories implicating the reticular activating system. Hutt and Hutt and their colleagues (Hutt *et al.*, 1964, 1965; Hutt and Hutt, 1970) suggest, from their EEG studies, that the phenomena of childhood autism are related to over-arousal.

The classic autistic child's ability to reproduce past experiences in the precise form in which they first occurred has already been commented upon in Chapter 2. Rimland (1965) suggested that the function of the reticular formation is to "unscramble" incoming messages and to imbue them with meaning, "so that they can trigger relevant memories in the mind of the listener" while the direct sensory tracts to the cortex via the thalamus transmit messages in concrete, literal, rather than coded form. The basic impairment in early childhood autism might be an abnormality, perhaps under-arousal, of the reticular system, so that it could code only in a limited, literal way. In such a child "only an exceedingly small range of neurones would be activated and only a very limited variety of responses would be evoked". The child's responses would be virtually identical to the original input. As mentioned previously,

Rimland thought that the basic cause of this abnormality might be a genetically determined over-sensitivity to oxygen inhaled at birth.

This is an interesting idea since it is an attempt to explain the cognitive and language abnormalities and perhaps also the unusual responses to sensory input described in Chapter 2. There is, however, no evidence to support it and Rimland's view of the function of the reticular formation is highly speculative and not in accordance with the views of most neurophysiologists.

Rimland's theory can be compared with that of Gellner (see above) who also tried to deal with the problem of how words and other sensory inputs are imbued with meaning. These ideas will be discussed in more detail in Chapter 4.

Hermelin and O'Connor (1970) discussed the problems inherent in attempts to relate elements of behaviour to central arousal in the present state of knowledge. In their own experimental work they recorded alpha waves from the occipital region in 10 autistic, 10 Down's syndrome and 10 normal children. As the authors explain, the 8–13 c.p.s. alpha rhythm recorded from the occipital region has been regarded as indicating the level of alertness. In a waking subject, the EEG pattern becomes faster and less regular with arousal. In a drowsy subject, however, slower EEG waves can be replaced by the alpha rhythm if interest or attention is aroused. There was no evidence for over-arousal in the autistic children's resting records. They showed a relative lack of sustained arousal to intermittent visual stimulation, but were relatively more aroused by a continuous sound than the other children. The authors concluded from this that to talk of a generally high or low level of arousal in autistic children is too simplified a view. They also point out that the EEG provides only one measure of arousal and it is not known whether, in autistic children, it correlates with other relevant indices, such as levels of activity in the autonomic system.

Arousal mechanisms have been associated with many other psychiatric conditions as well as autism, though so far rather non-specifically. There may well be abnormalities of arousal in autistic children, but these are as likely to be secondary to other abnormalities as they are to be primary. In any case it is difficult to explain the specific pattern of impairments and skills found in autism on the basis of anything as generalised as over- or under-arousal.

Retardation of maturation. Finally, under the heading of abnormalities of the central nervous system, the possibility should be mentioned that slowness of development of some brain function, rather than brain damage or other pathology, may possibly be the cause in a few children, especially those who make rapid progress after showing autistic behaviour in their early years.

Simon and Gillies (1964) found evidence of retardation in height, weight and bone age measurements in 44 psychotic children. Bender (1956) postulated that childhood schizophrenia might be explained by a maturational lag during embryonic development. Fish (1971) has carried out a series of investigations over more than 20 years, including prospective studies of children born to schizophrenic mothers. She reported an abnormally uneven development leading to disturbances of central nervous integration in infants who later became schizophrenic.

The problem in interpreting all this work is that the authors do not give clear descriptions of the children they are studying so that the diagnoses remain in doubt. With Fish's work, it is especially likely that the children studied were not classically autistic, since she studied children of schizophrenic mothers. As the work described earlier in this chapter has shown, the incidence of schizophrenia is not raised above the expected level in parents of typically autistic children, in contrast to the parents of those children who have schizophrenia following the pattern of the adult illness.

Biochemical abnormalities. Some investigations have been made in this field. Siva Sankar (1969) studied 30 different biochemical variables in a group of hospitalised children described as schizophrenic, 30 of whom were said to be autistic. The autistic children differed from the others on many variables and also differed from adult schizophrenic patients. They had more manifest biological deviations and had the lowest rate of variation of biological parameters with increasing age, suggesting continuing biological immaturity. The results must be viewed with caution because the children were all institutionalized, and no descriptions of the children's behaviour, or of their neurological and psychological impairments, or their skills were given.

Abnormal tryptophan metabolism has been reported by Heeley and Roberts (1965). Boullin *et al.* (1970, 1971) examined the ability to retain serotonin in the blood platelets in a group of children and found that it was defective in those who were rated as having Kanner's syndrome on Rimland's questionnaire (Rimland, 1968). Himwich *et al.* (1972) found urinary excretion of bufotenin in 5 out of 6 "possibly autistic" children.

Goodwin *et al.* (1971) noticed the occurrence of coeliac disease and similar disorders in some autistic children. They investigated a number of variables related to malabsorption and cerebral dysfunction in autistic children, their normal siblings, other normal children, adults with schizophrenia and with other psychiatric conditions, and normal adults. The results in the autistic children supported the hypothesis that this condition is different from schizophrenia and suggested a fundamental neurobiological dysfunction in autism with a possible correlation with malabsorption.

Rimland (1971) postulated that autistic children have markedly atypical metabolism with regard to vitamins. No proof of this hypothesis is available as yet.

DeMyer *et al.* (1971c) examined free fatty acid response to insulin and glucose stimulation and found significantly greater variability in psychotic as compared with emotionally disturbed or normal children. They suggested that the explanation might be "a deficiency of the regulatory feedback mechanism at a neurogenic or cellular level". They discussed the relevance of this finding in the light of the possible importance of free fatty acid for brain growth in the neonatal period.

The work in the field of biochemistry is at present hard to interpret because of the poverty of clinical data concerning the children studied, lack of repetition of experiments by other workers and the difficulty of knowing how to relate biochemical abnormalities to the details of the clinical syndrome.

Theories concerning impairments of psychological or psychophysiological functions

The ideas to be discussed in this section are not concerned with the primary causes of early childhood autism, but are attempts to define the functions that are impaired. Nevertheless they have a place in this chapter since, if the underlying impairments of function were to be accurately identified, this would provide valuable clues to the original aetiology.

Abnormality of emotional development

As discussed in Chapter 2, Kanner believed that an abnormality of emotional development was the fundamental impairment in early childhood autism. He considered that the children were born without the ability to make affective contact with other people, or, presumably, lost it if they had an early period of normal development before becoming autistic.

While there is no doubt that the children do have problems in relating to others, the concept of a deficiency of affect is much too global. The behaviour in the children leading to poor social relationships can be analysed in some detail. DeMyer *et al.* (1972b) pointed out that autistic children were co-operative in tasks when the situation was simplified so that they knew what was required of them. Hermelin and O'Connor (1970) found that young autistic children were just as likely as non-autistic controls matched for age and intelligence to approach and make physical contact with a strange adult, as long as the adult did not talk. Unlike the controls, however, the autistic children paid no attention to the adult when she asked questions or gave simple commands. So-called "gaze avoidance" loses its significance as evidence for emotional abnormality when it is seen to be part of a general problem of short visual fixation in relation to all visual input (O'Connor and Hermelin, 1967). The same authors noted the problem that autistic children have in executing expressive gestures as shown by the Illinois Test of Psycholinguistic Ability and concluded that "the absence of expressive gestures is not confined to the social situation, but must be regarded as a more general disability in performing a specific skill" (Hermelin and O'Connor, 1970).

Reichler and Schopler (1971) examined the level of relatedness to other humans and a number of perceptual variables in a group of psychotic children. Their results supported the view that impairments of human relatedness could be accounted for in terms of impairment in perceptual functions. Much of the inappropriate behaviour of the mothers could also be explained as a response to the perceptual abnormalities in the children.

Another quotation from Hermelin and O'Connor (1970) sums up the argument very well. "We would suggest that it might be fruitful to look at the social and interpersonal behaviour of autistic children in terms of the absence of simple skills which are basic to the more complex skills involved in social and linguistic behaviour."

Abnormalities of cognitive development affecting language and the ability to use symbols

Abnormality in the way language is used is one of the diagnostic features of early childhood autism. There is disagreement on the significance of this fact, and some authors (including Kanner, 1943) have suggested that autistic children are potentially able to understand and speak normally, but there is no disagreement on the observation that the children often fail to respond to speech and may be mute or use speech in abnormal ways.

A number of workers feel that cognitive problems leading to difficulties in handling symbols in any modality and in understanding and using language are the fundamental impairments which underlie the autistic syndrome. Their guess is that the basic pathology, when it is discovered, will be directly related to these abnormalities. This question will be explored in detail in Chapters 4 and 5.

Abnormalities of perception and attention

Another striking aspect of the behaviour of autistic children is the abnormality of response to all kinds of sensory stimuli. As emphasised previously, there are many points of resemblance between the behaviour seen in autism and that in the developmental receptive speech disorders and in congenital partial blindness combined with partial deafness, especially if due to maternal rubella (Wing, 1969). Autistic children, even more than these other groups, have odd and contradictory responses to sensory input, including inattention, fascination and distress which may all be seen in the same sensory modality and in the same child.

It is tempting to suggest that these odd responses are the outward signs of a fundamental impairment in the central reception of sensory information, particularly from the ears and eyes and that this impairment can explain all the other aspects of the syndrome. The difficulty with accepting this view is that autistic children seem to have problems in handling symbols and concepts even if they do learn to speak, read or write. A number of autistic children are able to acquire these mechanical skills, which argues against any marked perceptual problem, but they lack appreciation of the meaning of the symbols. This applies to any modality in which learning may take place (see Chapter 5). Furthermore, a small number of children with the classic features described by Kanner show only minimal evidence of abnormal response to sensory input but they still have the characteristic problems with handling complex symbols and fully understanding their meaning. Nevertheless, any theory of autism must be able to explain the behaviour suggestive of abnormality in handling incoming information, since it occurs so commonly among the whole group of affected children, especially in their early years.

Lovaas, Koegal and their colleagues have investigated problems of perception and attention in the course of their work on behaviour modification. They have found that "autistic children characteristically respond to only one component of a complex stimulus; that is, they operate on a very restricted range of stimulus control" (Koegal and Schreibmann, 1974; Lovaas and Koegal, 1973). Learning problems in autistic children, including problems in the learning of word meanings, might result from their stimulus overselectivity, since adequate learning in many situations depends upon the ability to respond to multiple stimuli.

Koegal and Covert (1972) found evidence that ritualistic

stereotyped behaviour, such as rocking, hand flapping, or twirling objects, interfered with learning. In attempting to interpret these results, they linked them to those of stimulus overselectivity and suggested that the children selectively attend to their own self-stimulation and not to the discrimination task. The almost perfect inverse relationship between the occurrence of self-stimulation and correct responding was in favour of this hypothesis.

These findings may well be related to the clinical observation that autistic children tend to select one trivial aspect of an object or a scene for attention and ignore the rest. One child who enjoyed assembling pieces of meccano often made shapes which he said were familiar objects but which were in fact only a small part of the whole. His duffle coat was represented by the angle where the arm joined the shoulder and a "dog" was an oblong for the body without head, legs or tail. Another child searched mail order catalogues for pictures of the on-off switches on electrical apparatus and a third was absorbed by church steeples and refused to look at any other picture. Stories of children becoming upset when adults they know wear a different necklace or use a different perfume, whereas other major changes pass unnoticed, may be due to this narrow concentration on one or a few stimuli.

The prevalence of this type of behaviour among autistic children, its relationship to other aspects of autistic behaviour and the underlying abnormality of brain function which could explain it, are all problems which would repay further exploration.

Problems of imitating body actions

The autistic child's problems in imitating movements made by other people is often in marked contrast to his relative adequacy in spontaneous movement. This may have a profound effect on the development of social relationships and ability to communicate. The earliest communication between a mother and child occurs in non-verbal ways, and the baby's ability to imitate the mother's movements, such as smiling, clapping hands and waving, reinforces the interaction (DeMyer *et al.*, 1972b).

The significance of the deficiency of imitation in autistic children and the possible relationship to the language and perceptual problems will be dealt with in detail in Chapter 6.

Conclusions

Environmental theories, although they have roused considerable interest especially among lay people, still have not been supported by any firm experimental evidence. This is in marked contrast to the findings in the field of delinquency. The importance of the family and social environment in the causation of anti-social behaviour has been clearly demonstrated in a large number of independent studies (Rutter, 1972a). No such consensus has been reached with regard to early childhood autism. In general, well-controlled studies have failed to show any specific abnormalities of personality or of child-rearing practices among groups of parents. On the other hand, there is a large measure of agreement that the autistic pattern of behaviour is associated with identifiable neurological abnormalities in a substantial minority of the affected children, even if the diagnosis is made using fairly strict criteria.

It seems likely that many different organic conditions can give rise to autistic behaviour, perhaps because they sometimes, by chance, involve a specific area of the brain or disturb a specific brain function. It may be that classic nuclear early childhood autism as described by Kanner represents the result of the smallest possible lesion, the nature of which is still in doubt. Other syndromes, including those found among severely mentally retarded children, may consist of the "nuclear lesion" associated with additional impairments, perhaps because the organic pathology has affected contiguous areas of the brain or closely related functions. It is also possible that there are a whole series of different syndromes, completely unrelated to each other, and that the behavioural resemblances are of spurious significance. The truth may, in the end, prove to be a mixture of both these hypotheses.

CHAPTER 4

LANGUAGE, COMMUNICATION AND
THE USE OF SYMBOLS

DEREK M. RICKS and LORNA WING

Definitions of Terms

The definitions of words such as language, speech and communication are still under debate among linguists (Mackay, 1972; Lyons, 1972). Different views are adopted depending upon the interests and purposes of the workers concerned. The issues are exceedingly complex and any system of classification that is used involves many assumptions. Nevertheless, when discussing abnormalities of language development in children, which can affect different aspects of communication independently of each other, it is necessary to accept a set of working definitions in order to avoid confusion. This can be done while still recognising that most of the subtleties and complexities of the subject have been by-passed.

The terms *symbol* and *symbolic* appear frequently in discussions of language. The *Shorter Oxford English Dictionary* (1968) gives several definitions of which the most relevant for the present purpose is "something that stands for, represents, or denotes something else, not by exact resemblance, but by vague suggestion or by some accidental or conventional relation".

The term *concept* will also be used in the discussions in this chapter. The most relevant definition given for this word in the same dictionary is "an idea of a class of objects".

Language will be used as defined by Sheridan (1972) to mean the symbolisation or codification of concepts for the purpose of self-communication regarding past, present and future events and for interpersonal communication, the latter involving both reception and expression. In order to merit the term "language" the symbols used must have a systematic relationship to each other, allowing for the creation of an infinite number of new messages which are understandable to all those with an adequate command of that language (Lenneberg, 1967).

The system of symbols making up a language can be received or expressed in various non-vocal forms as well as in sounds. These include written words, the Morse code, Semaphore, Braille, and the various systematic sign languages used by the deaf. Some of the systems, for example Morse, utilise visible or audible signs for letters so that individual words can be spelt out in ways that are analogous to conventional writing. Others, for example some of the sign languages of the deaf, have signs for whole words or concepts.

Vygotsky (1962) discussed an important aspect of language usually called *inner language* and defined it as "speech for oneself" which helps one to orient, to understand and to overcome difficulties. Sheridan (1972), describing inner language in children, referred to it as "that repository of concept-in-code upon which the decoding of incoming messages and the encoding of outgoing communications depend".

Speech is "the use of systematised vocalisations to express verbal symbols or words" (Sheridan, 1972). As Rutter (1972c) pointed out, speech may also be used to refer to the process of articulation, so it is necessary to make the distinction clear when discussing speech disorders.

When working with autistic children it is appropriate to distinguish between *spontaneous speech*, which will be used here to mean the vocalisation of concepts generated by the speaker and *echolalic speech*, which is the production of words that are an exact or partial copy of those originally spoken by another person. The echoing may be *immediate* or *delayed* for varying periods of time. It is sometimes difficult to tell whether speech is echolalic or spontaneous, especially when it is used in contexts where it appears to be appropriate (see below) but the distinction has to be borne in mind when evaluating the level of development of language in an autistic child.

The understanding and use of language involves a number of

different components, all of which must operate smoothly for perfect performance.

To illustrate this, the different ways in which the understanding and use of speech can be impaired will be summarized. Detailed descriptions of developmental speech problems have been given by Ingram (1959, 1969, 1972).

First of all, hearing must be adequate to cope with the variations in the pitch and volume of human speech. Then the brain must be able to recognise as words the sounds that are heard. Difficulties at this point are known as *receptive* speech problems.

The next stage is the linking of these words with the appropriate associations stored in symbolic form, which is necessary for complete understanding of the meaning of what is heard.

If a reply is intended, the words for this reply must be brought to mind in readiness for speaking. Problems in doing this are described as *expressive*.

Then the muscles of speech must be organised to *articulate* the words in a way which is intelligible to the hearer. Defects in articulation can be produced by a wide variety of abnormalities, including those affecting the brain, the motor nerves, the muscles used for speech, and the anatomy of the mouth.

A similar analysis could be made of the components of other forms of language such as writing or Braille. Impairments can occur at any point in the chain and may disturb one or more of the necessary functions.

Abnormalities may affect predominantly one aspect of language only, for example speech, or they may be more widespread. Diagnosis of language problems involves disentangling the different elements in order to identify which are impaired and which are still intact.

Communication is a more general term than language or speech and is used to refer to the transmission of information by any means, not only through a system of symbols. Mackay (1972) argues that the term should be restricted in certain ways, including limiting its use to interactions in which the signals from one organism are goal-directed towards another. Mackay acknowledges all the difficulties in deciding whether or not an act can be called "intentional" but believes that it is important to recognise the difference between directed and undirected activity even though the latter may have considerable effects upon other organisms. He suggests that goal-directed activity is distinguished by the fact that the organism emitting the signal evaluates the response produced in the target and then modifies its behaviour in consequence. A relevant example would be that of two children both of whom make the remark "Where's that ball gone?". Child A ceases to repeat these words, looks pleased and holds out his hands when his mother finds the ball and gives it to him. Child B, who has a severe language problem, continues to repeat the words regardless of the response they elicit. This behaviour may eventually be modified when the adults concerned work out the contingencies associated with it and carry out a programme aimed at its extinction. It would seem reasonable to define child A's behaviour as goal-directed communication, but to be extremely cautious about interpreting the "intentions" of child B although his behaviour did in fact produce responses in other people. This discussion is of interest because some people working with autistic children have been tempted to suggest that the children are intending to communicate by means of their stereotyped movements, their rituals or even their mutism. It is worth trying to estimate just how far these abnormal behaviour patterns are goal-directed even if the question is difficult to answer.

Communication includes both the use of language and of a variety of other signals, some of which are not sufficiently systematised to be classified as language, using the definition given above. The latter are often referred to collectively as *non-verbal communication*. Argyle (1972) classified the kinds of non-verbal communication used by humans under ten headings; bodily contact, proximity, orientation (the angle at which people sit or stand in relation to each other), appearance (including clothing), posture, head nods, facial expression, gestures, looking (eye contact) and non-verbal aspects of speech produced by variations in pitch, stress, timing and volume. He also suggested that non-verbal communication has three different functions; (a) to communicate attitudes and emotions and to manage the immediate social situation, (b) to support and complement verbal communication, with for example head nods, emphatic gestures, appropriate pauses while speaking, gestures illustrating size and shape, (c) to replace language. This last category cannot be accepted within the definition of terms used in this chapter without considerable qualification, since a systematised sign language with signs for letters or words should properly be called a *verbal*, although non-spoken, *language.* Some other sets of signs, such as the simple sign system devised for retarded, non-speaking, spastic children (Levett, 1970) are too unsystematic and limited in scope to be defined as languages, but are still *verbal*, because each sign precisely represents a word or a short phrase. On the other hand, gestures of greeting and goodwill made from a distance, or meaning looks exchanged by listeners when someone else is speaking could be called examples of non-verbal substitutes for language when they do not have precise verbal equivalents.

No system of classification is perfect, so it must be accepted that it is not always easy to draw the line between gestures which are "verbal" and those which are "non-verbal". The "thumbs up" sign, for example, always signifies that things are going well but, on the other hand, may convey approval, acknowledgement of information received, or that an action has been successfully completed, depending on the circumstance. This point may appear to be of academic interest only, but it has special relevance when considering children with language problems, some of whom use simple and limited forms of communication. It is of considerable interest to decide if any of these forms of communication have precise verbal equivalents. If a non-speaking child is using signs in this way he has achieved a most important step in his development which can be utilised for teaching and for management of behaviour.

Another important distinction to be made when observing children with language problems is that between non-verbal communication which is symbolic and that which is non-symbolic or *concrete*. Pointing to an object from a distance, to indicate interest in it or a desire to hold it, is symbolic though non-verbal. Pushing away or striking another person can, at least in some circumstances, be described as concrete, although these gestures can sometimes be used as symbols. Some severely handicapped children are limited to concrete gestures only, which is a very low level of development in the area of communication.

Aspects of the Development of Communication in Normal Children

Much work has been done on the development of language and social communication in normal children, especially in recent years when there has been a rapid expansion of interest in linguistics. Only those aspects which are of special relevance to language in autistic children will be mentioned here.

The descriptions of normal babies and young children are based on those by Sheridan (1973) and Egan *et al.* (1969); unless otherwise stated.

The development of non-verbal communication

Early vocalisation and gestures

Although children do not usually begin to use words before the second year of life, non-verbal communication is much in evidence in the first year. It may be difficult to determine just when in the early weeks vocalisations become "goal-directed" in MacKay's sense, but, by about 9 months, the normal baby is clearly using his voice to attract attention, express emotion and to engage in social exchanges with familiar adults. Crystal (1970) noted the use of intonation to convey meaning from about 9 months onward. Understanding of non-verbal communication develops earlier than its use and, by 6 months, response can be seen to the mother's tone of voice which may convey affection, irritation, an invitation to play, and so on.

The use of simple gestures for communication, such as smiling and pointing, waving, lifting arms before being picked up, also precede the onset of speech. By 12 months, for example, normal babies point to things that interest them, making excited noises and looking round to attract the attention of the mother.

Expression of emotion in sounds

Ricks (1972, 1975) investigated the way in which normal babies express emotional meaning in their intoned (not articulated) vocalisations. The sounds made by 10 babies aged 8 months to 1 year, whose development appeared to be normal, were tape-recorded by their parents. Six of the families were English and four were from non-English speaking countries. The parents of the latter spoke only their native tongue at home. Recordings were made in four types of situation which would be expected to elicit sounds with a specific emotional quality, as follows:

1. Requesting (e.g. seeing a meal being prepared),
2. Frustration (e.g. seeing a meal that was witheld),
3. Greeting (e.g. on first seeing mother in the morning),
4. Pleasant surprise (e.g. seeing a balloon or a lighted sparkler).

Each family persisted until satisfied that sounds had been recorded in all four situations. The English parents were then asked to listen to the tapes made from their own baby, two other English babies and one non-English baby. They were not told which was which but were asked to identify the meaning of the message, the situation in which the sound has been recorded, which was their own child and which the non-English child.

The parents accurately identified the sounds made in the four situations, that is to say, they understood the message conveyed. They had, of course, prior knowledge that there were only four possible choices, but, nevertheless, the results were very clear-cut. What was surprising was that they could not, from the individual sounds, pick out either their own or the non-English baby significantly better than chance. It could tentatively be suggested that the intoned sounds with which babies express needs and feelings are in-built and universal, not learned. How these vocalisations relate to the later development of non-verbal communication and to verbal language is still unknown, but the findings are of considerable interest, especially when compared with those in autistic children which will be described later.

The development of speech

Comprehension of speech

Normal babies begin to comprehend the meaning of words relating to familiar objects and events by the end of the first year. As mentioned previously they also begin to obey very simple instructions when accompanied by gestures.

Onset of speech

In addition to the noises expressing emotions, babbling involving the use of vowel and consonant combinations of increasing complexity develops throughout the first year. Towards the end of this time the normal baby uses jargon with intonation like that of conversation. The exact nature of the relationship between babble and speech is still a matter of speculation. Ricks (1972) described the onset of speech in normal children. He observed that the first words (excluding da da and ma ma sounds) appeared suddenly in the child's vocalisations and were associated with some definite and (to the child) striking event. The examples he gave included the child noticing an aeroplane, the pet dog or the noise made by a cuckoo-clock. The children who were observed produced an articulated sound in response to the particular event which excited them, such as "bow-wow" for dog or "uck-uck" for cuckoo-clock. These sounds did not appear in babble but occurred only when the relevant stimuli were presented. They were clearly used to indicate specific subjects although they were not conventionally accepted words. They will therefore be referred to as "sound-labels".

With repeated usage the sound-label was not modified to become the same as the adult word. Instead, the parents usually adopted the child's own pronunciation.

Once the sound-label had been used by the child, it tended, over a few days, to be generalised, suggesting that the child was forming his own concept or classification scheme, which was often different from any scheme adopted by adults. Thus "uck-uck" came to refer to any kind of dial and "bow-wow" to any four legged animal.

Jespersen (1922) described similar generalisations made by the young children he observed. He mentioned one child who used the sound-label "bing", thought to be a corruption of "bang", to mean a door, a brick, and any building made of bricks.

It was very noticeable that the children used these first sound-labels with enormous zeal and enthusiasm. If the same sound was spoken by an adult, the child at once alerted, looked round for the appropriate object, and said the sound himself. It may well be that the parents adopted the child's sound-label because this enthusiastic response was so delightful that it acted as a potent reward. In a further experiment, Ricks made tape recordings of the parents repeating their own child's first sound-labels and he also recorded a stranger imitating the parents. The children showed a more marked alerting response to the recording made by their own parents. In general, the children who showed the most obvious enthusiasm and excitement in relation to their first sound-labels were those who were the most chatty and the most generally responsive.

Development of grammar

By the age of 5 most normal children are able to use the basic grammatical structures, although they continue to widen their vocabulary and increase the complexity of their speech throughout childhood. It is suggested by some linguists that children become competent with language because the human brain has an in-built capacity to extract rules from the speech heard as part of everyday experience (Brown, 1965; Lenneberg, 1967; McNeill, 1966). Children have to learn the language of their own culture but these workers believe that the rules are demonstrably *not* learnt by a process of conditioning. They suggest that, at each stage of his development, the child extracts a different set of rules. Each stage is more complex than the previous one, but each is complete in itself and not just an incomplete version of adult grammar. Eventually, the stage is reached when the rules are the same as those adopted by the adults with whom the maturing child is in contact. Each child appears to make his own theories about the rules governing language on the basis of his own personal experiences. However, the stages of acquisition of grammar are similar among different normal children, suggesting that the human brain is organised to extract certain types of rules, which may possibly be fundamental to any human language. The rapid development of language in normal children, and their ability to use the more complex sets of rules to generate an infinite number of new sentences never used or heard by them before, fit much better with the above theories than with those of Skinner (1973) who argued in favour of the major importance of conditioning in the development of all human skills. One example of the difficulty of explaining language acquisition on operant conditioning alone is the ease with which normal children learn to use pronouns such as "you" and "me" appropriately. They can hardly do this by straightforward copying, since this would produce the pronominal reversal noted in the speech of autistic children. Neither do parents of normal children have to work out elaborate programmes of rewards and punishments to teach this remarkable skill.

The development of inner language

Sheridan (1969) suggested that the beginnings of inner language can be seen in the normal child around 12 months of age, at the same time as he is beginning to understand a few words in context. At this stage he shows that he understands the use of real everyday objects by applying them to himself, for example brushing his own hair with a brush. By 18 months he uses the objects appropriately in relation to other people or pets and, by 2 years he is able to use correctly miniature objects such as a doll's tea set.

The further development of inner language can be seen as play becomes more and more complex. It reveals the level at which the child is able to symbolise and abstract and how far he can understand new events by matching them against his coded store of past experiences, using this comparison as a basic for appropriate action.

In older children and adults this store of inner experience is no longer revealed in play, but may be judged on conversation, observations of behaviour and knowledge of the interests of the person concerned.

The Development of Communication in Autistic Children

The development of non-verbal communication

Although some mothers of autistic children report that they felt that there was something wrong almost from birth, a firm diagnosis of early childhood autism is rarely made before the end of the second year at the earliest. Therefore there are no reports of systematic observations on babies who later show the autistic pattern and the only evidence on behaviour in the first year of life is anecdotal and retrospective. This is a great pity, since details of the prelinguistic development of these children would be most valuable.

In a study of 27 autistic children aged 6 to 15 (Wing, 1971) parents completed a retrospective questionnaire concerning the children's behaviour in the first year of life. Fourteen were thought to have been abnormal from birth and of these 10 did not lift their arms to ask to be picked up, 7 showed little response to the sound of their mother's voice and 11 did not point things out for their parents to look at. The same problems were also reported in some of the children who were supposed to have had an onset of autism after the age of one year. These findings are in marked contrast to the normal baby's behaviour.

Expression of emotion in sounds

Ricks (1972, 1975) studied 8 autistic children aged between 3 and 5 years 11 months and 3 children aged 5 to 8 years who were retarded but not autistic. None of them had begun to use any verbal labels. The parents tape recorded the noises their children made to express the same feelings as in the study with normal babies described above; that is requesting, frustration, greeting and pleased surprise. The parents of the autistic children were then asked to listen to a recording of their own child, two other autistic children and one retarded but non-autistic child. As in the study of normal babies, the parents had to try to identify each of the four messages, which was their own child and which was the non-autistic child.

The results were very different from those found with normal babies. The parents could identify their own child with ease. They also had no problem in picking out which was the non-autistic retarded child whom they said "sounded normal". They understood the messages conveyed by their own child and the non-autistic child but not those of the other two autistic children. The sounds made by the autistic children were articulated, whereas those of the normal babies were intoned.

From this, it appears that autistic children can express at least the four emotions elicited in the experiment, but they have a personal, idiosyncratic way of doing this and do not use the expressive noises which Ricks' work suggests are common to normal babies.

This abnormality of expressive sound does not seem to be due to mental retardation since the retarded children who did not have autistic behaviour expressed their feelings in the same way as normal babies. It is impossible to say from these results whether the autistic children had had normal, intoned, expressive sounds as babies but developed the idiosyncratic, articulated methods of expression at a later stage. In the present authors' clinical experience, however, some parents do remember finding it difficult to interpret the sounds made by their autistic child when he was a baby, but eventually learnt what he meant.

Facial expressions

Autistic children are usually able to smile, laugh, weep and show fear or anger, but they tend to show only the extremes of emotions. Facial expression of finer shades of feeling, such as doubt, slight embarrassment, mild annoyance, are rarely seen. In fact, none of the types of non-verbal communication as classified by Argyle (1972) (see above) are used easily or naturally by autistic children. Even those who make the most progress have to learn the rules of non-verbal behaviour painstakingly by rote, instead of developing these skills naturally as part of the process of maturation.

Some autistic children and adults appear wooden and expressionless most of the time. Others frequently show the extremes of emotion in a way which is quite inappropriate for their age and the social situation. Parents and other close relatives usually learn to recognise how an autistic child or adult is feeling. Clinical impression suggests that the expression of emotion in the older age groups, including those who can talk, is just as idiosyncratic as in the pre-verbal 3- to 5-year olds studied by Ricks. Some children express themselves by singing different tunes. Parents get to know the sad song and the happy song although strangers cannot tell the difference in mood. Pleasure may be shown by covering the face with the hands and only the child's own family will know how to differentiate this from distress which is often shown in a similar way.

Gestures

Autistic children are late in beginning to speak and about half remain mute all their lives but, unlike children who are deaf or who have developmental receptive speech disorders, they do not use gesture as a substitute for speech.

Many autistic babies and toddlers show their needs only through crying and screaming. Their parents have to guess what is wanted, the sole guide being the volume of the noise. Once the children are able to walk, they usually develop the very concrete gesture of pulling an adult by the hand and placing it on the object that is wanted. This is done without looking at the adult concerned. Sometimes a child will push the adult's hand through a movement, for example turning on a tap when a drink is required. After this, the child may reach the stage at which he shows what he wants by taking the container and pushing it into an adult's hand. He may ask for a drink by getting a cup and a bottle of squash and giving these to his mother. Pushing people away when interaction and assistance are not wanted is also a characteristic action.

After the stage of concrete demonstration there may be the slow and imperfect evolution of the symbolic gesture of pointing. Nodding and shaking of the head to mean "yes" and "no" are rarely seen either as substitutes for, or as accompaniments of, speech.

Attempts have been made to teach mute autistic children to use gestural languages. This is extremely difficult to do, even if only a few simple and obvious signs are attempted. The children may learn, with suitable rewards, to copy the movements, but they tend to reduce them to the barest minimum. Thus the miming of the act of drinking to ask for a drink may be reduced to a quick lift of the hand without any movement of the head or lips. This reduction to a minimum is probably analogous to the tendency, seen in speaking autistic children, to reduce the number of words to as few as possible and even to contract down the words themselves. It is even more difficult to teach the children to use the signs to communicate, as distinct from copying them to order.

Any generalisations about autistic children have to be qualified, since one can always find exceptions. Rutter (1965) mentions one child who, though showing marked autistic behaviour when young, at the age of $10\frac{1}{2}$ was still mute but was able to communicate by gestures and signs. By this time he had lost all his autistic behaviour. Another child had very limited speech but communicated by drawings, gestures and some muttered comments. Children of this kind, though rare, are of considerable theoretical interest from the point of view of classification and aetiology.

Non-verbal aspects of speech are as abnormal in autistic children as other non-verbal communication. Vocal delivery tends to be jerky, with poor control of pitch and volume and odd intonation. In consequence, little information is carried by the sound of the voice. Some autistic children have speech which resembles that of children who are congenitally deaf. Facial expression, hand movements and bodily posture are not used to accompany speech as they are in normal people, which gives a curious impression of woodenness when the autistic child is engaged in social interaction.

Tubbs (1966) found that autistic children were particularly poor on the encoding sub-tests of the Illinois Test of Psycholinguistic Ability. These sub-tests are concerned with the *expression* of ideas. They performed least well on motor encoding which involves miming the use of various objects such as a hammer or a violin. Hermelin suggested that the apparent poverty of social response in these children could be related to a general disability affecting expressive skills. Bartak (personal communication) observed that autistic children use gesture very little even when they reach the stage of understanding other people's gestures fairly well. They tend to rely on speech if they can talk, without non-verbal supplements, however difficult they find it to express themselves. Wing (1971) also found that use of gesture changed very little with increasing age, although comprehension of gesture tended to improve.

Non-verbal comprehension

Understanding of facial expressions appears to be very slow in developing. Normal children seem able to pick up very small clues such as a slight frown or the lift of an eyebrow. Non-autistic mentally retarded children can also do this although they are slower to develop the skill. The behaviour of young autistic children cannot be controlled in this way. Eventually they may learn the meaning of exaggerated expressive movements combined with the appropriate tone of voice. When comprehension is beginning, an autistic child may study the face of his mother, evidently trying to find out what mood she is in before making a request. Sometimes a child will hold an adult's face with his hands while gazing intently, as if searching for a meaning which eludes him.

Development of understanding of other aspects of non-verbal communication is also delayed. Often the only way to teach motor skills to a young autistic child is to move his limbs through the action that is required, since he cannot follow instructions given in speech or gesture.

After a variable length of time, depending on the child concerned, it becomes possible to teach through concrete demonstration. This cannot be done until the child is using his eyes to obtain information. Some children are able to do this from early in life, but others seem to go through a phase in which visual input is as meaningless to them as the sound of speech. This may improve or disappear with maturation (Wing, 1969, 1971) and then teaching becomes easier.

Pointing is one of the earliest of the "symbolic" gestures which the children learn to understand. They may later learn to comprehend nodding and shaking of the head, even if they do not use these gestures themselves. It is usually helpful for teachers and parents to supplement speech with plenty of simple, obvious gesture used consistently.

Even those children who make the most progress have difficulty with the complexities of non-verbal communication which regulate all aspects of social life and may be teased by their normal companions for their gaucheness and naivety. They have to learn by rote both the meanings and the way to use them and this is a long, slow process which is never completed. Some bright autistic children make themselves conspicuous in public because they speak very loudly, regardless of the social situation. Those who have special subjects about which they like to talk fail to recognise the signs of boredom in their audience unless these are carefully described by an understanding parent. Life hardly seems long enough to give the autistic child all the detailed instruction he needs to learn the rules of social conduct.

The development of speech

Little is known about the way in which autistic children babble in the first year of life. Rutter *et al.* (1971) in a study of 14 autistic children and 11 children with development receptive speech problems noted that the parents reported diminution in amount or deviation in the quality of babble in about half of the former group and the majority of the latter. The parents of the autistic children in Ricks' study (1972) reported, on questioning, that their children had not developed normal conversational babble in their first year.

Ricks (1972) recorded the vocalisation of these autistic children when they were aged 3 to 5 years. He observed that their babble was monotonous like that of a normal baby falling asleep. He did not hear any of the lively babbling that normal babies produce in the early morning and the sounds did not have conversational inflexions.

Ricks also found that normal babies and pre-verbal children with Down's syndrome aged 3 to 6 years paid little attention to their own babble that was recorded and played back to them. The autistic children in the study, on the other hand, if they responded at all, did so by precisely imitating their own vocalisations. They ignored recordings of other autistic children. They also ignored a recording which was an imitation of their own babble made by a normal child. The possible significance of this finding will be discussed later on in this chapter.

Some autistic children remain mute all their lives. In Lotter's epidemiological survey (1966, 1967 a,b) 6 children out of a total of 32 (19 per cent) were still mute by the time they were 8–10 years old. A further 10 (31 per cent) had some words which were not used for communication or conversation. Each of the mute children in Lotter's study had an IQ below 55. In general, level of speech is closely related to intelligence as measured on appropriate tests (Rutter, 1965), but there is a small minority of mute children who score fairly highly on IQ tests and who have reasonable comprehension (Wing, 1969). Their lack of speech may be due to specific expressive or articulatory problems complicating the autistic pattern.

Although there are now many accounts of autistic children acquiring the ability to say words through operant conditioning (e.g. Lovaas *et al.*, 1966), there have been no systematic studies of the way in which the use of words develops without this formal training, as it does in the majority of those who acquire speech. Of the 63 children in Rutter's follow-up study (Rutter and Lockyer, 1967; Rutter *et al.*, 1967), only one had a history of a normal onset of speech. The children may begin to say words at almost any age, although the majority who acquire words do so by the age of 5. Some appear to be developing normally for a time and then lose speech as part of a general regression. The problems of organising a study comparable to that of Ricks' observations of the onset of speech in normal children are therefore formidable.

As with so many other aspects of the early development of autistic children, the only evidence available is retrospective and anecdotal and can often be obtained only if the clinician or research worker asks the appropriate questions. Parents with whom the present authors have discussed these problems do not recall any period in which their autistic child showed the exuberant joy in producing sound-labels that Ricks described in normal children. Instead, the parents recall a long period in which they tried all kinds of ways to persuade the reluctant child to say something. When a word did come, usually without any display of enthusiasm, there did not seem to be any rapid generalisation to cover a category of similar experiences. One child, for example, began to say "hegg" for egg, "me" for meat and "n-n" for "I want" at the age of 3, appropriately, but with a monotonous, unvarying inflexion. The first two words were strictly confined to the foods in question and never generalised at all.

Echolalia

The first speech may be meaningless echoing of the words spoken by other people. Rutter (1965) and Wing (1971) found that this was reported in at least three quarters of the speaking autistic children they studied when these children were young, although there is a tendency for improvement to occur with increasing age. For some children all speech is echolalic, but, in others, some spontaneous speech occurs as well.

Echoing is also found in young normal children who are in the early stages of speech acquisition but this is a temporary phase not lasting beyond about $2\frac{1}{2}$ years (Rutter and Bax, 1972). Autistic children, at least when they first begin to speak, echo in a parrot-like, meaningless way with no show of interest in what they are saying. They may repeat just the last words in a phrase or else repeat whole sentences, or even whole conversations. The words are often spoken with the inflexion of the original speaker, exactly imitating any regional or foreign accent.

Linguists studying the development of language in normal children have examined the way in which they imitate adult utterances (Brown, 1965). They have found that the young child translates the sentence to fit the particular set of grammatical rules with which he is operating at the time, or misses out the part that he is as yet unable to handle. This is in marked contrast to some autistic children who may be able to echo perfectly without changing what is heard at all.

Echoing can be immediate or it may be delayed for days, weeks or even years. A child may habitually repeat words or phrases originally spoken by other people while he is absorbed in some activity such as assembling constructional toys or making lines and patterns of objects. The words spoken are irrelevant to the activity and not an aspect of imaginative play. Parents listening in may be able to deduce the events of a school day and things heard at home may be repeated at school. Words spoken loudly and with emphasis are the most likely to make an impression and to be repeated (Hermelin and

O'Connor, 1970). This means that much of the echoed speech may consist of scoldings and expletives, and can cause considerable social embarrassment when spoken in public. A special voice different from the child's usual one may be used. Sometimes this can be identified as copied from someone else, but sometimes the source cannot be traced.

Meaningless echolalia may be the only kind of speech that is acquired, but a proportion of the children reach the next stage which is the *appropriate* use of phrases copied from others. The child usually begins by using his store of phrases to make requests. He reproduces exactly the words which he associates with occasions when his wants were satisfied. He therefore asks for a biscuit by saying "Do you want a biscuit" if this is what his mother says before opening the biscuit tin. The use of "you", "he", or the child's own name, instead of "I", has been interpreted as an unawareness of personal identity (Bettelheim, 1967; Creak, 1961). The fact that there is a high correlation between pronoun reversal and echolalia suggests rather that the former is a consequence of the latter (Rutter, 1965; Wing, 1969). Parents and teachers may utilise the tendency to echolalia to teach the use of "I". In a minority of children understanding of the use of pronouns eventually dawns and reversals diminish or disappear. In the rest, the phrases containing "I" which have been specifically taught (such as "Please can I have . . .?") are used appropriately, but in other situations copying of the "you" form still occurs.

The children's tendency to use echoed phrases, especially those that were first connected with an object or an event, can produce some strange effects. Kanner (1946) described a child who always said "Don't throw the dog off the balcony" to check himself from doing something wrong. This could be traced back to the time when his mother said the phrase with some irritation because he persisted in throwing his toy dog from the balcony of their hotel room.

Abnormalities in spontaneous speech

In parallel with, or occasionally replacing, the echolalia, some of the children produce a varying amount of spontaneous speech. This can often be recognised by the great effort with which it is produced and the immaturity or, in many cases, the abnormality of grammatical constructions. The immaturities are those described in the development of speech of young normal children (Jesperson, 1922; Brown, 1965) but they continue much longer than normal. One example is that of a child who, by the age of 9, grasped the rule that present participles are made by adding "ing" to the verb root and like a much younger normal child applied this to all situations. She described a picture of a man smoking a pipe as "Daddy piping" and of a boy blowing bubbles as "Boy bubbling". The same child later observed that people ended some sentences with phrases like "isn't it". She then added these indiscriminately, producing comments such as "We were sad, wasn't it?" and "She was a good girl, won't they?".

Abnormalities of grammatical construction like those in children with developmental receptive speech disorders are present in some speaking autistic children (Rutter, 1965). Wing (1969) found that just over half of a group of 20 speaking autistic children showed these problems in varying degrees of severity. They dropped out prepositions, conjunctions, and pronouns from phrases ("go walk shops") or else used them incorrectly ("you sit for chair in table"). Letter order in words and word order in sentences were confused ("pasghetti" for spaghetti; "pladding ploo" for paddling pool; "put salt it on"; "have you shake milk"). Words of similar sound or related meaning were muddled ("teapotmental" for "departmental"; "on" instead of "off"; "sock" instead of "shoe"; "mummy" instead of "daddy"). In some cases the children described objects by their use ("sweep-the-floor" for broom; "make-a-cup-of-tea" for kettle; "Mrs-Mend-a-Toof" for the dentist) or else coined words of their own ("cooshin" for stewed apples; "diddle-up" for shoe).

There is a marked tendency for the contraction of phrases and even words down to the barest possible minimum. One child when asked what he had done that day said "Hut-stick-walk" meaning he had gone for a walk to a hut and had found a stick on the way. "Home after bread" meant "Can we go home after we have bought some bread?" and "One more" was used to mean "I am tired of this task and will do only one more thing before I stop". When pressed very hard the child could produce longer phrases but always used this short-hand if no one corrected him.

A small proportion of autistic children eventually acquire the ability to use the rules of grammar correctly. Occasionally, though they may be late in speaking, they begin talking in complete sentences. In other cases some of the characteristic speech problems are seen in mild form and then disappear.

Despite the normality of their grammar, the autistic children in this group show their underlying handicaps through the content of their speech. They are still peculiarly restricted in the range of their conversation. Close acquaintance with them shows how much they, too, rely upon stereotyped phrases and repetition when they talk. Conversing with them is rather like holding a discussion with a well programmed computer or with a gramophone record. They are able to exchange concrete pieces of information about subjects that interest them, or else ask a series of questions, but once the conversation departs from this simple level the autistic child or adult becomes lost and may withdraw from social contact. There is a tendency to choose words without any feeling for colloquial speech (for example, "I wish to extract a biscuit from the tin") which gives an air of pedantry. This is exacerbated by the lack of variation in tone of voice. If the autistic person has a special interest he is inclined to talk about this *ad nauseam* but without actually being able to discuss and explore any new angles on his subject. The same pieces of information tend to recur whenever the same subject is raised. One young man, when telephoning his aunt, always began by saying "This is Charles Smith, your nephew, speaking". He liked music and enjoyed talking about it but his contribution invariably consisted of a list of all the records he owned and all the conductors he had heard, although his grammar was impeccable. He was unable, for example, to say why he enjoyed the interpretation of a particular piece of music by one conductor more than another, although he knew which recording he preferred.

As mentioned previously, the non-verbal as well as the verbal aspects of communication are as poorly developed in this group as in more handicapped autistic children. This, combined with their apparent ability to use speech normally, can be very puzzling to other people who sense that something is wrong but are unable to define precisely what gives this impression of strangeness.

The understanding of speech

There is, in most autistic children, a marked lack of interest in speech. In the early years some of the children show no response at all even when their parents speak to them. They may later begin to understand a few single words which have specific associations. At this stage, parents may complain that their child understands what he wants to, because they know that he responds when for example they say the words "chocolate" or "orange juice" but ignores his parents when they give him instructions. Careful observation shows that the children's understanding is genuinely limited and that they have learnt the meaning of a few words through a process of accidental operant conditioning because these words are closely connected with rewards, especially food.

If comprehension improves with increasing age, it becomes clearer that the children perform poorly because of their language impairments and not with intent. They try to obey instructions but make characteristic mistakes, such as the child who was sent upstairs to fetch the pullover from the chair in the bedroom and came down with the chair.

The growth of understanding of speech is characteristically slow. Severely retarded autistic children may never develop any awareness of the meaning of speech. Other children who are less handicapped develop comprehension to a varying degree.

The group of children who make the most progress and who develop grammatically normal speech have good understanding for all practical everyday purposes, but show their remaining handicaps when they become involved in conversations on complex, particularly abstract, issues outside their own limited experience.

Even the children who do develop enough comprehension of speech for simple practical purposes still show many characteristic problems. Replies to questions tend to be concrete and limited to the here and now. Thus a child may be able to give a list of items in response to a simple question; ("What did you have for dinner?" "Meat and cabbage and potatoes and gravy and salt and jam tart and custard and orange juice and cup of tea"), but it may be virtually impossible to obtain a reply to enquiries concerning his own feelings, or his likes and dislikes.

Autistic children often have difficulty in understanding when they are asked to make a choice. If they are echolalic they may automatically repeat the name of the last object mentioned whether or not that was their preference. They show by their behaviour that they have strong likes and dislikes but they fail to understand the meanings of sentences which ask them to choose.

Words are used and responded to in a very limited way. An autistic child who always referred to the dog's dinner plate as a "dish" was confused when asked to put some scraps in the dog's "bowl". She solved the problem by giving the food to the dog in the washing-up bowl.

Slapstick comedy and very simple, obvious jokes involving words may be much enjoyed, but humour depending upon the multiple associations of words is greeted by blank incomprehension or by a totally literal interpretation without any realisation that the anecdote was intended to be funny (Dewey, 1973a).

Idiomatic expressions can be very confusing for even the brightest autistic child, and parents and teachers learn through experience to choose their words with care. One child was terrified when her mother used the familiar phrase "crying her eyes out". Another, when asked if he had lost his tongue, started anxiously searching for it.

Bartak (personal communication) pointed out that the autistic child's biggest problem is in understanding and using those parts of speech which change with the context and with the speaker, such as pronouns and prepositions. These words describe relationships rather than concrete objects or events. The tenses of verbs also have the disconcerting habit of changing with circumstances and autistic children have problems with these as well. It is of interest that Jespersen (1922) discussed the words that change their meaning according to the situation, which he called "shifters", and he described the problems they present for young normal children who are just learning to speak. The difficulties are more severe in autistic children and tend to be permanent rather than temporary, but may not be different in kind.

Parents tend to develop a way of communicating with their children which circumvents some of these problems. They give instructions one at a time; they avoid complex grammatical constructions; they supplement with concrete demonstration and gesture; they speak clearly, loudly, with a rising inflection; they repeat as often as necessary and they know that they have to allow time for the message to sink in and be understood.

Executive speech problems

Problems of pronunciation are common in young autistic children (Rutter, 1965). Wing (1969) found that these were reported in three-quarters of a group of 20 speaking autistic children when they were under 5 years old. There was some improvement with increasing age. The difficulties are like those found in some young normal children and in children with developmental expressive speech problems. There may be a marked contrast between the clearly enunciated echolalic speech and the poorly pronounced spontaneous speech.

The problems vary in severity in different children. Some may be unable to produce any intelligible words, some may miss off the beginnings or ends of words ("wee" for "sweetie"; "na" for Ribena; "bi" for bicycle), while others have comparatively minor problems with only certain sounds ("doup" for "soup"; "glubs" for "gloves"; "fumb" for "thumb"). This aspect of speech may, in some autistic children, be affected far more severely than comprehension. There are, however, some who have never shown any difficulties in pronunciation.

Development of inner language

Poverty of development of inner language is an important characteristic of autistic children. In the early years this is shown by the quality of their play. Most young autistic children handle toys and other objects as if they are seeking sensory stimuli. They do not use them for their proper purpose or for imaginative play. They may be able to do jig-saw puzzles and assemble constructional toys, so long as they require only visuo-spatial or mechanical skills and not imaginative understanding.

A very few autistic children do reach the stage of imitative play. They may line up their dolls and talk to them as if they are playing school, but this tends to be an exact repetition of their own experiences and does not contain any novel invention.

The more competent children may learn to read but parents often complain that their children take no pleasure in this activity. Those who read from choice tend to use this skill to acquire more facts about the subjects that specially interest them. Works of fiction have little appeal, probably because a rich inner life, dependent upon inner language, is necessary for their enjoyment.

Parents of the brighter autistic adolescents are often worried because they see no signs of appropriate planning for the future and no interest in the realities of adult life. This type of foresight depends upon the existence of inner language which can be used for thinking and planning.

Theoretical Implications

In the light of the definition given at the beginning of this chapter, autistic children could be said to have impairments affecting all aspects of communication, not just speech or language. This may sound simple in theory, but, in practice, there are many difficulties in defining the nature of these impairments, because of the remarkably wide variation to be found in the severity with which the autistic behaviour pattern is manifested in different children. Each time it seems that the essence of the problem has been grasped, and that the primary features of the syndrome can be defined in such and such a way, other children are found without these particular features and yet who clearly show the behavioural patterns of early childhood autism.

Formation of concepts

At the lowest end of the scale, among the children who are severely mentally retarded as well as showing autistic behaviour, there are some who appear to have developed no concepts at all.

They show no sign that they differentiate between the people with whom they come into contact and they cannot perform the simplest task requiring any kind of classification. It is tempting to explain their lack of response, their stereotyped movements and other abnormal behaviour by their total inability to comprehend their environment.

The majority of autistic children however, *are* able to form some concepts. These may be limited to the simple ones of size, shape, colour and number, but, in the brighter children, the concepts are sufficiently advanced to allow for the correct classification of the more familiar contents of the environment, including people, other animals, plants, means of transport, and may even include such complicated abstractions as the characteristics of different human age groups.

Problems arise, even for the most able autistic children, at the level where concept formation depends upon the ability to *manipulate* instead of just storing linguistic symbols.

Comprehension and use of symbols

Among the most severely impaired autistic children, there are some who have no ability to understand or use symbols. These obviously include the children who have no demonstrable concepts, but there are other children who can, for example, match on size, colour or shape when shown how by concrete demonstration, but who do not seem to have any appreciation of even the simplest symbols in whatever sensory modality they are presented. They do not respond to their own names nor to any other words or gestures. It may be possible to condition some limited response to a simple stimulus but nothing higher than this can be achieved. These children are presumably unable to store or reproduce even the simplest linguistic codes.

Children who have meaningless echolalia seem to be able to store the sounds of words and to reproduce them in vocal form when the appropriate stimulus recurs, but without any understanding. The process is an automatic response and not a symbolic activity.

Echolalia used purposefully may indicate that the child concerned treats each whole phrase as a symbol for a person, object or event without extracting from it the features which it has in common with other symbol phrases. There is no recombination of the individual words to form new phrases.

Those children who produce at least some spontaneous, non-echoed speech are clearly using words as symbols. This can occur at different levels of complexity but even the brightest autistic children and adults tend to be limited and concrete and inefficient in their response to and use of words. This will be discussed later in this chapter.

The comprehension and use of grammatical rules

The difficulties which many speaking autistic children have in understanding and producing grammatical language have already been described in some detail. The problems are very similar to those found in children with developmental receptive speech disorders and it could therefore be suggested that developmental "aphasia" was one of the essential impairments in early childhood autism. Its frequent presence in the condition is of considerable importance when considering the possible aetiology, but, as emphasised in Chapter 2, in the discussion of differential diagnosis, developmental receptive speech disorders can occur on their own without the additional features of the syndrome of early childhood autism. The main differences stem from the fact that purely receptive "aphasic" children can understand and use non-spoken (for example, gestured or written) language, whereas the impairments of autistic children affect *all* forms of communication.

It might be suggested that autistic behaviour results from a combination of developmental speech disorders plus equivalent disorders affecting the comprehension and use of language expressed in non-spoken ways. This seems a plausible hypothesis, but it cannot be accepted without qualification since the abnormalities found in the developmental receptive speech disorders are not present in all autistic children. There is a small group of children with a clear history of the classic autistic syndrome who, at least when seen in later childhood, understand and produce sentences without any evidence of problems in using grammatical rules. Despite this apparent competence, conversation of more than a few minutes' duration with such a child or adult will bring out very marked limitations in the way he uses language.

The central problem

The central problem, which is present in even the most mildly handicapped autistic people, appears to be a specific kind of difficulty in handling symbols, which affects language, non-verbal communication and many other aspects of cognitive and social activity.

A theory of language acquisition in normal children

Ricks' work suggests that, in normal children, the first sound-labels, like the pre-verbal vocal signals indicating emotional states, owe virtually nothing to social reinforcement. These labels do not necessarily relate to objects pointed out to the child, nor to the objects whose labelling might be expected to secure parental approval. The sound used may be unlike any real word and may be adopted by the parents before they teach the child the socially accepted label. Furthermore, when generalisation occurs, the child often uses a method of grouping different from that adopted by the adults in his culture. (For example, one normal child had the same label for light bulb, aeroplane, moon and bird.)

Ricks' postulated that the growing normal brain is organised so that it is constantly scanning, checking and looking for similarities and also that labelling the concepts derived from this process is an inborn activity. The earliest categories seem to be self-generated but the criteria for classification are constantly changing in the light of experience, including conversation and social interaction.

This mechanism for scanning, classifying and reclassifying may well be the basis of the later development of the ability to organise verbal symbols according to sets of grammatical rules which change and become more complex as the child matures.

The concept of "inner language" fits neatly into this formulation.

This has already been defined as the store of concepts in code which grows as the child acquires competence in understanding and using language. In the normal child and adult, the symbols in the store must be readily available for the purpose of comparison with current experiences and must be modifiable in the light of new information. The acquisition of such a store of symbols allows the child to form new categories (concepts) not only from concrete experiences, but also by recombining and reshaping ideas already stored in symbolic form. Thus one can imagine a series of new abstractions based on previous abstractions, curtailed only by the capacity of the person concerned to marshal and handle all the necessary coded material. The practical relevance of these abstractions can be tested by a return to concrete experience, but there is no absolute limit to the possibilities of abstract theorizing.

Language acquisition in autistic children

Learning by conditioning. The process of language acquisition, if it occurs at all, seems to be quite different in an autistic child. It appears that in such a child the mechanism underlying the normal active scanning, checking and classifying of experience is either absent or severely limited. In consequence, words (if they are acquired at all) are learnt passively by operant conditioning, instead of as an integral part of an active "processing" of experience.

As the normal child matures, the words in his vocabulary subtly expand and change their meaning. They acquire overtones and ambiguities as well as their original meaning. For an autistic child, words tend to retain the precise meaning they had when first learned. Thus errors in naming and classifying tend to be perpetuated for many years instead of being rapidly modified as they are by a normal child. Although they may be able to understand and use verbal symbols for practical purposes, autistic children and adults, however high their tested intelligence, do not seem to be aware of the undertones and overtones, the many associations, some clear and obvious, others fleeting, hard to grasp, but none the less capable of evoking ideas and emotions, which give words the power and significance they have for normal people. An autistic child lacks any feeling for the poetry of language, even when his grasp of vocabulary and grammar is adequate.

The problems with "inner language" can be predicted from this hypothesis.

Autistic people do not seem to be able to use their store of concepts in code in order to modify their ideas or to form complicated abstractions. As has been emphasised throughout this discussion, it is not a question of an absolute lack of abstracting ability. Apart from the profoundly retarded children with autistic behaviour who appear to have no concepts at all, autistic children can classify on the basis of their concrete experience. Those who are only moderately or mildly handicapped may have the ability to abstract on the basis of remembered experience, providing that this does not involve any complicated associations. Thus one very competent child was able to choose the cheapest offer when buying groceries and could go to more than one shop to find the best bargain, showing that he could retain and use his recent observations.

The problems arise when such children or adults have to make further abstractions from material that is already abstract and to appreciate complex relationships between a series of different categories held in the mind. This is the function of "inner language" in the normal person, shown in, for example, the appreciation of subtle verbal humour; the expression of a reasoned opinion on any subject; working out the future consequences of a series of events; or inventing an imaginary story. These skills are all virtually unattainable by autistic people. They have especially severe problems in understanding other people's feelings because this requires the reading of many subtle non-verbal signs which have to be interpreted, linked to the context, and matched up with past experiences of the particular way in which people show emotions. Thus one finds autistic adults who can, for instance, tune a piano to an unbelievable degree of accuracy, but cannot hold down a job because of their total social naivety, arising from their inability to understand social cues.

Abnormalities of memory storage. The other part of the picture of early childhood autism, and one which allows for some measure of compensation for the basis impairments, is the excellent memory which characterises those who are moderately or mildly handicapped. Experiences appear to be stored exactly as they occurred, as programmes are in a computer, and can be reproduced, unchanged, in response to the appropriate stimulus. Some autistic people can do lengthy numerical calculations in their heads and a few can play chess. These activities involve the use of symbols, but in each case they follow strict, inflexible rules which, once learnt, can be applied without the need for variation. The type of memory described would be of obvious advantage in these fields. Autistic children in normal schools may appear to be making good progress because they can reproduce all the material learnt from text books on request. When they reach the stage at which they are asked to discuss the implications of the facts they have learnt, their handicaps become apparent.

The pleasure and excitement which autistic people find from listening to music and looking at symmetrical or regularly repeated patterns is probably related to these basic impairments and the remaining abilities. It may be that, although they cannot derive interest and satisfaction from stories, poetry, new ideas and all the other activities needing a wealth of associations for their appreciation, the autistic person's high level of ability to detect and remember patterns rather than meanings allows them to enjoy repetitive experiences. Ricks' observation that young pre-verbal autistic children sometimes precisely imitated their own vocalisations which had been recorded and played back to them (a response never observed in normal babies) may be another example of the interest in a *pattern* of sound as opposed to its meaning.

Comparison with severely retarded children and adults

It can be argued that severely mentally retarded people are also poor at verbal abstractions and reasoning. In order to deal with this point, it is necessary to emphasise, once again, that the term mental retardation is a general one which covers many different patterns of impairments. In particular, three patterns need to be distinguished here. In the first place, there is a group of very severely retarded children who are at the pre-verbal level of development but who differ from autistic children in that *all* their functions, including motor skills, are equally retarded. This group should be differentiated from the second group comprising those with little or no language development but whose motor and visuo-motor skills are comparatively more advanced. These are the children who have either the full picture of childhood autism or who have marked autistic features (see Chapter 2).

Finally there is a third group of children without autistic features in whom language has developed to about the same level as would be expected from their motor skills. These children can use verbal symbols more or less as flexibly as a normal child of the same language age. Words have some associations for them, as shown by the appreciation of the cruder forms of verbal humour in the older children; they can give opinions and discuss ideas among themselves, albeit at an immature level; they can give a narrative account of their experiences and tell an imaginary story even if this consists of a string of loosely associated events without an overall plot. All of these skills can be observed for example, in older children with uncomplicated Down's syndrome with an IQ between 30 and 50, but would be beyond the grasp of classically autistic adults even with an IQ in the normal or superior range.

Comparison with normal children and adults

The relationship between the autistic syndrome and normality is also of interest. To a certain extent all normal people have to rely upon automatic rather than thought-out responses in order to carry out routine activities without wasted effort, for example the polite exchange of standard remarks about the weather, or the bus conductor's request for "Any more fares please". Young normal children enjoy the precise repetition of songs and stories and may have uncannily accurate memories for certain things that interest them. The point is that normal people, unlike those who are autistic, have the possibility of thinking spontaneously and flexibly as well as producing habitual responses. It may be that there is a continuum between mild autism and normality (see the discussion of Asperger's syndrome in Chapter 2) and that the position of any individual on this continuum depends upon the degree to which he is able actively to categorise his experiences and call, in a controlled way, upon all the associations, as opposed to storing them in the precise form in which they first occurred. Perhaps the most gifted normal people have both types of ability developed to a high degree.

Relevance for theories of normal language development

The characteristic problems in using language found in autistic children are of relevance for theories of language development in normal children.

In the opinion of the present authors, the purely behaviourist model does not provide a satisfactory explanation for the ability, observed in normal children, to categorise objects and events in the environment and then to enlarge and change the system of classification in the light of new experiences. This behaviour strongly suggests that the human brain actively imposes order on incoming information and is not just a passive recipient waiting to be conditioned into storing the appropriate data.

The latter description does, however, fit the pattern of language learning in the autistic child who provides a sad demonstration of the inadequacy of this method of functioning. Even the most competent autistic child or adult is limited to those concepts which can be learnt through the conditioning provided by his own practical experience. This experience can be enlarged by sympathetic and skilful teaching but the inevitable result is a patchy and distorted picture of the world.

Brown (1965), in his discussion of the process of language acquisition in normal children, suggested that language is but one example of the way in which human beings are able to organise all information according to complex rules. He pointed out the analogy between the rules governing language and those governing social behaviour.

This idea is of considerable interest in the present context, since clinical observation shows that the inflexibility characteristic of an autistic child's language spreads to all aspects of his life. It is particularly clearly demonstrated in his inability to understand and use the rules of social conduct, thus providing some indirect support for Brown's hypothesis.

Even for the most competent autistic adults the daily programme depends upon the observance of a series of habitual actions and any unexpected occurrence is liable to cause confusion and anxiety. Sometimes an adult who has been autistic as a child is able to live an independent life because he has unvarying routines for self-care, for getting to work and carrying it out, for evening interests and even for holidays. People of this kind are usually known by their colleagues and neighbours to be eccentric and rather unsociable but utterly dependable. It is when changes occur in the environment which directly affect their routines that their basic lack of adaptability becomes a problem which other people have to solve.

Aetiological theories

It must be emphasised that the foregoing is a tentative formulation of the central problem and not an aetiological explanation. Many suggestions as to the basic cause of autism have been put forward, some of which are dealt with in Chapter 3. In most cases the theories of aetiology are not worked out in sufficient detail to show how the problems described in the present chapter could be produced. In this section, only those hypotheses which seem to have a direct relationship to the abnormalities of language and symbolic functioning will be discussed.

Sub-cortical lesions

Both Gellner (1959) and Rimland (1965) have suggested neurological mechanisms whereby sensory experiences are invested with meaning. Gellner hypothesised that the connections between sensory pathways and the autonomic system have to be intact in order for words to acquire emotional significance. Rimland's view is that the reticular activating system imbues incoming messages with meaning so that relevant associations can be invoked from the listener's memory store. Both authors have suggested organic lesions (described in Chapter 3) which could interfere with the postulated brain functions and thereby cause the impairments found in early childhood autism.

Gellner's hypothesis allows for abnormalities in the encoding and transmission of information as well as its reception. This might link with Ricks' (1972) findings of abnormalities in the vocal expression of emotional states in pre-verbal autistic children and with Tubbs' (1966) study which showed that autistic children are particularly poor at expressing ideas in words or gestures.

Ricks' studies of the idiosyncratic noises used by autistic children may provide support for the theories which implicate sub-cortical rather than cortical lesions as the primary problem, especially if it can be shown that typical autistic children never go through a phase in which they use the intoned emotional signals common to normal babies.

Lack of cerebral dominance

Hermelin (1966) and Ricks (1972) have both suggested that there may be an abnormality of the function of the dominant hemisphere in autistic children. Sperry (1968), in his work with patients who had had extensive midline sections of the cerebral commissures, showed that the minor hemisphere, at least in some patients, though unable to understand verbs, can comprehend written and spoken nouns and phrases describing objects, although the understanding cannot be expressed in words. It is superior to the major hemisphere in tasks involving spatial relationships and block design.

Kimura (1964) found that the right temporal lobe plays a greater part in non-verbal auditory perception than does the left. Shank-weiler (1966) showed that the ability to discriminate auditory patterns and tone quality was reduced in patients with right temporal lobe damage. He also noted that the same patients had problems in identifying or interpreting complex visual forms and patterns of a non-verbal kind, although they could still recognise letters of the alphabet.

The functions attributed to the minor hemisphere are very like the abilities which remain intact in typical autistic children. It could be said that the children function as if they have two minor hemis-

pheres. However, there is evidence that, following hemispherectomy in the first year of life in cases of infantile hemiplegia, the
remaining hemisphere, right or left, is able to develop both its own
functions and those of the one that was removed, although the
development of intellectual, especially verbal, function is likely to
be mildly or moderately retarded (McFie, 1961 a,b). If the impairments underlying autistic behaviour are due to lack of hemisphere
dominance the pathology must be of a kind which prevents the
non-dominant hemisphere taking over the language functions.

Abnormalities of the speech areas

The theory of lack of cerebral dominance leaves many points
unexplained. In particular, the available evidence suggests that the
minor hemisphere is "non-speaking", but about half of all autistic
children do learn to say words, even though there are the problems
already described affecting the way in which speech is used.

Geschwind (1968) discussed the literature on the anatomical basis
of echolalia following brain injury. This occurs if the speech areas
and the afferent auditory connections are intact, but isolated from
much of the rest of the cerebral hemispheres. "There is no comprehension because language arouses no associations; there is gross
disturbance of spontaneous speech, since the speech areas receive
no information from elsewhere in the brain".

It is interesting to consider whether congenital abnormalities
causing complete or partial disconnection of the speech areas could
allow the development of the peculiar type of word storage and use
seen in classic early childhood autism, plus the general problem of
interpreting, coding and using experiences in every other modality.

Stengel (1947) described the characteristics of echolalia. He noted
that, in its most severe form, there is automatic repetition of words
without understanding, although this occurs in a conversational
setting and not randomly in response to any words heard. The
patients will also finish sentences left half completed. If improvement occurs, the parrot-like echoing changes to a repetition as if the
meaning is being queried, which may be followed by a spontaneous

correct response. After this, exact repetition may be replaced by changing the pronouns appropriately (e.g. Examiner: "Do you want tea?" Patient: "Do I want tea?"). With complete restoration of comprehension the echoing disappears. Stengel pointed out that, if recovery is not complete, the patient's speech may become fixed in any of these stages.

Stengel remarked that the clinical phenomena of echolalia were the same whatever the aetiology. He noted that it could be associated with a variety of conditions including schizophrenia, epilepsy, mental retardation, following encephalitis, the recovery stage after coma, and in some, but by no means all, young normal children in the early stage of language development. This brings up the question whether the echolalia in all these conditions, and in early childhood autism, is caused by related types of neurological disturbances. It is also legitimate to ask the further question as to whether the adults who show echolalia and stereotyped movements and who have been diagnosed as having chronic schizophrenia are not, in reality, unidentified cases of early childhood autism.

Nature of the "processing" problem

Hermelin, in Chapter 5, gives more detailed consideration to the precise nature of the problem which autistic children have in "processing" incoming information. This type of analysis is obviously necessary before reasonable suggestions can be made as to the possible neurophysiological mechanisms involved in the central abnormality.

Can the problems of symbolic functioning explain the full clinical picture of early childhood autism?

As emphasised in Chapter 3, any theory concerning the aetiology or the nature of the impairments in early childhood autism, if it is to be acceptable, must provide an explanation of all aspects of the syndrome and not just one or a few selected features. The hypothesis concerning abnormality of symbolic functioning must therefore be examined critically to see if it can be related to the other impairments and behaviour problems characteristic of the condition which were described in detail in Chapter 2.

Speech problems

It has already been noted that problems closely resembling the developmental receptive and expressive speech disorders are often found in association with early childhood autism. It appears from clinical and epidemiological studies (Lotter, 1966, 1967 a,b; Morley, 1967; Rutter and Lockyer, 1967; Rutter *et al.*, 1967; Wing, 1969) that the combination of autism and developmental receptive speech disorder is more common than either of the two syndromes in pure form. Since either can occur without the other, the hypothesis of a global abnormality of symbolic functioning in autism cannot be used to explain the receptive speech disorder or vice versa. The frequency of association, however, suggests that there is a close anatomical or functional relationship between the different aspects of language and the handling of symbols which are disturbed in these two conditions.

Poverty of non-verbal communication

Superficially, it may seem that the marked poverty or even absence of non-verbal communication in autistic people needs no special explanation, since it can be viewed as one aspect of the global problem affecting symbolic function of all kinds. Looked at in more detail, it is not so clear why the use of gestures should lag so far behind the development of speech even in the least handicapped. If an autistic child or adult can use the words "yes" and "no" appropriately, why does he not accompany them with a nod or a shake of the head as happens with normal people?

The relationship between the verbal and non-verbal aspects of communication is not yet clarified. Schaffer (1974) and Trevarthen (1974) have described mouth movements and gestural behaviour, during interactions with the mother, in infants under 12 weeks of age, which show the temporal patterning and other features of adult conversational behaviour. During these "conversations" the mothers tend to imitate their infants and not vice-versa. It could be suggested that non-verbal methods of communication precede but are intimately linked with the development of language. The poverty of gesture in autistic children could therefore be more evidence of the abnormal way in which language develops in this condition.

In Trevarthen's view, normal human infants are endowed with the ability to differentiate between persons and physical objects and to interact and communicate with the former from a very early age. It may be that the mothers of autistic children who were uneasily aware that something was wrong with their baby from the time of early infancy may have noticed the absence of this early communication skill without being able to put their observations into words. Follow-up studies of language development in children who did not "converse" with their mothers from the early weeks onwards would be of obvious interest in this context.

Other impairments

The other impairments found in classically autistic children are the abnormal responses to sensory experiences (distress, fascination, ignoring); the problems of imitating movements; problems of motor control, which include the odd posture and gait, the tip-toe walk, and the flapping of the arms and facial grimaces which accompany excitement; lastly the abnormalities of autonomic function, vestibular control and physical development which can be observed in many of the children.

It is not at all clear how these additional impairments can be related to the problems of symbolic functioning. It could be suggested, for example, that the abnormal responses to sensory stimuli are due to a lack of ability to interpret their symbolic significance, or that the odd gait and posture are further expressions of the poverty of non-verbal communication, but such explanations are *post hoc* and lack experimental validation. Complete understanding of the connection between different aspects of the autistic syndrome must wait on advances in neuroanatomy and physiology.

The difficulties that autistic children have in imitating movements made by other people are explored in more detail by DeMyer in Chapter 6.

Secondary behaviour problems

The majority of the behaviour problems listed in Chapter 2 can more easily be attributed directly to the problems of symbolic functioning and non-verbal communication than can the additional impairments mentioned above.

The social aloofness seen in most young autistic children, the intense resistance to change and attachment to objects and routines, the inability to play imaginatively, and lack of understanding of abstract pursuits have all been discussed earlier in this chapter. The tendency to select for attention one aspect instead of the whole of a person, object or scene can also be explained by the problem of understanding the symbolic meaning of experience, as can the inappropriate emotional reactions.

The impression of an odd, mechanical voice, gait and posture seems to arise from a combination of the poverty of non-verbal communication and the general problems of motor control.

Absorption in stereotyped movements and simple sensory stimuli could be explained as the only activities available to a child who could not obtain pleasure from communicating with others or from activities involving understanding of complex abstractions.

The socially immature and difficult behaviour seen in many young autistic children is similar to that which can be observed in any condition which interferes with maturation and social learning and is not specific to early childhood autism.

General mental retardation

As discussed in Chapter 3, general mental retardation is a frequent, though not an invariable, accompaniment of early childhood autism. The retardation cannot be explained on the basis of the impairments typical of autism. It seems reasonable to suggest that the classic autistic syndrome may be produced by a circumscribed lesion of the brain but that this limited abnormality can also occur as part of much more widespread damage causing general mental retardation as well as autistic behaviour.

It is possible that some of the conditions which lead to mental retardation, such as phenylketonuria or encephalitis in the first three years of life, are especially likely to include among their effects damage to the areas of the brain which are relevant to the autistic syndrome.

Ricks (1972) discussed the possibility that there may be two different ways in which autistic behaviour could be produced. The typical syndrome could, as suggested here, be due to an impairment of the mechanisms for scanning and classifying experiences and making creative use of the store of symbols. In other children, similar behaviour might occur because of multiple impairments which interfere with the perception of the environment, thus blocking any possibility of classifying experiences appropriately. This type of "secondary autism" might be especially likely to occur among children who are severely generally retarded. There is as yet no evidence for or against this hypothesis but it could perhaps explain some of the clinical differences found among children with autistic behaviour.

Special skills

The combination of impairment of symbolic function and an accurate memory for objects and events as they were first experienced provides a plausible explanation for the special skills found in the more able autistic children. Their ability with visuo-spatial tasks, the accurate verbal mimicry in those who can speak, the memory for music and, in some, for lists of names or facts in the absence of true comprehension are all predictable. It is possible that the precision with which the autistic child manipulates objects and remembers visual displays is a consequence of his lack of grasp of the symbolic meaning. The types of skill shown by autistic children and the significance of their peculiar form of memory are explored further in Chapters 5 and 6.

Conclusions

The picture of early childhood autism which emerges from this discussion is that of a series of jig-saw puzzle pieces which have not yet been fitted together. It is probable that many of the pieces which are needed to complete the pattern are still missing.

All that can be said with certainty at the present stage is that abnormalities in the handling of symbols and in the development of language and other forms of communication are prominent features in early childhood autism. They may be the primary problems which explain all the other aspects of the syndrome, but, until more facts are available, the question must remain open.

The formulation suggested by Wing and Wing (1971) still remains the most reasonable one in practice. That is, early childhood autism can be regarded as a condition in which a number of specific impairments, already described in this and other chapters, occur in combination, giving rise to a recognisable pattern of disturbed behaviour. Partial forms of the syndrome can occur as well as the complete picture and both partial and complete forms can be associated with other types of handicaps. Of all the impairments, those affecting language and communication in general have the greatest importance in practice since they determine the type of education and management needed by the child.

CHAPTER 5

CODING AND THE SENSE MODALITIES

Introduction

This chapter discusses the coding of sensory stimuli by autistic children; how far this is affected, on the one hand, by the sensory modality and, on the other, by stimulus configuration independent of modality.

Different sensory channels may have different facilities for dealing with certain kinds of information. But though presented in the same modality, different stimulus displays also have different underlying structures, which may lead to their specific and modality independent coding.

Results from the experiments which will be presented tend not to support the frequently made suggestion that children with autism are specifically impaired in processing information from some sensory channels, such as the auditory one, while being better able to deal with other, for example, tactile information. Rather, they seem to have specific difficulties in recognising redundancies and rules in sequences of stimuli, regardless of their modality.

On the other hand, in contrast to temporal-sequential structures, autistic children can deal relatively efficiently with the spatial framework and with information which refers to fixed positions in space. This is so regardless of whether such spatial cues are provided through vision or through the kinesthetic sense.

Our results also show that the interrelationship between the sensory modality of stimuli and the code used to deal with them is a complex one. Language impairment, whether caused by autism or deafness, seems to predispose children to extract spatial rather than temporal structures from ambiguously ordered items. This indicates an association between impairments in the auditory-verbal channel and difficulties with the extraction of temporal-sequential patterns from stimulus displays.

It is conceivable that the processing of sequential information depends particularly on the efficient use of redundancies and on appropriate information reduction. It may be the impairment of these processes which underlies much of the cognitive pathology of childhood autism.

Definition

In the context of the following chapter, childhood autism will be regarded as a condition which has developed on the basis of a central disorder of cognition. This working definition does not, of course, deny the presence of other aspects of the syndrome, such as an emotional or motivational malfunctioning. But a complex and multidimensional condition such as this cannot be fruitfully investigated in its totality. As we cannot tell in advance where a scientific advance will occur, the specific features which are selected for investigation will be determined as much by the biases and inclinations of the investigator as by any assumed order of predominance. We do not as yet fully understand the normal processes of perception, memory, language development or reasoning, so the specific characteristics of the cognitive pathology of childhood autism still remain undefined. Explanations offered in terms of a single underlying lesion accounting for such a multidimensional impairment are probably misleading, regardless of whether one implicates such diverse processes and mechanisms as, for instance, language disability, over-arousal or an abnormality in the hippocampus.

Achievement levels versus strategies

Much research in abnormal psychology has been concerned with describing deficits and disabilities associated with a particular diagnostic entity. It has been established that most intellectually retarded children can solve the problems, or learn the tasks, which can be mastered by normal children of comparable mental age. It has also been found that autistic children, while particularly impaired in language functions, generally perform better on visuo-spatial tasks, or on those in which immediate rote memory is involved. Such findings tell us what particular groups of children can or cannot do. They are concerned with levels of achievement, rather than with the way in which these levels are reached. In contrast, in the studies to be reported here, we have attempted to analyse the coding of stimuli and the strategies which autistic children employ. We concentrated mainly on those areas in which there seems to be relatively little impairment, namely memory and spatial ability, and asked whether there were any particular characteristics in the way in which the children achieved the relatively high levels of perfor-mance in these areas. We adopted two procedures for this purpose. One was to match autistic children, not only with younger normal groups of the same mental age, but also with retarded children, who had the same chronological age as well as the same mental age as the autistic children. With this procedure, any result which simply distinguished the normal from the two retarded groups would probably be due to IQ, and therefore of only limited interest, but if the results of such studies fell into any other pattern, something specific to autism could possibly be concluded.

Perceptual impairments

Another approach to the question of how autistic children organ-ise information from the world around them is to compare them with those whose supply of such information is limited because of some perceptual impairment. Though autistic children seem to see and hear adequately, their behaviour often resembles that of children whose vision or hearing is severely impaired. Though they can hear and see, it appears that they may not listen or look, and the consequences for information processing of not looking and listen-ing may be similar to those of not seeing or hearing. But rather than simply concluding that the behaviour of autistic children frequently resembles that of children who are blind or deaf, we should ask the more precise question: in what way and under what conditions does information processing in deaf or blind children resemble that in those who are autistic? For instance, does the lack of coded information from one channel affect in any way the manner in which the remaining information is processed? We therefore also compared autistic children with those with the specific handicaps of blindness or deafness.

The tasks we used in this series of experiments have usually been well within the capacity of the children we tested. Where possible, the experiments were designed in such a way that they did not elicit either correct or incorrect responses. The aim was rather to elicit the predominant strategy from amongst all those that were available. In other studies we matched the total level of performance of the autistic children with that of the control subjects, and tried to discover whether the pattern of results suggested that different strategies were used to achieve these levels. As already mentioned, we were not concerned with the question of whether certain groups of children could or could not do certain things, but with the way the children did them.

Information reduction

In order to deal effectively with information about the environment, structuring and reduction of the incoming data is essential, because of the limited capacity of the human organism for information processing. One device which helps to overcome such limitations is to make use of redundancy in the information. In listening to speech, or in reading, not every single phoneme or letter needs to be perceived. The listener or reader supplies much of the necessary information by using his knowledge of the nature of the language which is used. Another way to make economical use of limited capacity is "chunking", that is treating many items such as words as a unit such as a sentence, and many letters of the alphabet as word units. Capacity limitations may also be overcome by reducing the input through condensing and categorising. This involves the induction of rules, so that, for instance, a memory span of seven for randomly arranged digits can be increased considerably by having a series in which any subsequent number is twice as large as the preceding one. All that needs to be remembered in this case is the rule, which of course first has to be stated or induced. It is no exaggeration to say that virtually all cognitive operations involve such "pattern perception". Pattern perception means that the organism processes input as if most of the input was lawful and predictable. In his series of experiments on time perception, Wundt, as early as 1896, found evidence of subjective structuring that was in no way warranted by the stimuli. When presented with a monotonous, perfectly regular series of clicks, observers found it extremely difficult not to perceive various rhythms of stresses. Wundt called this the subjective element in perception.

Miller (1967) has summed up the issue by stating: "It seems that the very fact of our limited capacity for processing information has made it necessary for us to discover clever ways to abstract the essential features of our universe". Different aspects of this universe may need different codes, in order that they can be dealt with most effectively. In order to cope with the stream of successively occurring events, information reduction according to appropriate rules seems particularly essential. Because memory capacity is limited, retention of very large numbers of separate items would not be possible, so contraction and "chunking" into larger units is necessary. The best example of this process probably comes from the area of language. Comprehension depends on making use of the redundancies of language and the way in which we have learned to compensate for our limited memory capacity may be related to our capacity for language.

This process of information reduction may not apply in quite the same way to spatial as it does to temporal patterns. Of course, a great deal of abstraction and feature extraction also occurs when spatial information is stored. But information about items in space is often simultaneously available. This means that a lot of going over and reviewing can be done during the actual process of perception. Similarly, memory images often enable one to re-evoke an entire scene. It is different for temporal sequences, such as words in a sentence. These are perceived and recalled successively, and, after an event has occurred, one often remembers also its temporal place in the sequence. As has already been pointed out, this capacity to remember temporal sequences is limited, as everyone knows from, for instance, trying to recall a long telephone number. We deal with this problem by using rules to reduce the information load.

In the experiments to be reported here, we investigated the effect, in autistic children, of the sensory quality of the information. We also asked whether input restriction from one sense affects information processing from other senses. In addition to this we were concerned with the kinds of codes which are necessary for dealing with different aspects of the environment, and with the abilities and disabilities of autistic children in handling such codes. All the experiments which follow have been carried out in collaboration with my colleagues N. O'Connor or Uta Frith.

The children

The autistic children taking part in the present series of experiments came from a sample of children who conformed to the diagnostic criteria described by Rutter (1968). All attended special schools. All showed language abnormalities with associated cognitive disorders, some degree of autistic withdrawal and various forms of repetitive and obsessional-ritualistic behaviour. The average chronological age of the main sample was 10·4 years (6·10 to 15·6), the mean social age as measured by the Vineland Social Maturity Scale was 6·4 years (3·4 to 10·6), the mean WISC Verbal scale IQ was 48 (35 to 79) and the WISC performance scale IQ was 65 (44 to 115). A few experiments also included a group of autistic children who functioned at a considerably lower intellectual level. These subjects had IQ's below 40, and were mute or had only a few words of speech. Onset in all cases was reported to have occurred before the age of 18 months, and no child showed signs of any gross neurological abnormality. Retarded children were matched for mental as well as chronological age with the autistic group. These non-autistic retarded children came from schools for the educationally subnormal or from E.S.N. (Severe) schools. Normal controls covered a wide age range from 3 to 15 years.

In the experiments in which autistic children were compared with those with specific perceptual impairments, blind or deaf children were selected as control groups. Their mental and chronological ages ranged from 10 years to 15 years. These children attended schools for the totally blind or deaf. Onset of blindness or deafness in all cases had occurred at birth or during the first 18 months of life.

The Experiments

Spatial location

The first series of studies to be reported here concerns the way in which autistic children deal with some aspects of spatial organisation. In an early experiment we tested very retarded autistic children on two discrimination tasks. The subjects all had IQ's below 40 and had very little or no speech (Hermelin and O'Connor, 1970). In one condition a reward was obtained for selecting one of two boxes marked with a particular shape, and for disregarding the box's left- or right-hand position which was varied from trial to trial. In the other task the choice of a spatial position rather than that of shape was rewarded. We found that autistic children learned the second task much faster than the first.

It may be of interest that, at least in the case of some non-human mammals, evidence points to a different visual system for providing the organism with information about the qualities of objects, as distinct from their location (Schneider, 1967). The findings indicated that the visual cortex permits the distinguishing and identifying of visual stimuli, while certain midbrain structures aid the animal in locating visual targets. In any case, our results indicated that autistic children of low intelligence found it easier to locate than to identify a stimulus cue. This and similar findings led us to hypothesise that one area in which such children functioned relatively well was concerned with the spatial framework and with spatial position.

An organism experiences space not only through vision, but also through other senses. Attneave and Benson (1969) who investigated the role of sensory specific processing of information, stated that space was primarily represented in visual terms, regardless of whether the input was from vision or from another modality. From their experiment on the learning of associations between words with a particular location in space, and words with a particular body location touched, the authors concluded that the subjects "mapped" stimuli into an imagined visual space. They suggested that different modalities might have qualitatively different facilities for data handling, and that sensory information might be transferred to the modality best able to process and store it. On this assumption, temporarily blindfolded subjects should respond like the sighted, by utilizing a conceptualized visual space. On the other hand, subjects without sight or without the ability to process visual information adequately might use a different code for spatial organisation.

We compared normal, blind and autistic children to test this hypothesis (Hermelin and O'Connor, 1971). The subjects of this experiment were 10 autistic, 10 blind and 20 normal children. Ten of the normal children were blindfolded. The onset of the autistic syndrome for all 10 children occurred before the age of 18 months; their behaviour included social withdrawal, language abnormalities, repetitive "rituals" and stereotyped movements. None had detectable neurological impairment. They were aged between 11 and 15 years and were matched for mental age with the other groups.

Seven of the 10 blind children were congenitally blind, while onset in the remaining three occurred within the first year of life. All attended a school for the totally blind. Their IQ's on the Williams (1950) test ranged between 100 and 142 (mean 118). Like the normal children they were aged between 8 and 10 years.

Subjects were tested individually. They were first told that they had to learn four words. These were "run", "sit", "walk", "stand". The index and middle fingers of each hand were then placed on a $6 \times 16\frac{1}{2}$ in. board, as shown in Fig. 5.1. One half began with the right hand extended in front of the left, and for the other half of the children these positions were reversed. The top of a finger was then lightly touched with a brush while E said "This is 'run'", or, while touching another finger, "This is 'sit'", etc. Care was taken not to indicate whether "This" referred to the stimulation of a particular finger or its particular position. After this demonstration, the child had to learn to respond to stimulation with the brush by uttering the correct word. Stimulation was administered in a predetermined

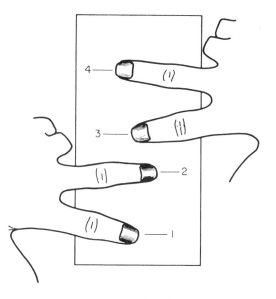

Fig. 5.1

random order, with the proviso that each tactile-verbal stimulus-response pair occurred equally often over a series of 40 trials. A learning criterion of 19 correct out of 20 responses was adopted. Incorrect responses were corrected by E saying, for example: "No, this is 'stand'". Correct responses were reinforced by saying "good".

After the associations had been learned to criterion, E changed the position of subject's hands, so that those fingers initially at positions 1 and 2 were now in positions 3 and 4 respectively, while those which had been in positions 3 and 4 during learning were now at 1 and 2. While E was altering the position of subject's hands, he said "We will just go on". No further instructions or corrections were given over the 40 transfer trials.

After the hand reversal, two alternative strategies were available to the child. He could maintain a fixed spatial framework so that location became independent of the finger touched. Thus, if the word "run" had been associated formerly with the finger in position

4, this finger now occupied position 2, but the response to its former spatial position could be maintained. Alternatively, location might be regarded as relative, and attached to a particular finger. Thus "run" which was initially given in response to stimulation at one point in absolute space might now be given to the same finger occupying a different position in space. The first type was termed "location" and the second "finger" response.

The results showed that the location responses dominated in those subjects who performed the task with vision, while finger responses were more frequent for those without. Sighted autistic and sighted normal children did not differ significantly from each other in response distribution, nor did the blind children differ significantly from sighted blindfolded children. Those who performed the task while looking, differed significantly in their response pattern from those who did not. Thus, in this task children used the most immediately available sensory data for organising their responses. Blindfolded normal children did not respond in terms of a conceptual spatial framework which was organised in visual terms. Rather, they behaved as if they were blind. On the other hand, autistic children responded in a similar manner to other seeing children, and did not organise the stimuli in terms of a relational, tactually, determined, spatial or "finger" code. They used an absolute visual-spatial framework to determine location. This shows that it is an oversimplification to assume an overall abnormal hierarchical structure of sensory channels in childhood autism, and to assume, for instance, a general dominance of touch over vision. When visual information is codable for autistic children, as when it refers to spatial location, they use it like other sighted children and do not behave like the blind or blindfolded.

Kinesthetic information

That it is the code used, rather than the stimulus modality, which determines the way autistic children deal with information was also shown in another study where kinesthetic instead of visual cues for spatial location were available. In a recent experiment we compared normal, blind and autistic children on their ability to remember and reproduce an arm movement. The children were aged between 10 and 15 years. The normal and blind groups were matched for verbal mental age which had a mean of 12 years and 8 months. The mean verbal age of the autistic children was 7 years and their mean performance mental age was 11 years. Normal and autistic children were blindfolded during the experiment. All were tested individually.

Information about movement arises from the kinesthetic sensory system, which is concerned with the perception of the position of parts of the body relative to each other and to the entire body (Howard and Templeton, 1966). Physiological evidence indicates that the kinesthetic receptors are located in the joint capsule (Mountcastle and Powell, 1959). Information from these receptors reaches the sensory cortex and thus provides conscious awareness of movement.

Obviously, different aspects and components of movement, such as its location, direction, speed and acceleration have to be coded. The experiment dealt with the differentiation between location and distance cues. A further question, which was investigated in this context, was whether blindfolded sighted children would use visuo-spatial imagery, and whether the availability of such images was advantageous for the memory and reproduction of previous location reached or distance travelled.

The apparatus used was a vertical rod, on which a lever could be moved up and down. A centimeter scale running along the rod enabled the experimenter to determine accuracy. Sighted children were blindfolded before seeing the apparatus.

In the procedure used for movement reproduction, a stop was set at distances of 10, 15, 20 or 30 cm from the bottom starting position. The subject then moved the lever up to the stop three times for a given distance. After this, the stop was removed, the lever was put back at starting position, and the child was required to attempt to reproduce the movement, approximately 3 seconds after having carried out the standard movement. For distance reproduction the same initial standard procedure was used, but, after the stop was removed, the lever was put at a different starting position from that used in the training trials. The subject attempted to reproduce the same amount of movement, that is to cover the same distance as initially, but from a different starting point. In location reproduction the lever was also moved to a new starting position after the removal of the stop, and the child attempted to stop at the same location as he had in the training trials when using a different starting point.

Thus, in the first condition a vertical arm movement was experienced, and had then to be reproduced. In the second, the amount of movement, that is the distance covered, had to be reproduced when starting location was altered. This would of course also result in an altered end position. Finally, the amount of distance to be covered had to be ignored in order to arrive at the same end location as in the training trials, but after starting from a different point.

There was an additional refinement in the experimental procedure. The question could be asked whether a movement made with one arm could be reproduced better with the same arm than with the contralateral one. Over a short time period, information may still be available from muscular feedback, and reproduction with the arm that performed the standard movement may be more accurate than that attempted with the other arm. To investigate this, half the children used their preferred hand for the training trials, where movement was terminated by the level reaching the stop, and then the same hand for reproduction when the stopper was removed. The other children used their nonpreferred hand for the training trials and the preferred hand for the test trials.

Movement reproduction

There was an overall tendency for all children to make larger errors when a longer than when a shorter movement had to be reproduced. This tendency was least marked for the autistic children. Shorter distances tended to be overestimated and longer ones underestimated. All children performed as well when one as when both hands were used, and the groups did not differ from each other in the degree of accuracy.

Distance reproduction

Autistic and blind children were less accurate than normal children in reproducing the same amount of movement from a new starting position. The two handicapped groups showed more undershooting for long distances. No difference according to hand use was found.

Location reproduction

There was no difference between the groups in degree of accuracy, nor was the use of one hand different from that of two. As with movement reproduction, normal and blind children tended to make greater errors with longer distances, while this was not the case for autistic children.

The autistic children therefore could reproduce experienced movements at least as well as blind and sighted normal children, and could also isolate location cues, and use them as adequately as the other groups. This implies not only that autistic children have good short-term memories for simple movements, but they must also have a code which enables them to deal with kinesthetic-spatial cues in a flexible manner.

These conclusions may account only for the results of simple reproduction, and reproduction of end location, and may not apply to the attempts to reproduce distance independent of starting and stopping positions. Particularly at the more extended heights the amount of error for this last task increased sharply, due to marked undershooting. This was particularly so in the blind and autistic children. The experiment had been designed in such a way that, in the distance reproduction task, the target point was always higher than that for the corresponding distance in each of the other conditions. It is possible that the direction, and perhaps even the size of the errors, might have been dependent on the extent to which the child had to reach upwards in order to complete a movement ending near the top of the scale. It seems that the blind children in particular were reluctant to extend their arms to such a degree. But it is also possible that distance information is best handled by reference to the visual system, and that particularly the blind, but also the autistic children, were handicapped in this respect. In the case of the blind children, the reasons for this are obvious. As far as the autistic children are concerned, we have shown previously that integration between different modality systems seems to be impaired. Even when visual cues were provided, autistic children seemed to rely mainly on motor feedback, ignoring the visual information (Frith and Hermelin, 1969).

Marteniuk and Roy (1972), from the available physiological evidence (Mountcastle and Powell, 1959; Smith, 1969), suggest that distance information is not very precise, or perhaps is even uncodable when it is the only information available regarding limb displacement. In our results this became evident only when the target reached a point at which the arm had to be extended above the head. With shorter movements the relation of the arm to the body may have provided a reference point, but it seems that, at the more extended heights, the normal sighted children may have utilised additional remembered visual imagery as a reference to gauge distance. As the blind children were unable to elicit these additional cues, their performance at the extended heights on distance reproduction deteriorated. The autistic children, though not having any visual impairment, nevertheless seemed unable to refer kinesthetic information to a visually derived spatial framework. They therefore resembled the blind in their performance on the distance task at greater heights.

Experiments with visual sequences

We shall now turn to those experiments which are concerned with memory of temporally distributed series of events. Objects and events are located not only in space but also in time, and memory for temporal order may be particularly important for successively presented items of information, such as speech. As we want to investigate whether disabilities in using certain codes are or are not modality specific, we shall first report some studies in which sequences of items were visually presented. This makes the terms "temporal" and "spatial" somewhat ambiguous, but the emphasis here is on the sequential character of the presented material, and on the rules which govern these sequences.

The first experiment in this series of studies (O'Connor and Hermelin, 1965), compared autistic with normal and retarded children in three tasks, using the material illustrated in Fig. 5.2. This material was used to test matching, memory and seriation.

The autistic children who acted as subjects were similar to those described in the first spatial study (Hermelin and O'Connor, 1970). Their chronological ages ranged from 10 to 15 years. They had low intelligence test scores and no, or little, speech. Their mean performance mental age of about 5 years was matched with the chronological age of the normal children. Retarded children matched for chronological age with the autistic children were also tested. They

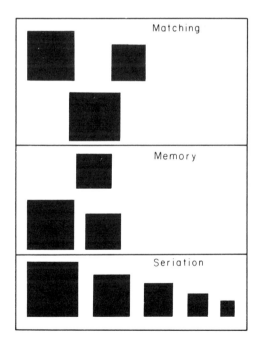

Fig. 5.2

had a mean performance mental age of 3 years, which was lower than that of the other groups.

The first task in the experiment was concerned with matching from cues. Two squares of different size were presented, together with one cue card. The square drawn on this cue card matched one of the object squares. Selection of this matching square was rewarded. The second task tested immediate memory. The subject was required to choose between two squares, one of which had been shown to him 3 seconds beforehand. Correct matching from memory was rewarded. The third test, seriation, consisted of presenting five squares of decreasing size. The experimenter set these out in order of size, and invited the subject to look at the series. The arrangement was then destroyed and the subject was instructed to reconstruct it.

The results showed that all groups were equal on the matching tasks, suggesting that they could all differentiate perceptually between the items. The autistic and normal children also performed equally well on the memory task, whereas the retarded children performed significantly worse. On the other hand, while the normal and retarded groups achieved a good performance level on seriation, the autistic children's scores were significantly lower on this test. Immediate visual memory seemed related to performance intelligence, as only the retarded children, who had lower performance test scores than the other graphs, performed badly in this task. For the seriation task the retarded children did not have to rely on memory for the absolute size of the items. All they had to do was to extract the rule that the squares formed a series of decreasing size, and it seems from the results that they were able to do this. The autistic children did not seem able to extract this rule, but appear to have treated the series as a number of unconnected items. As they could not always remember the order of each of the 5 items they were often unable to reconstruct the series.

True seriation, according to Inhelder and Piaget (1964) does require more than simply the ordering of elements. The operation consists of a systematic method of seeking first the largest element, then the largest of those left over, and so on. But this implies also that a given element will be simultaneously smaller than the preceding items and larger than those following. Inhelder and Piaget suggest that this is a form of reversibility or reciprocity, a concept which normal children acquire only at about age 7.

Binary patterns

It might be argued that the previous seriation test involved more than the simple appreciation of order. The next study to be reported (Frith, 1970a) used simple binary sequences, where two items, in this instance red and green counters, were arranged in a pattern which the child had to reproduce. The simplest patterns which can be formed with such material appear to be repetitions such as: "red, red, red, green, green, green", or alternations, such as: "red, green, red, green, red, green". If a child is presented with a series in which the number of items it contains exceeds his immediate visual memory span, he has to extract the dominant rule governing the pattern in order to reproduce it correctly. In the case of a regular alternation or repetition series, this is relatively easy. In the case of more complex structures, such as "red, green, green, red", it is more difficult. The more irregular the pattern becomes, the more difficult it will be to extract the dominant feature. The patterns used in the experiment contained either predominantly repetitions or alternations. Also, some patterns were very regular while others were not. The dominant feature of a pattern could be clearly identified in terms of "Alternation" or "Repetition" rules as could the degree of regularity or irregularity it contained.

Young normal children aged 5 to 6 years were matched for chronological age with the mental ages of a group of autistic children. Each child had to learn to make up four patterns with green and red counters of 3·6 cm diameter, which they placed in a row inside a groove on a board, just wide enough to hold a counter. The patterns were never shown beforehand, so that they had to be constructed gradually, aided by corrections. Each session, which lasted about $\frac{1}{2}$ hour, started with a sorting task to make sure that there was no difficulty in colour discrimination. For this the subjects had to sort green and red counters into two boxes. There were 36 counters of each colour.

The instructions for the experimental task relied mainly on a demonstration and a practice trial. The counters from the two boxes had to be placed one by one in a row, so as to make a certain pattern. If the wrong colour was chosen, this was at once corrected by the experimenter. As soon as one pattern was completed it was covered by a lid. The subjects had to repeat each pattern nine times, but as each time the just-completed pattern was covered, copying was impossible and the pattern had to be remembered.

Rule extraction

Error scores indicated how often a subject had used the incorrect colour in any position in a given pattern. Analysis of variance showed a significant interaction of Groups by Pattern. This interaction demonstrated that the numbers of errors made by the normal children were clearly different for the four patterns, while the error scores of the autistic children were similar for all patterns. Normal children learned the two regular patterns faster than the more irregular ones, while the autistic children did not.

Another analysis investigated whether the errors were random or whether they were systematically related to the dominant feature of a given pattern. Errors in "repetition-dominant" patterns should be due to excessive application of the repetition rule and errors in "alternation-dominant" patterns should be due to excessive application of the alternation rule.

An error due to alternation in an alternation-dominated pattern was considered a positive instance of feature extraction, while an error due to repetition in such a pattern was considered a negative instance. The reverse was the case for repetition patterns. An analysis of variance showed that normal children made more errors which were in accordance with the dominant feature of the pattern; errors not complying with the dominant features were significantly less frequent. For autistic children both types of error were equally frequent, and were independent of the dominant features of the given pattern.

The performance of normal children on this task indicated that for them the four patterns were not equally easy to learn, but autistic children did not perform differently with the different types of patterns, in spite of their differing degree of regularity. This finding is consistent with the hypothesis that autistic children are less sensitive to the structural characteristics of sequentially ordered stimuli than others of equal mental age. Even more support for this hypothesis was provided by the error analysis. Most errors made by the control groups were consistent with the predominant rule of the given pattern.

This indicates that feature extraction did occur. In autistic children little evidence of feature extraction could be found. Most of their errors were not consistent with the predominant rule of the pattern as given.

Thus, in the seriation and the colour sequence tasks, autistic children did not seem to use the redundancy of information which was provided. Instead of extracting the structure of the patterns, thereby reducing the memory load, they treated the material as a series of distinct items to be retained by rote memory.

Redundancy in a jig-saw puzzle task

These results confirmed findings from a previous study (Frith and Hermelin, 1969) which had also demonstrated that autistic children tend not to make use of redundancy. Children of different levels of cognitive ability were tested, but as the task was a relatively easy one for the more intelligent children, scores differentiated only between the younger and more backward groups. Therefore only the data from these latter groups will be presented here.

The subjects were 10 autistic, 10 retarded and 10 normal children. The autistic children were selected according to psychiatric diag-nosis, which in all cases included onset in the first 18 months of life. All showed absence or impairment of speech, stereotyped move-ments and a low level of cognitive functioning. All the autistic children had at some stage in their lives been described as socially aloof and unable to form adequate human relationships. The retarded children all had IQ's below 50 and were free from autistic symptoms. These two groups were matched with each other and with normal children in terms of their level of performance on visuo-motor items

(Subtest I) from the Frostig Test of Visual Perception. This requires the child to draw a pencil line between two printed lines and to connect dots with a straight line. The performance was assessed in terms of accuracy, and the derived mean perceptual age for all three groups was 4 years, which was also the chronological age of the normals. The chronological age of the retarded and autistic children ranged from 6 to 15 years.

The material used in the experiment resembled a jig-saw puzzle. It was selected because observation suggested that autistic children are often surprisingly efficient with constructional tasks of this type, sometimes performing as well when presented with the pieces face-down as when they are face-up. Such tasks therefore present few additional problems of motivation, attention, frustration or communication of instructions. Different forms of puzzles were presented to each child. These are illustrated in Fig. 5.3.

For each of the sets, 6 cards measuring 10 cm × 7 cm were used. They were made of 2-mm thick cardboard covered with a translucent film. All cards of a set contained pictures of trees, flowers or houses, so that the vertical orientation of a card was immediately

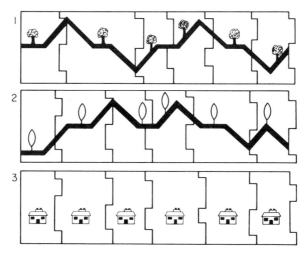

Fig. 5.3

recognisable. Cards for the first two sets contained line segment patterns. In addition, when placed together correctly, the cut-out edges of the cards interlocked as in a jig-saw puzzle. Only the length and not the shape of the interlocking edges varied between the cards, in order to make discrimination of this feature difficult. As illustrated in Fig. 5.3, the line pattern in set 1 repeated itself, that is, it contained a high degree of redundancy. Set 2 also had a line pattern, but this was less redundant. In set 3 only spatial and not sequential information was given. The correct succession of the cards was determined by the fit of the interlocking edges, as there was no continuous line pattern.

The analysis of the data was carried out using error scores, that is, the number of times a child picked up an incorrect card and was corrected. Two aspects of these results are of interest. The first is concerned with a comparison of conditions where sequential as well as spatial cues were present in the material (Sets 1 and 2) and that where only spatial information was provided (Set 3). Normal as well as retarded children made fewer errors with the sets which provided both types of information, while for the autistic children this was not the case. They were not helped by the presence of continuous line segments on the cards.

The second analysis of the results compared the effect of redundant sequential cues (Set 1) with Set 2 which had less redundancy. Normal and retarded children made fewer errors with the regular than with the irregular line pattern, while there was no such difference for the autistic children.

It is of importance that overall performance level was equal for all three groups, and differences became apparent only in the different patterns of scores for the various conditions. This suggested that these differences were due to different strategies used by the children, and not to different levels of ability. Strategies adopted by the normal and retarded children alike included the use of sequential as well as of spatial information, and pointed to the extraction of the feature of redundancy in the line patterns. The autistic children did not make use of this redundancy, and did not perform better with sets in which the line pattern repeated itself than with those where it did not. They seem to have used the spatial information provided by the cut-out edges rather than the sequential cues, even when the latter were present.

Auditory-verbal sequences

So far this section has dealt with studies in which visually presented sequences were used. For such material the terms "spatial" and "temporal" are ambiguous, as any one item occupies a place in space as well as in a temporally sequential order. In this context it may be more precise to distinguish between stimuli which occupy a single fixed position in space, and those which are interdependent and consist of items which are sequentially ordered. Auditory stimuli are more clearly temporally structured, and the next experiment is concerned with tasks in which stimuli and responses are auditory-verbal.

The procedure in this study (Frith, 1970b) resembles that used in the experiment with colour sequences (Frith, 1970a). Normal, retarded and autistic children were selected and matched for their immediate memory span for digits. The children then had to recall word lists that were longer than their immediate memory capacity. For example: "mouse-mouse-mouse-bag-bag-bag" or "spoon-horse-spoon-horse-horse-spoon". All children could remember the two words in each list, and they knew which one came first and which second. To obtain a high recall score, it was necessary to remember the arrangement of the words.

As in the experiment with binary visual patterns, the analysis of recall was done in two stages. First, the number of correctly recalled words (that is, the right word in the right place) was examined. This showed that simple, high redundant patterns like "mouse-mouse-mouse-bag-bag-bag" were recalled much better by the control groups than by the autistic children. With less redundant patterns of quasi-random arrangement, such as "spoon-horse-spoon-horse-horse-spoon", the autistic children did at least as well as the controls.

The second stage of the analysis was concerned with the types of errors which were made. As previously, the predominant rules which governed the structure of the sequence were either alternation or repetition. These rules could be used to reconstruct the original sequence with minimal loss. For example, the sequence "one-two-one-one" contains predominantly alternations. If this rule is used in recall, the sequence "one-two-one-two" is obtained, which is almost correct, except for one error. It was determined whether or not the dominant rule of the originally presented sequence was also the dominant rule of an incorrectly recalled sequence. The results showed that the rules: "mainly repetitions" or: "mainly alternations" were extracted and correctly retained by normal and by retarded children, even in otherwise incorrectly recalled messages. Errors made by these children were in accordance with the dominant feature of the sequence. The rule, which was correctly extracted, was incorrectly applied, that is, applied in an exaggerated form. Instead of three repetitions following one alternation ("one-two-two-two") there would be, say four repetitions but no additional alternations ("two-two-two-two") or ("one-two-two-two-two"). On the other hand, if a given sequence contained predominantly alternations, the recalled sequence tended to contain even more alternations. For example, "one-two-one-one" was often recalled as "one-two-one-two". The non-dominant rule was hardly ever exaggerated by the normal and retarded children and was sometimes even omitted, as in the previous example.

Autistic children performed quite differently. They also showed rule exaggeration, but they tended to apply almost exclusively the repetition rule, whether or not this was the dominant rule in the presented sequence. For example, the sequence "spoon-horse-spoon-horse-horse-spoon", containing four alternations and only one repetition, was recalled as "horse-horse-horse-spoon", containing only one alternation but two repetitions. In this case the non-dominant rule was exaggerated.

It can be concluded from these results that normal and retarded children were able to extract either one of the two important rules present in the input, but that autistic children have a bias towards applying only one rule, that of repetition, regardless of the input.

Temporal and spatial ordering

As the results from the two experiments with binary sequences were so similar, regardless of whether the material was visually or verbally presented, it does seem that it is the coding process rather than the stimulus modality which is crucial. Nevertheless, different sensory channels may have different facilities for dealing with certain kinds of information. Space is a framework which is constructed mainly through visual and motor feedback information, but things and events are located in time as well as in space. Appreciation of temporal sequences may be specially related to the sense of hearing and in particular to the language system. The auditory system seems predisposed to organise items in a temporal sequence (Hirsh, 1967). Deprivation experiments by Hirsh, Bilger and Deatherage (1956) indicated that temporal judgments were most disturbed by restriction of auditory input and little disturbed by restriction of vision. Paivio (1971) suggested that the visual system is specialised for storing spatially organised objects and events, while temporal sequential processing is primarily a function of the auditory-vocal system.

If this is true, what will happen if verbal stimuli are visually presented in such a way that either temporal or spatial organisation is possible? In reading, spatial and temporal orders normally coincide. For many languages the temporally first occurring word is printed on the extreme left-hand side of a page, the temporally second on the second position from the left, and so on. In other languages, for instance Hebrew, the spatial order runs from right to left, and in others, such as Chinese, it is from top to bottom. In all instances a correspondence between temporal and spatial order is maintained.

If visual displays tend to be spatially ordered, whereas auditory and particularly verbal stimuli are temporally organised, one might investigate whether children with and without intact language systems would use different strategies with ambiguously ordered, visually presented, verbal material. In the previous studies, which were concerned with spatial organisation, we have compared autistic children with others, who were either temporarily or permanently deprived of sight. The next series of experiments used deaf as well as autistic and normal children to investigate temporal coding and its relation to hearing and language (O'Connor and Hermelin, 1972).

The basic procedure for the study was to present three visually exposed digits successively from a display box with three apertures.

The display of digits was arranged on a panel at eye level with three windows, each 4 cm square and 12 cm apart from centre to centre. Digits appeared in these windows successively and were themselves 2·5 cm high. Subjects were shown three digits which occurred successively in such a way that the second, i.e. the "middle one" from the temporal point of view, always occurred in the left- or right-handed positions on the display box and never in the centre. The digit which occurred in the spatial middle of the three display windows was therefore always either the first or third in temporal succession. The display is schematically presented in Fig. 5.4.

If a subject was asked which of the 3 digits was the "middle one", he would thus have to select 1 of 2 digits, that which occurred in the spatial or that which occurred in the temporal middle. Instructions were "You will see 3 numbers, wait till you have seen them all, then tell me the middle one". If a subject asked which middle number he was to choose, he was encouraged to make a free choice. Of 45 children, only 2 asked this question. The temporal and spatial order of digits was randomised over trials using Digits 1–9 inclusive. The 3 digits were presented over a 2-second period, and the average pause between any two displays of 3 digits was 8 seconds with a range of 6 to 12 seconds. The actual digits displayed were set by the operator during the pause between trials by means of 3 rotary switches for left, centre and right digits respectively. Intensities were 1·2 log fl.

The results from this experiment showed that all children who

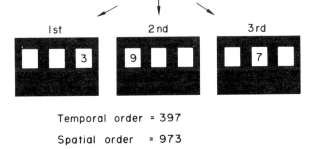

Fig. 5.4

were presented with this incongruously ordered display, whether they were normal, autistic or deaf, ignored temporal succession and selected the spatially central digit as the middle one. All children responded similarly, whether deaf or hearing, normal or autistic.

Essentially, our results indicated that visual input modality induced a spatial set. Though two alternative response strategies had been possible, temporal sequential order had been ignored. However, the experiment had used a single item selection task, which put no load on the memory system. Experiments on short-term memory for *verbal* input lead one to expect that here the coding of items to be remembered does include information about temporal order. Tulving and Madigan (1970) noted that the temporal code of verbal items in short-term memory becomes part of what the subject remembers, even when no specific instructions to retain order information are given. Conrad (1962) and Morton (1970) have shown that, when verbal material has to be remembered, it is almost always stored in a speech code, regardless of whether it was present acoustically or visually. Such a code would be expected to have temporal-sequential characteristics. It therefore might be predicted that, in contrast to the previously reported task where memory was not involved, incongruently ordered material would be coded temporally if it had to be recalled. In memory tasks normal children might be expected to change from a modality determined spatial code to a language determined temporal one. Would deaf or autistic children also use a temporal-sequential ordering strategy? If such a strategy was language dependent and was a function of a covert speech code, other forms of organisation might occur in these language impaired groups.

In our next experiment (O'Connor and Hermelin, 1973) digits were again presented visually in such a way that their organisation in memory could follow a spatial, left to right or a sequential, first to last order, but this time all 3 digits had to be remembered.

The display apparatus was the same as that used in the previous study. As before, in any one display the spatial and temporal orders of digits were incongruent, so that they never appeared in a left-to-right succession. For instance, if the numbers occurred in a temporally successive order, e.g. 3 9 7, the spatial order might be 9 in the left-hand window, 7 in the middle one and 3 in the right-hand one. Sixteen sets of 3 digits in non-corresponding temporal and spatial order were then presented to each child. The children were given the following instructions: "You will see 3 numbers coming up in these windows. When you see all 3, I want you to tell me the numbers you saw".

Temporally organised responses were obtained from almost all normal children. This response distribution in favour of temporal as compared with spatial organisation was statistically highly significant. In contrast, while nearly all normal children recalled the digits from first to last, nearly all the autistic and most of the deaf recalled them from left to right. Normal children switched their strategy from a spatially organised one in a single item selection task, to a temporally ordered one if recall was required, but most of the subjects from the other groups retained a spatial, left-to-right order for the memory tasks. Within the groups, neither language ability in the autistic, nor degree of articulation ability in the deaf children distinguished the spatial from the temporal coders.

It could be argued that recall allowed the subject to select either one of two available ordering strategies, a temporal or a spatial one. In recognition, on the other hand, such a choice could be excluded, and it would be possible to test whether the material was accessible to the subject exclusively in either the temporal or the spatial order. In the next part of the experiment we therefore used a forced choice recognition procedure. As previously, 3 digits were displayed visually in an incongruent spatial and temporal order. The subject was then immediately presented with a card measuring 5×10 cm. On each card 2 sets of 3 digits were printed. One set corresponded to either the temporal or the spatial order of the preceding display. The other set consisted of the same 3 numbers, but ordered randomly in a manner which did not correspond to either the temporal or spatial sequences. If the temporal sequence of exposure had, for instance, been 3 5 9 and the left-to-right exposure 5 3 9, one card would show 3 5 9 (temporal) together with 9 3 5 (random) and another card would show 5 3 9 (spatial) with 9 3 5 (random). On half the cards the randomly ordered set was printed above and on half below the temporally or spatially ordered set. Each subject was tested for 32 trials, and for 16 of these he tried to recognise the temporal and for the other 16 the spatial order of the previously displayed digits. Instructions were: "You are going to see 3 numbers. After this you will see a card with 2 sets of numbers. Point to the one you have just seen".

The results obtained from normal children indicated that only the temporally ordered digits were recognised successfully. If the digits shown were in a spatial order, responses were at a chance level, that is, the random arrangement was pointed to as often as the spatially ordered one. On the other hand most, though not all, autistic and deaf children, in recognition conditions, used a spatial (left to right) rather than a temporal (first to last) organisation of the memory code. It can therefore be assumed that temporal ordering is in some way related to, or dependent on, hearing or listening which in turn may be important for the adequate use of language as a storage code.

Summary and Conclusions

It now remains to summarise the results which have been reported here, and attempt some interpretation. But first we must draw attention to the restricted nature of the findings, which are derived from a small number of experiments with a particular sample of subjects. One of the most important qualifying factors for the generality of any conclusions drawn from these studies is that most of the autistic children who took part were functioning on a relatively high intellectual level. Except in one experiment dealing with spatial location, and in two dealing with sequential order, all subjects had some speech and some comprehension, and all had IQ's above 50, with some subjects being in the normal range. Less than half of all children diagnosed as autistic function at these levels, and the findings may not be representative of the whole autistic group.

Even in regard to the particular group of children tested here, the experiments were confined to a single well-delineated area of behaviour and represent only one aspect of a multifaceted syndrome. Our concern was mainly with the relationship between specific sensory input, and the codes used to interpret this input.

From the results we have reported, our conclusion is that the autistic syndrome does not include abnormal functioning of some sensory channels. Autism cannot justifiably be regarded as being based on a multiple but selective perceptual impairment, where the children do not respond to some sensory stimulus modalities while preferring others (Schopler, 1965; Hermelin and O'Connor, 1970). It is possible to recognise, even without results from experiments, the oversimplification such statements represent. How, for instance, could the relative lack of responsiveness to speech and the often reported strong responsiveness to music be reconciled with a general auditory imperception? The central problem in autistic children appears to involve not stimuli in a particular modality, but stimuli requiring organisation into particular codes which are modality independent. Such codes are used by the normal child to reduce the information load and enable him to integrate stimuli and interpret the environment appropriately through the extraction of rules and redundancies.

Storage systems which are modality specific are assumed to contain information in a relatively "raw" or unprocessed form. Such modality specific short-term stores have been proposed for vision and audition (Neisser, 1967) and more recently for touch (Schurman *et al.*, 1973). It is assumed that information in these stores decays rapidly, unless it is encoded and transferred to a non-modality-specific "abstract" short-term memory store.

Autistic children have very good short-term memories, but the system seems to have retained many of the characteristics which, in normal people, are associated only with a very brief, sensory specific, memory trace, which is assumed to be uncoded. Much of the encoding and restructuring of information, which apparently occurs normally in the short-term non-modality-specific, abstract memory store, may be absent in childhood autism. Instead, the children tend to use an extended form of the uncoded immediate memory system. This leads to good results with material which needs little subsequent coding, but depends on distinct item retention, such as sequences with little redundancy or regularity. The process is also an efficient one when precise location of objects, or position of limbs in space, have to be remembered.

The frequently described musical ability of the autistic child also provides an illustration of these characteristics of memory storage. Kozloff (1973) has recently reported that of the four autistic children he investigated, three had a remarkable memory for songs and music. These three children were also alleged to have had absolute pitch, though no details of how this fact was established are given. In any case, what seems to occur is that tones or tunes are stored by autistic children in the identical manner in which they were initially heard. They often react with anger or distress if music familiar to them is transposed into a different key, or is played at a different speed or pitch. The so-called musical ability seems to share many characteristics with the autistic child's tendency for verbal echolalia, that is, the precise storage and reproduction of unprocessed material over relatively long time periods.

The system breaks down when the amount of information to be retained exceeds the immediate memory span, and when limited capacity would normally force the system to use appropriate information reduction. As recording becomes increasingly necessary, and as rules have to be generated, the autistic child's behaviour will become increasingly incoherent and inappropriate.

This interpretation of the nature of memory in autism may go some way to account for the particular impairments in the areas of social interaction and language, where transformations and the extraction of flexible rules are crucial for comprehension and production. If autistic children stored such information in a manner similar to that usually found only in normal immediate memory lasting a few seconds, this would result in just the type of "parrot" language and the complete social naivety which one can observe in these children.

As certain aspects of autism have been compared to those of developmental "aphasia" (developmental receptive speech disorder) it is relevant to note that difficulties with temporal sequencing have also been observed in aphasic children (Stark, 1967; Poppen *et al.*, 1969). Lowe and Campbell (1965) had found that "aphasoid" children were impaired in judging which of two rapidly presented

tones came first, and concluded that impairment in temporal ordering might be crucial in the communication difficulties of such
children. Other investigators, such as Doehring (1960), Stark (1966),
and Withrow (1964) found that visual sequencing and visual memory
were also impaired, though in a careful investigation Tallal and
Piercy (1973) did not confirm this. Tallal and Piercy showed that
children with development aphasia were not only deficient in
perceiving order of rapidly presented auditory stimuli, but were
equally inferior to controls in discriminating other aspects of rapid
auditory input. Processing difficulties were apparent with shortening
interstimulus intervals, decreasing the duration of stimuli and increasing the number of stimulus elements in a series. With increasing tone duration or interstimulus interval the aphasic children's
performance was significantly improved.

The relation of the aphasic children's deficit in rapid auditory
processing of non-verbal material to their language impairment
remains obscure, as slowing down speech rates does not seem to
improve their comprehension. Therefore, despite some obvious
overlap between aphasic and autistic symptoms, it is necessary to
beware of oversimplifying the similarities. For instance, Griffiths
(1972) remarks that the poorest performance of aphasic children is
found in areas of short-term memory and in Tallal and Piercy's
experiment the aphasic children remained inferior to controls for
auditory serial memory involving four or five elements, even when
interstimulus interval and tone duration were long.

Autistic children, on the other hand, perform particularly well on
memory tests, where their performance tends to be equal to that of
normal controls. We have also shown (Hermelin and O'Connor,
1970) that the autistic child's language deficit is only one aspect of a
more general inability to use signs and symbols, and is related to
other coding impairments. There are no such indications in aphasic
children, and the nature of the connection between the two conditions must be regarded as an unsolved problem.

In contrast to the autistic child's inability to process complex
temporal sequences, codes which relate to the spatial framework
seem less affected. This can be observed clinically as well as
experimentally. Autistic children tend to do well on spatial tests in

intelligence scales, and are often very adept in solving jig-saw puzzle type tasks. In our experiments the children could deal with visual information when it referred to spatial location, and they could also use kinesthetic cues flexibly and efficiently.

Why are these codes, which deal with the spatial rather than the temporal framework, relatively more intact? Perhaps spatial coding depends to a lesser extent on the extraction of rules and the use of redundancy than does the processing of temporally ordered sequences. Particularly in relation to spatial location cues, less processing and more precise memory images may be needed. Space may also be a more concrete structure than time, as it can be directly perceived, while time has to be inferred. It seems likely that concepts about the structure of space occur developmentally earlier than those relating to temporal structures, and it may be relevant that motor development, on which the construction of a spatial framework may be based, is often reported to be normal in childhood autism.

There still remains a considerable problem in relating the experimental findings to the clinical picture of childhood autism and discrepancies are glaringly apparent. One of the most persistent features of the autistic syndrome is the tendency for rigid, stereotyped and repetitive behaviour, relating not only to temporal but also to spatial arrangements. The "insistence on sameness", to use Kanner's original term, shows itself in an obsessional regard for the arrangement of objects in space, as well as for the succession of events in time. If one argues that this type of behaviour is related to the child's inability to perceive or generate more complex varied and flexible patterns, it is difficult to maintain at the same time that he possesses codes for such patterns when they refer to spatial structures.

One possibility is that these results reflect our omission of any attempt to equalise for the level of difficulty in the temporal and spatial tasks we presented. There might be temporal sequences which are easier to process than those we have used, just as there will be spatial patterns which will be more difficult to deal with. One indication that this may be so comes from an early experiment (Hermelin and O'Connor, 1970). In this we presented a series of temporally related pictures, such as a candle gradually burning down, instead of meaningless squares or discs as in the present series of studies. We found that the children could order such a sequence rather well and did not show the difficulties which they had with the more abstract material. Order of succession in experiences related to reality may be quite different from, for instance, the word order in a sentence. While the first could be described as "necessary" the second, though commonly agreed on, is arbitrarily determined.

Another indication that the level of difficulty in a task may determine whether it is appropriately coded comes from the relatively good results obtained with behaviour therapy. The success of these methods depends on the ability to form temporal associations between specific behaviour items and their contingencies of reinforcement. Kozloff (1973) has recently shown the importance of absolute consistency of these contingencies for autistic children, and the disintegration of the trained behaviour patterns when these contingency schedules are not strictly adhered to. Nevertheless, the success of the method depends on the ability of the children to recognise the lawfulness of certain temporally ordered events.

There is no easy way in which the levels of difficulties of different mental operations can be equated, and the picture remains somewhat contradictory and obscure. It is not the purpose of science to ignore complexities and contradictions where they exist. Oversimplified explanatory theories are usually short lived, and may hinder rather than help progressive understanding. It is the nature of such an approach as has been presented here, that no final answers emerge and that each question as it becomes answerable produces several new ones in its turn.

In spite of these and other qualifications which can be put forward, our results have gone some way in delineating the nature of the central disorder of cognition on which, as was hypothesised at the beginning of this chapter, autism is based. This cognitive pathology seems to consist largely of an inability to reduce information through the appropriate extraction of crucial features such as rules and redundancies. The impairment in these processes imposes well remembered, stereotyped and restricted behaviour patterns, which become increasingly inappropriate as the requirements for complex, flexible codes increase. It is in the areas of language development and social interaction, which are governed by such complex and flexible rules, that the autistic child's cognitive impairment becomes most evident.

CHAPTER 6

MOTOR, PERCEPTUAL-MOTOR AND INTELLECTUAL DISABILITIES OF AUTISTIC CHILDREN

MARIAN K. DeMYER

After infantile autism was first described by Kanner (1943), the motor, perceptual-motor and intellectual abilities of these children were thought to be basically normal in most cases. The reasons for this belief were the rarity of motor signs such as involuntary movements, the ability of the children to walk with an ostensibly normal gait, and their skilful use of some objects. For example, some could spin objects or climb gracefully and easily. In addition, autistic children were said to have "intelligent" faces and most were free of the obvious facial stigmata seen so commonly in other groups of developmentally delayed children. Their failure to perform age-appropriate items from intelligence tests was believed to be due to negativism and not inability. One widely held theory advanced to explain these "facts" was that most autistic children had anatomically normal brains and that the relatively high splinter skills (also known as "islets of intelligence") were a "true" reflection of their potential intelligence. Their severe verbal disabilities were thus seen as a failure to learn communication skills because of parental failures. If the right treatment key could be found, the hypothetical "locked-in" verbal intelligence would advance in an accelerated fashion to catch up with the splinter skills and with the norms for the child's age.

Results of Intelligence Tests

A series of I.Q. and neurological studies by the staff of the Clinical Research Center for Early Childhood Schizophrenia located at Carter Hospital, Indiana University Medical Center failed to support the idea that most autistic children have basically normal biological intelligence. Early studies (DeMyer *et al.*, 1971b; Alpern, 1967) showed that the non-performance of autistic children in age-appropriate standard intelligence tests was related to task difficulty. They could perform items designed for infants and showed high test-retest reliability. In a survey of 155 autistic children, mean age 65 months, we found an overwhelming incidence (94 per cent) of IQs below 68 and 75 per cent below 51 (DeMyer *et al.*, 1974). While the verbal IQs were the most severely depressed, the mean being 35, the mean performance IQ was also low, namely 54. In contrast, a control group of 47 non-psychotic retarded children, mean age 60 months, had significantly higher IQs, with a mean of 56 on verbal tests and 70 on performance tests (see Table 6.1).

Table 6.1
Comparison of initial IQ scores of all consecutive referrals

Diagnostic group	No. subjects	Mean age in years	Mean general IQ	Mean initial perf. IQ	Mean initial verbal IQ
Retarded	47	4·95	65·4	70·3	55·7
High autistic	26	6·62	61·0	67·0	51·1
Middle autistic	63	4·67	43·7	57·1	28·1
Low autistic	66	5·03	29·7	37·4	19·7
(All autistic children	155	5·44	44·8	53·8	34·9)

NOTE: All group means differ significantly, p > ·01, except for the retarded and high autistic groups.

The IQ study was empirical and all consecutive referrals diagnosed as autistic or non-psychotic retarded were included. The non-psychotic retarded comparison group (to be referred to for brevity as the retarded group) was selected from two sources: (1) centers in the city which trained preschool children who had the use of their arms and legs, but who had a general or specific learning deficit (Down's syndrome children were excluded); and (2) children referred directly to the Research Center for evaluation of speech and emotional problems, who were diagnosed as retarded in a specific or general way but did not have psychotic behavior.

Because these initial evaluation IQs were derived from so many different test sources, we retested the children a mean of 6 years later and found high correlations with the original IQs. General IQs correlated ·700, performance IQs correlated ·577 and verbal IQs ·630 ($p < ·001$ all three correlations) (DeMyer *et al.*, 1974).

In addition to predicting later IQ scores, we found that the IQ at the initial evaluation predicted how well the autistic child would do in school at follow-up 6 years later and that it was related to symptom severity and response to treatment. The higher the IQ, the less severe was the social withdrawal and the less severe the speech abnormalities. Treated autistic children with initial IQs over 50 showed a greater increase in IQ over time than did untreated children in the same IQ range. Those children whose IQs were initially under 40 showed no differential IQ effect with treatment (DeMyer *et al.*, 1974).

While these IQ studies were useful because they revealed that nearly all autistic children were testable and that the resultant IQ was a good predictor of outcome, they told us little about the cause of the low-measured IQ in 94 per cent of the children. Results of other studies at the Research Center suggested that autistic children probably were neurologically disabled and that their nurture had been quite similar to a group of extensively matched normal children*.

*Matched with the autistic children for age, sex, social class, number and sex of sibs, position in family, and race and religion of parents.

Evidence for Neurological Dysfunction

Let us look briefly at the evidence for neurological dysfunction in the majority of the autistic children. They had significantly more pathological signs on the neurological evaluation than the matched normal children and nearly as many as the retarded children. Seventy five per cent of autistic children had Brain Dysfunction scores (DeMyer *et al.*, 1973) more than 2 standard deviations from the same scores for normal children. Through a process of combined assessment and treatment we found that autistic children demonstrated insurmountable blocks to learning even though they developed high motivational levels through operant conditioning techniques. While the type of learning dysfunction varied from child to child, it was remarkably stable over time in the same child. Whatever neurological modalities were involved, there was a profound language dysfunction in each autistic child (Hingtgen and Churchill, 1969). Even if the mechanics of speech were present, symbolic language processes were deficient (Churchill, 1972). The perceptual deficiencies remained in nearly all the treated children although some improvement was possible for most.

Indirect evidence for a disordered nervous system came from a study of parental child-rearing practices in the infancy of the autistic children (DeMyer *et al.*, 1972c). While we had to rely on the parental memories of this period, we could find no important differences in how the parents of autistic and normal children related to their infants. Instead we found that 36 per cent of parents of autistic children and 44 per cent of parents of retarded children had observed less mental alertness and slower motor development in their handicapped offspring during infancy as compared with the normal siblings.

These are symptoms of neurological dysfunction. In every study of neurological status, including the EEG, intelligence, and motor function, the autistic children were quite different from the matched normal children but were similar to the retarded children who were age matched and had the use of all four limbs.

Investigation of the Causes of Social Withdrawal

In view of the neurological similarities of autistic and retarded children, we had to attempt to explain their behavioural differences. Given a group of children alike in signs of neurological dysfunction, how can we explain that some, called "autistic", were socially withdrawn* and non-communicative, while others, called non-psychotic retarded, related warmly, even being overly dependent, and used such speech as they had for communication? Three possible answers suggested themselves:

1. The environment provided by the parents of the autistic children in the first years of life was less supportive of close emotional relationships.
2. Since the autistic group as a whole was more depressed intellectually than the retarded group, the decreased capacity of the autistic children to understand the complexities of living accounted for social withdrawal.
3. There was a difference in the types of neurological modalities affected.

Our evidence is against the first possibility because parents of

---

*A description of severe social withdrawal is given in this extract from Allen *et al.* (1971), quoted to show the criteria used for rating:

"The child did not habitually stay near people, especially other children. Eye contact was of short duration, and the child looked through people rather than at them. He did not imitate their physical actions or play with other children even though he may have hovered at the edge of a group. He did not respond to other people's attempts to engage him in a simple conversation, although he may at times have given a clear indication of understanding uncomplicated speech, especially when it related to food, a favored object, or routine. Parents frequently described this child as one who stays in 'his own little world,' needing his parents only when in physical distress or if he wants or dislikes something. His signaling system under these conditions was rudimentary—only a cry, a tantrum, or leading the parent by the back of the hand. He did not signal by pointing or by serial pantomime as an aphasic child would. Between episodes of displeasure or pleasure, the child had a flat affect described by parents as a 'don't care' attitude. At times, he 'did not want his mother out of sight,' and sought physical contact (clinging behavior) at every opportunity."

retarded children were judged to be less warm and less social than parents of autistic children during the handicapped children's infancy, when etiological factors could have been operating in the environment (DeMyer *et al.*, 1972c). (Ninety five per cent of the children in both groups were reported to be abnormal before their third birthdays.) The evidence is more compelling that the chief difference between the autistic children and the group of non-psychotic retarded children such as those who have "aphasic" speech disturbances may be in the greater degree of central language disturbance, that is a poorer capacity to deal with abstraction, in the former. Churchill (1972) had argued cogently for this cause. Such differential disturbance should be reflected in a lower mean IQ, especially verbal IQ, in the autistic group, and the results of our tests have, in general, confirmed this.

More detailed examination of the children has, however, shown that the situation is more complicated than the above results suggest. In our series of studies, we divided autistic children into three groups. The *high* group was characterised by a mixture of communicative and non-communicative speech and some islets of social relatedness in a background of withdrawal. The *middle* group of children showed severe withdrawal, no communicative speech but some adaptive behaviour that approximated to their chronological age level. The *low* group showed the same features as the middle group with the exception that all their verbal and adaptive behaviors were below that expected for their chronological age. When we looked at the IQs of these three sub-groups of autistic children, we found that one group, the high autistic children, had similar IQs, including scores on verbal tests, to the retarded children. However, we again found that in comparison with the retarded children, the high autistic group were more withdrawn, used less communicative speech and failed to use objects symbolically. Symptomatic differences from the retarded children could not be explained on the basis of EEG or neurological findings or parental differences any more in the high autistic group than for the middle and low autistic groups. Therefore, we decided to look for evidence of qualitative differences in the neurological modalities affected.

Because the nervous system is nearly impossible to examine directly, we have sought evidence, from a detailed examination of the motor, perceptual-motor, and verbal intelligence test responses, that retarded and autistic children differ in their patterns of learning assets and liabilities. Our studies to date show that, in addition to more severe language deficiencies, many autistic children have more severe problems than retarded children in certain visual-motor tasks. The difficulties they show are akin to dyspraxia (DeMyer *et al.*, 1972a). The remainder of this chapter presents results of testing autistic and retarded children, using items gleaned from the literature on standardised tests, which suggest some differential visual-motor and language features.

Some of the specific questions we asked of the IQ data were:
1. Given similar IQs and neurological status in high autistic and in retarded children, are there specific intelligence test items that differentiate the two groups? Specifically, do high autistic children, in comparison with retarded children, obtain:
   (a) Lower scores on verbal abstraction items and higher scores on rote verbal items such as digit span and word repetition?
   (b) Lower scores on certain visual-motor items such as hand-finger imitation?
2. Do any individual verbal or perceptual-motor items differentiate the middle and low autistic children from each other and from the high autistic and retarded groups? By definition, we distinguished the middle and low autistic groups on the basis of splinter skills present in the former and absent in the latter. We had observed clinically and in experiments on a small number of children that these splinter skills were often in fitting and assembly tasks whereas the most marked disabilities often involved verbal abstraction and motor imitation. Thus the questions we wished to help answer by examination of IQ items were:
   (a) Do middle autistic children generally have splinter skills in fitting and assembly tasks which are characterised by the fact that the object remains in the child's visual field at all

times and specific disabilities in motor imitation or in tasks that must be *remembered* visually, *conceptualised* visually, or related to the child's own body?
(b) What kinds of verbal items account for most of the verbal disability in middle and low autistic children?
3. The ultimate and most interesting questions about which we hoped to gain more insight concerned the nature of the social withdrawal and the non-communication of autistic children:
(a) Why are autistic children so much more withdrawn and non-communicative than non-psychotic retarded children?
(b) What accounts for the differences in degree of seriousness of symptoms among the three groups of autistic children?

Comparison of verbal and performance profiles

A series of verbal, motor, and perceptual-motor tasks were administered to 66 autistic children, mean age 5 years, and to 29 retarded children, mean age 6 years. The derivation of the test items and procedure are described fully in DeMyer *et al.* (1972b). Diagnostic criteria (DeMyer *et al.*, 1971a) for infantile autism included severe and sustained social withdrawal, reduced communicative speech, and non-functional object use. We divided the autistic children into the three subcategories, high, middle and low, as described above (see Table 6.2).

The retarded children, in contrast to the autistic children, were not socially withdrawn, although nearly all of them were over-dependent on their parents and had other behavior problems such as irritability and negativism in relating to people. In addition, their general intelligence was either borderline or in the mentally retarded ranges or they had a specific learning disorder such as dysphasia.

Verbal profiles

Four types of verbal tests were used at the initial evaluation:

1. Verbal memory as tested by word and digit repetition from the

Table 6.2
Description of subjects for verbal and performance profile

Diagnostic group	Total (N)	Mean CA*(mos)	Mean BDI†	% Abn. EEG	Mean gen. IQ‡	Mean Vineland social age
Retarded	(29)	71·8	58·8	75	70·3	63·8
High autistic	(11)	93·8	51·1	82	58·5	56·5
Middle autistic	(20)	56·4	30·8	75	47·2	54·8
Low autistic	(35)	59·2	55·4	79	28·9	37·9

*Chronological age.
†Brain Dysfunction Index.
‡Cattell–Binet.

Stanford–Binet test battery (Terman and Merrill, 1960) and the Wechsler Intelligence Scale for Children (WISC) (Wechsler, 1949).

2. Number concepts from Bayley (1969), Gesell *et al.* (1940, 1946, 1965) and WISC (Wechsler, 1949).

3. Word recognition as tested by the Peabody Picture Vocabulary Test (Dunn, 1965).

Because many of the basement* mental ages were beyond the abilities of many children, performance cannot be reported for all children (see Table 6.3).† All scores are expressed as mental ages corrected for chronological age.

*The term "basement" mental age, as used here and following, refers to the lowest possible mental age for that particular series of items. For example, no test item in the standardized psychological test literature contains a number concept item that is mental age graded below 30 months. The lowest mental age graded visual memory item (searching for a disappearing spoon) is by contrast 8 months. Other types of items have other basement mental ages. The upper mental age limits also differ between tests. These varying characteristics point up the roughness of our measures and the need for more specific, experimentally designed test items to answer some of our questions. Also new tests should be devised and standardized to test specific modalities as they progress in complexity with increasing chronological age, because there are serious gaps in our tests especially between infancy and early childhood.

†A fuller discussion of results of verbal testing is given in DeMyer *et al.* (1974).

Table 6.3
Comparison of verbal profiles in four diagnostic groups

Tests from which items were derived	Rep. of words, digit span, Stanford–Binet and WISC	Bayley, Gesell, and WISC	Peabody picture vocabulary and Bayley	Comprehension questions from Stanford–Binet, WISC & Denver (For retarded and high autistic)
Basement mental age of items	12 mos.	30 mos.	6 mos.	30 mos.
Modality	Verbal memory	Number concept	Receptive word skills	Abstract/creative language
Retarded N = 29	63·9	70·5	62·2	53·0
High autistic N = 11	33·0	76·8	55·6	45·7
Middle autistic N = 20	46·0	57·6	37·0	29·5*
Low autistic N = 35	24·6	—†	21·8	14·3*

Note: Displayed are mean group quotient scores.

Results of T-tests

Retarded × High autistic	p < ·01	p < ·01	
Retarded × Middle autistic	p < ·01	p < ·01	p < ·01
Retarded × Low autistic			p < ·01
High autistic × Middle autistic			p < ·05
High autistic × Low autistic		p < ·01	p < ·01
Middle autistic × Low autistic	p < ·05	p < ·01	p < ·01

*Middle and low autistic groups were tested chiefly by means of sentence length and number of words spoken since they did not reach the basement abstraction mental age of 30 months. Thus for most of the middle and low autistic children, these means do not reflect abstraction levels.

†The number of low autistic children passing basement number concept items was too small to compute a mean.

4. Comprehension as tested by age-graded items from the Denver (Frankenburg and Dodds, 1967), Stanford–Binet (Terman and Merrill, 1960), and WISC (Wechsler, 1949) test batteries.

The low verbal intelligence of autistic children was again demonstrated by group mean scores in the retarded ranges for all three groups. The retarded children and the high autistic children who generally scored in the borderline to mildly retarded ranges were about equal in number concepts, word recognition, and language comprehension items. Contrary to original expectation, the retarded children scored higher in verbal memory items than the autistic children. Most middle and low autistic children, even though their chronological ages surpassed the mental ages required for the basement items, could not be scored on verbal tasks. The single exception was word comprehension from the Bayley Infant Scales or the Peabody Picture Vocabulary Test which required no expressive speech.

Because so many of the low and middle autistic pre-school children failed to pass basement verbal abstraction items, we studied the problem again when the children were older (mean follow-up time 6 years) and more speech had developed. The WISC, which measures both the rote and the more abstract aspects of language, was administered to 46 children in later childhood or teen-age. Of these 46 subjects, 33 had been originally diagnosed as autistic and 13 had been diagnosed as retarded. Sixteen children originally diagnosed as autistic, with a mean chronological age of 11 years, were no longer socially withdrawn. All of the 13 children (mean chronological age 10 years) originally diagnosed as retarded remained non-psychotic, and all but one were still retarded in one or more ways. Of the 17 originally autistic children (mean CA $13\frac{1}{2}$ years) who remained withdrawn, ten had some useful, communicative speech and seven were either mute or used only a few words (see Table 6.4).

The results of the later verbal subtests are given in Table 6.5. For this table, the children were divided into three groups: firstly the 13 retarded children; secondly 16 originally autistic children who on follow-up were no longer socially withdrawn; and thirdly, 17 autistic

Table 6.4
Subject description for follow-up WISC profiles by change of diagnostic group

| Change in diagnosis | Total (N) | Follow-up mean CA (mos.) | Mean BDI | Mean initial IQ | | |
				Perf.	Verb.	Gen.
Retarded–Retarded	13	119	56·2	71	52	63
Autistic–No longer withdrawn	16	133	40·7	67	50	61
Autistic–autistic	17	162	40·9	65	33	47

children who remained withdrawn on follow up. Those children remaining withdrawn achieved the lowest scores (see Table 6.5) with their poorest verbal score in Comprehension (mean IQ equivalent 29) and their best verbal score in Digit Span (IQ equivalent 59). Those children who were originally autistic but who were no longer withdrawn at follow-up also had their lowest verbal score in Comprehension (mean IQ equivalent 71) and their highest score in Digit Span (IQ equivalent 93). In contrast the lowest score for the retarded group was Vocabulary, 60, and the highest Similarities, 74. Their Comprehension was about midway of the verbal scores, namely, 68. Thus the autistic children who ceased to be withdrawn and those who remained withdrawn had WISC verbal profiles which were nearly the same in configuration (see Fig. 6.1) except that the scores were all about 30 to 40 IQ points apart. The verbal profile of the retarded children was different in that Comprehension was not the lowest score. In fact the Comprehension scores of the retarded children and the autistic children who ceased to be withdrawn were quite similar (67 and 71 respectively). The other WISC verbal scales that might be expected to test thinking ability, namely, Arithmetic and Similarities, were little different from those scales that tested the more rote aspects of language such as Digit Span and Information.

The one interesting finding that seemed to point to lesser abstracting ability in the autistic children who had improved to the point that they were no longer socially withdrawn was that Comprehension scores were 15 IQ points lower than other subtest scores, with the exception of Vocabulary which differed by only seven IQ points.

Table 6.5
WISC scores at follow-up testing

Change in diagnosis	Mean IQ equivalents for scaled scores WISC verbal subtests											
	Info.	S.D.	Comp.	S.D.	Arith.	S.D.	Simil.	S.D.	Vocab.	S.D.	Dig. Sp.	S.D.
1. Retarded-retarded N = 13	73	±20	68	±24	67	±17	74	±21	60	±18	65	±17
2. Autistic-no longer withdrawn N = 16	90	±36	71	±26	87	±39	85	±35	77	±27	93	±25
3. Autistic-autistic N = 17	51	±22	29	±16	54	±29	48	±25	39	±14	59	±28
Significant difference:												
1 × 2	p < ·05		p < ·01						p < ·05			
1 × 3	p < ·01		p < ·01				p < ·05		p < ·05		p < ·01	
2 × 3					p < ·05		p < ·01		p < ·01		p < ·01	

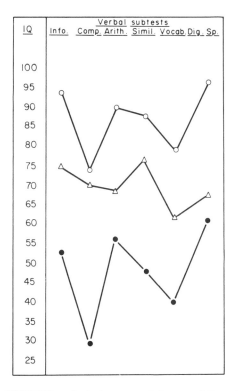

Fig. 6.1. Profiles of WISC IQ equivalent scores at follow-up. △ Retarded–retarded, ○ Autistic–no longer withdrawn, ● Autistic–autistic

The Vocabulary subtest, of course, tests expressive speech as well as verbal abstraction capacity. In contrast to the finding at initial testing, at follow-up this group of children had higher Digit Span (verbal memory) scores than the retarded group.

We looked at the Comprehension mental ages on the later tests of the autistic children who ceased to be withdrawn and found the lowest were in the range of 40 to 50 months. This suggested the interesting possibility that a Comprehension mental age of 40 months represented a threshold below which the type of social withdrawal found in early childhood autism was likely to occur. However, this idea is obviously an over-simplification. Although a

Comprehension age of below 40 months was characteristic of most of the autistic children who were socially withdrawn when tested, there were five children who remained withdrawn on follow-up but whose Comprehension ages ranged from 50 to 77 months. Another problem in accepting the hypothesis of a threshold of 40 months for level of comprehension of speech is that normal children below this mental age level do not have autistic behavior and are not socially withdrawn.

In any case the values for the Comprehension mental ages as measured in the autistic groups must be taken with caution and regarded as speculative. Not only were the groups small, but we modified the handling of the scaled scores. Because several of the lower functioning children obtained zero or less-than-zero scaled scores, all scaled scores were converted to IQ equivalents and extrapolated downward when necessary in order to score all children (DeMyer *et al.*, 1973). However, this finding pointed to some potentially useful research in regard to an important modality to be measured while following the progress of autistic children. The principal abilities measured by the WISC Comprehension scale should be defined, new tests for low mental age children devised and carefully followed in autistic, retarded and normal children. Such a study would not only define more precisely the nature of the abstraction disturbance but also the Comprehension mental age most likely to be associated with a change from social withdrawal to more normal interpersonal relationships.

For many autistic children, their very low or non-existent verbal abstraction abilities may be sufficient to explain in large measure their social withdrawal, their non-communicative speech, and their non-symbolic use of objects (Churchill, 1972). However, it is clear that the autistic children with the higher abstraction or comprehension ages should, in theory, on an analogy with normal children, be able to relate well emotionally, especially if the people caring for them understand their limitations yet push sufficiently for intellectual and emotional growth. When a retarded child is in the region of about 40 to 66 months in terms of speech comprehension (abstraction) ability, other special disabilities may complicate his capacity to understand and communicate and tip the child into serious social withdrawal.

In an experiment (DeMyer *et al.*, 1972a) it was found that the autistic children's imitation of body motion was more deficient than object imitation, which was, in turn, more deficient than their ability to assemble objects that suggested their own solution. The body imitation skills of the autistic children were less mature than those of the retarded children. Body imitation requires that the child should remember a quickly disappearing motion, or perceive that his body is like that of the demonstrator and transfer the remembered motion to his own motor system. Experiments by Bryson (1972) suggested that some autistic children had a poor visual memory. Other autistic children may have had relatively good visual memories but could not transfer visual percepts to the motor system. Either deficit may result in visual-motor non-performance which borders on dyspraxia. The low level of the abstraction abilities combined with the motor imitation difficulties can be used to explain the autistic child's social withdrawal. The child would have neither verbal nor non-verbal communication pathways open to other people. If a retarded child is particularly low in abstraction capacity he may still have sufficient visual-motor skills to participate in non-verbal communication with others and thus would not be likely to be socially aloof.

The performance profile

The motor and perceptual-motor performances might offer some clues to special disabilities in autistic children in addition to those affecting verbal comprehension. Those same 66 autistic and 29 retarded children whose verbal skills were measured were also given visual-motor items that tested the adequacy of both their upper and lower limbs (see Fig. 6.2).

All mean scores (expressed as mental age corrected for chronological age) are listed in Table 6.6. The overall perceptual-motor intelligence of most autistic and retarded children was in the borderline* to retarded* range, albeit generally higher than the

*In this chapter, the grades of mental retardation are defined by the following IQ limits: Borderline normal, 68–83; Mild retardation, 52–67; Moderate retardation, 36–51; Severe retardation, below 36.

I. *Upper Limbs*
  A. Motor skill required remains constant at 12 to 15 months.
    1. Model present during whole of task completion:
       (a) Matching coloured discs to coloured discs (Gesell, 1940)
       (b) Placing geometric forms in formboard (Seguin Formboard)
           (Stutsman, 1948)
    2. Partial visual cues present:
       (a) Problem solving (Manikin and object assembly
           puzzles)—shape and lines are the visual cues (Stutsman,
           1948); (Weschler, 1949)
       (b) Ring stack set (Fisher–Price)—size is the visual cue (unpub-
           lished data)
  B. Motor skill required advances with task complexity.
    1. Model present during whole of task completion:
       (a) Geometric drawing-exact model present (Beery, 1967)
       (b) Imitation of object use—use of object leaves some "perma-
           nent" environmental change (e.g. stringing beads, cutting
           with scissor) (Stutsman, 1948)
    2. Model disappears and no "permanent" environmental change
       results:
       (a) Imitation of hand-finger movements (Stutsman, 1948; Sloan,
           1955; Bergès and Lézine, 1965)

II. *Lower Limbs*
  A. Motor skill required advances with task complexity.
    1. Model disappears and no "permanent" environmental change
       results:
       (a) Imitation of standing on one foot, jump, hop, skip, run
           (Bayley, 1969; Frankenburg and Dodds, 1967; Gesell, 1940,
           1946; Sloan, 1955)
    2. Partial visual cue available:
       (a) Use of object (stairs) in stair climbing and descent (Sheri-
           dan, 1960)

III. *integration*
  A. Motor skill required advances with task complexity.
    1. Partial visual cue available:
       (a) Ball play—coordination of arms, hand, trunk, legs, feet and vision
           (Gesell, 1940, 1946; Sloan, 1955)

Fig. 6.2. Visual-motor profile test

verbal intelligence. As usual the low autistic children performed
more poorly than the other groups, with one interesting exception,
namely gross motor tasks involving the lower limbs (that is,
stair climbing and hop/skip/run/jump). Again the retarded and high

Table 6.6
Profiles of visual-motor skills in retarded and autistic children*

Diagnostic group	Upper limbs							Lower limbs		Integration
	Colour match	Form-board	Problem solving	Ring stack	Geom. draw	Fine motor w/obj.	Fine motor imit.	Gross motor imit.	Gross motor w/obj.	Complex motor ball play
Retarded N = 29	79	78	77	65	61	50	56	54	58	72
High autistic N = 11	63	75	63	62	55	60	54	42	41	47
Middle autistic N = 20	83	85	64	63	51	55	38	50	65	48
Low autistic N = 35	50	46	35	39	29	31	28	45	52	35
	Exact model available		Partial visual cue available		Exact mode available		No visual cue remains	Partial visual cue available		
	Motor skill required remains constant at 12–15 months							Motor skill required advances with task complexity		

*Displayed are mean age corrected (Quotient) scores.

autistic groups were alike in performance except that the retarded were more adequate in ball play and stair climbing (p < ·05). The middle autistic children obtained similar scores to the retarded and high autistic groups except that hand/finger imitation was significantly lower, falling in the low moderate* to severely retarded* range (IQ mean equivalent score 38) (p < ·01). Hand/finger imitation was the lowest visual-motor score of both the middle and low autistic groups. Gross motor scores for the lower limbs and ball play were the lowest for the high autistic children while ball play was one of the higher scores of the retarded children.

When the nature of the task was clear from the appearance of material presented, which remained in the child's view throughout the test, and the motor age required to complete the task was not above 12 to 15 months, then all four groups performed at their highest level (see Fig. 6.3). The score for matching of colours and shapes was borderline normal for the retarded and the high and middle autistic children (75 to 85 IQ equivalent) and in the moderately retarded range for the low autistic children (50 IQ equivalent). When partial, or more abstract, visual cues were available to the children during task performance and the motor component remained at infancy levels, all groups showed a decrease in adequacy of performance. Examples of this type of task were the Merrill–Palmer Manikin, the WISC Object Assembly (both involving the assembly of cut-up pictures) and the Fisher–Price ring-stack. When the task called for increasing motor skill as well as increasing complexity of visual percept, that is, drawing geometric figures (Berry, 1967), then performance decreased again. In object imitation tasks (e.g. cutting with scissors, stringing beads) which left some sustained visual pattern for the child to copy, the effect was the same as in geometric drawing. When the imitation task required a copy of a hand/finger motion, (which left no sustained visual pattern) the effect was to decrease performance of the middle and low autistic groups. Lower limb tasks (stair climbing and hop/skip/run/jump) caused a decrease in the performance of only

*In this chapter, the grades of mental retardation are defined by the following IQ limits: Borderline normal, 68–83; Mild retardation, 52–67; Moderate retardation, 36–51; Severe retardation, below 36.

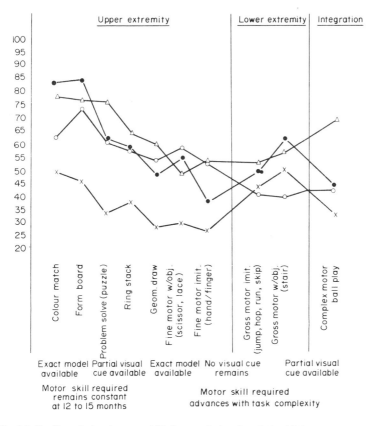

Fig. 6.3. Profiles of visual-motor skills in retarded and autistic children. △ Retarded, ○ High autistic, ● Middle autistic, × Low autistic

the high autistic children. In contrast, gross motor performance was as high as colour and shape matching tasks for low autistic children (IQ equivalent 45 to 52). Ball play, which is a complex task involving coordination of vision, arms, hands, trunk and legs, was done best by retarded children (IQ equivalent 72). This task was performed at the moderately retarded level (IQ equivalent 48) by high and middle autistic children and in the severely retarded range (IQ equivalent 35) by the low autistic children.

Comment

The results of analysing detailed verbal and perceptual-motor testing show clearly that autistic children as a group had scores within retarded ranges on nearly all types of tests. When the autistic children were subdivided into three groups chiefly on the basis of severity of social withdrawal, the IQ also differentiated these groups: the high group had the best scores, the middle were intermediate and the low group had the poorest scores. A control group of non-psychotic retarded children of similar age and possessing the use of all four limbs resembled the high autistic group in overall performance and verbal IQ. These two groups were of particular interest since it was difficult to see any reasons for more severe social withdrawal and less communicative speech in the high autistic than in the retarded children. Their neurological examinations, EEGs and family status did not differ.

The questions we asked were, in some instances, answered rather definitely by the data but in other instances only a hint of the answer was given, thus pointing the direction to continued study. One question that seemed fairly clearly answered was the type of splinter skill most commonly present in autistic children, namely fitting and assembly tasks. This was also one of the most common splinter skills in non-psychotic retarded children. Not only was this true at initial evaluation when most of the children were pre-school age but it was also true at follow-up 6 years later when Block Design and Object Assembly were the best performed subtests of the WISC (unpublished data). Normal or near-normal performance on fitting and assembly tasks does not appear to be a sign that other types of intelligence such as verbal abstraction and different kinds of visual-motor tasks are at the same level. Instead, fitting and assembly tasks may just be the easiest kinds of tasks for developmentally retarded children to perform. The reason for this easier performance is not known definitely but an analysis of the tasks on which top performances were generally obtained gives a clue. In matching colours and fitting form-boards together, an exact visual cue was available to the child at all times. In addition, the motor component of these two types of task was within the capacity of a 12- to 15-month-old infant.

Very few of these children had motor symptoms *per se* and so the picking up and releasing of one object and putting that object in an exact matrix would be logically within their capabilities.

The type of task affected the scores in other ways. If either the visual or motor component of the task was made more difficult than the simple matching of like objects, then adequacy of performance again dropped in all four groups of children. However, in addition, there were some differences among the four groups in visual-motor performance. These involved chiefly motor imitation and ball play. Middle and low autistic children had particular difficulties when memory of a motor cue was required in the upper limbs only. The high autistic children had more difficulties in imitating movement of the lower limbs only. All three autistic groups were less capable in ball play than the retarded children.

The answer to our most intriguing question as to what made one group of neurologically disabled children withdrawn and unable to communicate by speech or by sign and the other group socially relating and communicative were clearer for the two lowest functioning groups of autistic children than for the high autistic group. The test results for the low autistic children showed severely retarded verbal skills. Even word comprehension was about 1 to 2 years in mental age while abstraction skills were so low as to be untestable. Visual-motor integration skills were so low that depriving these children of an exact visual cue, or increasing the motor component above 12 months made the task generally impossible for them to do. Even with an exact visual cue and with only infancy motor skill required, the low autistic group performed like children 2 years younger than the mean chronological age of the group. No amount of treatment or education that we have tried has succeeded in enabling the low autistic child to progress in an accelerated fashion. The passage of time, as the nervous system myelinates and nerve cells branch, enables the low autistic child to acquire increased complexity of performance. In other words this type of child does increase in mental age as time passes, but not in IQ. He may acquire the ability to draw a circle (36 months mental age) by the time he reaches the chronological age of 7 years whereas at the age of 4 years he was merely able to scribble (18 months mental age).

However, the mental age line of the low autistic child does not advance any faster than his chronological age line. Only in gross motor skills of the lower limbs do these low functioning children approach the non-psychotic retarded group and such relative adequacy is apparently unrelated to speech adequacy.

Low autistic children perform better than infants only in matching like objects and in the use of their lower limbs. Their ability to use language and to integrate visual memory with fine motor skills remain at the infant level. These children can handle only the simplest Gestalten of the natural environment. They could not be expected to learn the significance of a smile or frown in their preschool years or understand the complex language of other people. They could not be expected to use other humans as helpful interpreters of the environment except in the most simple cir-cumstances. We found the symptom of severest social withdrawal, namely, not differentiating the parents from other people, only in the low autistic group. These children were also the lowest performers, with IQs in the below-25 range. Only in use of lower limbs did their IQ equivalent approach 50. Their repetitive non-functional use of objects would be a natural response of a child who could understand neither the symbolic properties of a toy nor its structural arrangement.

Except for use of the lower limbs, the middle autistic children performed all tasks at a higher level than the low autistic children; albeit their performances were retarded. The one type of task that they performed at close to normal or even at normal levels in some cases, was matching that required only infantile motor skills and either full or partial visual cues that stayed in the child's field of vision at all times. Having to remember a visual cue and relate this cue to his own body elicits the middle autistic child's lowest visual-motor performance. This type of skill is of utmost importance in learning body language. The other extremely low skill in middle autistic children is abstract language comprehension. The only verbal skill that is available is word comprehension. Like the low autistic group, these middle autistic children would have difficulty in handling the complexities of the natural social or physical environ-ment. They do have one skill which apparently had led many observers to think of the middle autistic child as "intelligent". They can often handle complex visual stimuli, particularly if these stimuli do not leave the child's field of vision and do not demand complex motor integration. Again, as with the low autistic children, these splinter skills are not indicative of the ability to think abstractly with either words or objects except at extremely simple levels. The reasons for social withdrawal and non-functional object use would be the same as for the low autistic children.

More difficult to explain is the social withdrawal of the high autistic children whose general intellectual levels on both verbal and performance tests are much like the non-psychotic retarded children. Also their verbal abstraction and upper limb imitation levels are similar to the retarded children. The chief difference between high autistic and retarded children comes in ball play and performance of tasks involving the lower limbs. Most high autistic children show more severe visual-motor integration difficulties than retarded children in ball play and in tasks involving the lower limbs. This finding suggests that the high autistic children may have a disability akin to a dyspraxia that complicate their use of the environment to a more severe degree than the retarded children. This inability to plan and carry out many visual-motor activities might tip a child who is only moderately retarded in verbal comprehension skills into partial social withdrawal.

The highest functioning autistic children, which in our series comprised only 16·8 per cent of the whole autistic group, did appear to benefit the most from treatment and education (DeMyer *et al.*, 1974). While about 8 per cent advance from a subnormal measured intelligence to either a verbal or a performance IQ in the normal range, the overwhelming number of autistic children remain in the retarded ranges. Intensive treatment and education for those children with initial IQs below 40 seems to enhance their performance and verbal intelligence no more than the passage of time would be expected to do.

PART TWO

EDUCATION, MANAGEMENT AND SERVICES

THE PRINCIPLES OF REMEDIAL EDUCATION FOR AUTISTIC CHILDREN

LORNA WING

Aims

The aims of education for any handicappe. child are: to help overcome or compensate for the primary disau ...es; to reduce or remove the secondary behaviour problems; to improve the level of self care; to teach practical, academic and occupational skills; to help the handicapped person to derive as much satisfaction and enjoyment from life as possible.

In the first edition of this book published in 1966, it was noted that, unlike teachers of the blind and deaf, for whom the rules of teaching are fairly well laid down, teachers of autistic children had to "make it up as they go along". Since that time, some progress has been made and a few guide-lines are beginning to emerge. The practical details of teaching techniques are described in Everard (1975). In this present book, the emphasis will be on the principles on which these techniques are based.

Comparison of Educational Approaches

Bartak and Rutter (1973) and Rutter and Bartak (1973) compared three different educational settings in which autistic children were taught. Unit A used regressive techniques and was directed by a child psychotherapist. The approach was consistently sympathetic and non-directive. Each child had only two 20-minute sessions with a teacher each week. Otherwise, the children were cared for by untrained helpers. Unit B was the only one which accepted disturbed but non-autistic children as well as those who were autistic. A fairly permissive classroom environment was used to combine special educational methods with regressive techniques. Unit C was a school for autistic children in which the environment was structured and organised and in planning teaching much emphasis was laid on the children's perceptual, motor and cognitive handicaps.

The interaction between teachers and children and the progress made by the children was observed over a period of 3 years. The results were complicated and raised a number of different issues, but some of the important points can be summarized. Improvement in use of speech, reading accuracy, reading comprehension and arithmetic were greater in Unit C (with the structured regime) than in Units A and B. Social behaviour in the classroom, as measured by concentration on the task in hand instead of engaging in irrelevant activities, stereotypies, or doing nothing, was most appropriate in Unit C, less so in Unit B, and least in Unit A. The difference was mostly due to the children with IQs of less than 50, who were particularly difficult to motivate to attend to tasks. There was more parallel or co-operative play in Unit C than in the others, although this occurred for only a small percentage of time in all the units.

Social behaviour at home and during psychological testing by the experimenters improved in all the units but, unlike the other measures mentioned above, there were no significant differences between the units.

The authors concluded that education, especially with a structured regime geared to the children's specific handicaps, does produce academic and social improvements in autistic children, although it must be pointed out that the extent of progress is comparatively small and is least marked in the children with the lowest IQs.

Schopler *et al.* (1971) also demonstrated the advantages of a structured environment, especially for the less able autistic children. Rutter and Bartak (1973) defined a structured situation simply as one in which the adult determines what the child should be doing. They pointed out that the use of the term should not imply rigidity, rote learning, or forcing the child to perform.

Churchill (1971) confirmed experimentally the clinical observation that the abnormal behaviour of autistic children becomes more marked under conditions of failure. He found that crying, temper tantrums, visual avoidance and problems such as self-biting and stereotyped movements all increased when the children were presented with tasks too difficult for them to perform. These behaviour problems became even more severe if the experience of failure was prolonged.

The author suggested that the brain dysfunction in autism may so reduce the child's ability to meet even the ordinary demands of everyday life that he lives in a condition of perpetual failure. This is made even worse when he is faced, in a teaching situation, with yet more tasks which are outside his specific range of abilities. So-called negativism is a predictable result. In contrast, when an autistic child is given tasks within his capacity, he is likely to be co-operative and responsive (Alpern, 1967; DeMyer *et al.*, 1974).

These observations have obvious relevance for the planning of teaching programmes. Teachers experienced in this field are usually well aware of the necessity for starting with tasks that an autistic child can perform, giving him a positive attitude towards learning, and then helping him to acquire new skills in a series of steps small enough for him to accomplish without too much difficulty.

The Content of Educational Programmes

When their basic lack of creative imagination is considered, it is not surprising that autistic children benefit from a structured rather than a permissive "free exploration" approach and that they are disturbed by failure, but these findings do not help to decide what should be the nature and content of the educational programme. Should an attempt be made to overcome the primary impairments, or should education be mainly compensatory—that is organised to teach the practical skills which the children find fairly easy to acquire because of their ability to learn by rote?

The most structured approach of all is that of operant conditioning. Programmes have been devised to teach skills such as speech by building up from individual sounds, to words, phrases and then sentences. It was hoped that this mechanical approach would enable each child eventually to develop the ability to use language rather than just to use words parrot fashion. It was also hoped that other skills would be learnt in the same way and that they would generalise so that eventually the child would have a complete repertoire of normal behaviour, remaining stable when the treatment ceased. Sadly, these hopes have not been realised. Operant conditioning gives some children some useful skills, but it does not make them normal.

Lovaas *et al.* (1973), in an interesting account of a 1 to 4-year follow-up of a series of 20 autistic children who received behaviour therapy, noted that the continuation of the initial improvement, which had been found in varying degrees in all the children, depended upon the post-treatment environment. Those who were institutionalised regressed, while those at home with parents who had been trained to carry out behaviour therapy continued to improve. The children who had regressed returned to the previous higher level of function if behaviour therapy was reinstated.

As discussed in Chapter 4, it seems likely that the operant model for the acquisition of language and other cognitive skills is a considerable over-simplification of the way in which these abilities develop in normal children. If any method could be found to free the autistic child from his stereotyped responses and to encourage the development of inner language, this would, in theory at any rate, be far more likely to produce a genuine and lasting improvement.

In practice, as things are at present, it would seem best to attempt a combination of both approaches—that is to use operant techniques and rote learning when necessary, but also to try to encourage development along more normal lines.

Before anyone can begin to teach an autistic child, it is necessary to deal with the behaviour problems which prevent him from attending to the task in hand, such as restless wandering, screaming, destructiveness, and stereotyped movements or obsessional activities which may occupy his whole attention. At this stage, the common-sense techniques of behaviour management, such as ignoring undesirable behaviour and positively rewarding behaviour that is constructive, are of considerable value.

Once the behaviour problems are, to some extent, under control, teaching can begin. With most of the children it will be necessary to help them to learn the basic self-care skills such as dressing, toilet training, washing, and the use of a knife and fork. Some autistic children are very late in learning to use a spoon or even to move their jaws for chewing. In Chapter 10, Janet Carr discusses the way in which such skills can be broken down into tiny steps and taught by techniques of rewarding.

A very useful approach with autistic children is to teach the steps needed to accomplish practical skills by guiding the child's limbs through the necessary movements. An autistic child finds it difficult to watch other people perform and then translate the movements on to his own body; he cannot understand verbal instructions, but he can learn through feeling his own muscles move. Initial resistance or complete passivity may be met, but, if the teacher perseveres, the child eventually begins to perform. He may continue to demand the touch of the adult hand and refuse to do anything by himself, but this can be overcome by reducing the amount of contact very slowly until finally there is no touching at all.

The two areas in which teachers have concentrated their attempts to overcome primary disabilities are first, the difficulties with expressive movements and second, the problem of using language flexibly and creatively. With regard to the former, Sybil Elgar emphasised the importance of physical education, swimming and dancing (Elgar and Wing, 1969). Other workers have devised programmes to encourage miming and expressive movements in autistic children and many use movement to music. It would be most helpful if this work could be evaluated and useful programmes published for others to follow.

In the field of language, techniques are being developed for teaching through visual analogies of linguistic processes (for example, Fraser and Blockley, 1973). Joan Taylor describes her approach to this problem in Chapter 8. These new ideas are of considerable theoretical as well as practical interest. They are being used with children who have developmental language problems of all kinds, as well as those who are autistic. Experimental evaluation of the results of controlled trials with carefully selected and matched children would be particularly valuable.

Although it is clearly worthwhile to try these special methods of teaching directed at the primary impairments, it is also clear that many children are too handicapped, or have grown past the stage of development when they could be expected to benefit. It is necessary to teach these children, by rote, to respond to and to use a range of useful phrases and to perform practical tasks, even if they have only limited understanding. The main purpose is to allow the child to fit more easily into his family or residential community and to take part in any social activities which he enjoys, even though his primary impairments remain unchanged. This solution is very much second best, but is infinitely preferable to leaving the child without any skills at all. Least progress can be expected in the most severely retarded autistic children (see Chapter 6) but efforts to improve difficult behaviour and to teach some basic self-care are worth while. The problems of this group are discussed in Chapter 10.

Involving the Parents

The difficulty that autistic children have in generalising has already been mentioned. Rutter and Bartak (1973) noted that improvement in social behaviour found in autistic children in the classroom did not generalise to other situations. They therefore felt that involvement of the parents was essential if the children were to make the same progress at home as at school. Schopler, in Chapter 9, discusses the theoretical and practical aspects of using parents as therapists for their own children.

Evaluation of Results

The results of treatment, education and management techniques must be evaluated in the light of the outcome which occurs in the absence of any specific intervention. A small proportion of autistic children do show marked improvement by the time of adult life, although they could not be called normal. Any method of treatment that is advocated must produce a result which is better than the natural outcome, if it is to be accepted as useful.

Careful diagnosis and description of level of handicap is also of primary importance in considering the results of treatment. Widening the definition of autism to include children with much milder handicaps will give too optimistic an impression, while the inclusion of large numbers who are profoundly generally retarded will have the opposite effect.

Up to the present time, the best that can be offered in the way of treatment is the painstaking long-term process of management and education to reduce behaviour disturbances and to increase useful skills. This process is undramatic and modest in its aims but is of great value to the parents and families of the children concerned.

CHAPTER 8

AN APPROACH TO TEACHING COGNITIVE SKILLS UNDERLYING LANGUAGE DEVELOPMENT

JOAN E. TAYLOR

The major difficulty in teaching autistic children is helping them to understand instead of learning by rote. This chapter will present a method designed to encourage the acquisition of skills needed for the development of comprehension and flexible use of language and which can also be used to assess the level a child has reached in the basic cognitive processes underlying language.

Problems in Forming Associations

The impairments of symbolic function characteristic of early childhood autism are described in Chapter 4. Certain aspects of these problems will be mentioned again here in order to give a context for the specific teaching techniques.

Autistic children, if they have any speech at all, can imitate sound sequences in the same way as a mynah bird or budgerigar. Some of them advance beyond this stage and can link the word labels with objects, actions or familiar situations. It is possible for the more able child to have stored up hundreds of stock words, phrases or sentences which he brings out automatically as labels for all familiar occasions. Often the remarks appear to be appropriate, but the limitations of this process are demonstrated at times when the label is unexpected or bizarre. It is as though the autistic child who has reached this stage has the bricks of language but no plan for building with them.

It would seem that there are processes which underlie the building of cognitive schemata which the normal baby uses from birth but which are, apparently, unavailable to the autistic child. A normal child can scan a visual display, then focus his attention on details which are significant to him because of their association with previous memories, then scan again and so on, until he has noticed the important points. The autistic child spends less time in looking than the normal child and tends to fix on one detail, relevant or irrelevant, to the exclusion of other information.

Normal babies and children can associate two items of perceptual input, but the items can be easily separated, or associated with other items. For the autistic child, once two items have become associated with each other they are indissolubly glued together. The label is pasted on the object and will not come off. In this situation, when one of a pair of associated items is presented to an autistic child, he can retrieve the other from his memory store with ease, but that is all. For example, if such a child is shown a picture made of gummed coloured paper, the sight of the gummed paper may evoke the remark "Don't pull it off," while the content of the picture is ignored. In contrast, in the normal child, any item of perceptual input will trigger off many associations among which he can choose those most appropriate for the situation. Furthermore, he can hold an idea in his mind, scan his memory for any relevant items in the store and recognise them when he finds them. He can create mental images, fit these into his schemata and compare them with reality. If an adult, when playing with a young normal child, pretends to make a stool gallop along, then pats it and strokes it and imitates the sound of neighing, the child would produce his word for "horse" but would also laugh at the joke. The adult's actions would have elicited the idea of a horse but at the same time the child would also be aware that the stool was not a real horse but only a pretend one.

The autistic child's memories appear to be tied up in fixed associations and are not retrievable in the flexible way enjoyed by normal children. They are not available for building complex schemata, making analogies, seeing and making jokes, understanding or using figures of speech, or for pretending or inventing.

A normal baby or young child seems to be protected against too much teaching. At an early age a child imitates words said to him, but, a little later, when words begin to have meaning for him, this echoing ceases. Attention to meaning takes precedence over the automatic response to a stimulus which is the basis of parrot-like imitation, so the echoing is inhibited. In general, the young normal child does not learn from teaching by others until the items he is being taught will fit into the mental schemata that he is building for himself. As described in Chapter 4, he infers the rules of language for himself and has to go through all the stages of modifying and expanding these rules, despite any adult attempts to help him make short cuts.

In a normal child, there is an interplay between flexibility and temporary rigidity. He can scan, stop to notice, then scan again; he can retain or alter any item in his information store; he has the binary choice of "hold or change", so that both consolidation of learning and further progress are possible. There is an equivalent interplay between a young normal child and his parents; he can retain his own rules despite their best efforts or he can, at the right time for him, learn from their instruction.

If it were possible to start these processes in a young autistic child he might eventually develop more fluid, less rigid, thinking. The first step is to try to help the child to pay focussed attention to perceptual input as will be described below. It will be recognised that a programme of this kind would not be suitable for the most severely retarded autistic children. It may be thought too easy for children with the milder handicaps who are willing to work and can do these simple tasks without much difficulty. However, the preliminary activities are intentionally simple, being carefully chosen and presented so that the child can understand that he is to work on his own without specific adult direction. The simplicity of the first tasks has the added advantage that observation of the way the child manages them allows for an assessment of his attainments and difficulties and his response to the demands of a new situation.

Teaching Techniques

The tasks are presented in visual form which confers obvious advantages for autistic children and others who have problems with the temporal sequencing inherent in spoken language (see Chapter 5). Also, the teacher is able to observe the child's strategies for performing and the types of errors he makes far more easily when working with concrete, visible materials rather than the intangible spoken word. The materials hold the child's visual attention and give him time to grasp the basic ideas, whereas auditory stimuli can more easily be ignored by a child who does not comprehend them. Spoken instructions and other auditory input are cut down to a minimum while the child is attending to the visuo-motor task. Continual vocal encouragement, correction of mistakes or urging to greater efforts are all to be avoided. Too much reiteration of, for example, "that's right" or "good boy" may result in the child relying on his teacher's approval so that he constantly hesitates to act on his own initiative; he may alter his first choice if it is not immediately approved, taking "no comment" to mean disapproval. The teacher's role is quietly to encourage the child's persistence and, when he has finished, to show appreciation of his success.

The method of presentation of the material says, in effect, to the child, "Here is something. What can you do with it? Take your time, it is all yours." The child is required to observe, scan, see what can be done and then do it, working out the little problems that are presented. I usually prefer to call the exercises "games" since this conveys the feeling of an interesting or enjoyable occupation pursued in a relaxed atmosphere, which should give the child a positive attitude rather than a feeling of stress, resistance or boredom. Since the teacher needs to know if the child can learn and whether he can modify his behaviour in response to experience, she must let the child do the work of observing, selecting and manipulating the materials as he thinks fit. She should not interfere. She should sit close enough to maintain her quiet supervision but far enough away for the child to feel that he is doing the tasks on his own. It is often better for the teacher to sit to one side of the child so that left and right are the same for both. Some children are disturbed by having an adult sitting facing them. They may glance at the teacher for cues instead of paying attention to the task. One little girl, instead of working, would stare at the teacher's face and say "Eyes, eyes."

Careful observation of the child's performance is important.

Notes should be written up immediately after the end of the session, since writing while working with the child would disturb the rapport with him.

Visuo-motor skills

The simplest games in the series require the child to engage in repetitive, mechanical activities needing visuo-motor coordination; for example, the child is given a tray of beads and a wooden posting box with one hole large enough to take any of the beads. Another similar task is that of putting rings on suitable wooden pegs. The apparatus is given to the child who is not told what to do but is encouraged to try for himself.

There are several ways in which a child may fail to do these simple tasks. He may do nothing at all, or act only if he is repeatedly told "You do it," "Do another one." He may put his hand out to the teacher as though soliciting help. He may select four items, put them before him on the table and contemplate them, or pick up handfuls and drop them, or put a few in the posting box and then do no more. He may arrange them in a line, ignoring the box.

If he fails, in these or other ways, to link together the materials and apparatus, he needs more of these simple mechanical activities. He should not be shown how to perform, since this strengthens his dependence on other people and gives no information on whether or not he could do the tasks himself if given time. The same task should not be presented repeatedly; instead, different tasks that are based on the same simple principles should be tried. The aim is for the teacher and child between them to establish that the child makes an attempt to work with the material, that he sees for himself what needs to be done and does it by himself. Once this has happened, the child can progress to the next step in the series of games.

Forced choice tasks

These games give the child the opportunity of learning that there are rules governing the relationships between objects. The observation of these rules modifies the child's actions.

The child can be given a dish of round beads, some of which are large and red and the others small and blue. The structuring apparatus is a wooden posting box with a hole in the lid which accepts only the small beads. Another example of the same kind of task consists of long and short sticks of various colours and a small wooden box into which only the small sticks will fit.

With these tasks, the child is confronted with a situation which requires him to pay attention to the materials and the apparatus. In the first example, the single hole invites him to put the beads in, but, at the same time, limits the choice to one kind of bead. If he quickly learns the rule that only the small blue beads go into the small hole, he can be given large blue and small red beads to see how quickly he can change to the new rule.

Working from left to right

Sequencing from left to right is a habit so firmly ingrained in adults in our culture that they may expect a child to work in the same way by instinct. The left to right rule, is, of course, completely arbitrary, is not shared by all human beings, and has to be learnt by children. It is important in our culture, because it underlies reading, writing and many other forms of visual sequencing.

The materials used may be collections of mixed beads, blocks, rings, or similar objects. The structuring apparatus can be a long strip of wood or metal with holes or pegs along its length or a strip of paper with divisions drawn on it.

The teacher structures this game by giving the initial visual, not verbal, cues. As soon as the child picks up one item from the material given to him the teacher points to the first hole on the left. If the child places the bead or other material in this hole the teacher points to the next hole and so on for the first five holes. She then says "You do it" and leaves the child to finish the row for himself, noticing if he continues to work in the left to right sequence. Two or three different strips are given, each time with different materials. The child receives less and less help from the teacher until finally he is left to complete a sequence entirely on his own.

These tasks are suitable for assessing whether or not the child has the left to right rule, or can learn it very quickly. If he does not pick it up easily, it is not useful to try to train him by using these arbitrary tasks. It is much more helpful for the child to learn the rule in its real life context, with the guidance of the adults who care for him, and as part of the other games in this programme.

Making choices

If his performance on the first three series of games shows that the child is willing to try to use the materials offered, that he can observe the rules that relate objects and modify his behaviour appropriately, and has some awareness of the custom of working from left to right, then he is ready to proceed a step further.

The tasks of matching and sorting require the child to make a choice. There are different ways of presenting such tasks, which affect the degree of difficulty experienced by the child. One of the simplest ways is to present a row of items, then give the child the duplicates, one at a time, to place beside the items they match. In this situation the teacher does most of the work. The child's part is reduced to the more or less mechanical task of scanning and placing. This could be described as the visual analogy of the verbal echo.

Another method of presentation is to scatter several items on the table. The child is shown the duplicate of one of the items and must scan the display to select the one that matches. The onus is on the child to scan and perform the deliberate act of picking up the item he chooses from a distracting display, which is harder for him than the first task described above.

The game is made more difficult still if pairs of items are randomly scattered on the table and the child has to find two alike. He has to understand the concept "two" and has to make a deliberate choice of one pair amid a distracting display of many potential pairs.

A child may fail to complete a task of matching similar items for several reasons: he may be unable to engage himself with the task; he may not understand what he is to do; he may be confused by the total visual display; or he may not be able to make up his mind to a deliberate choice.

To help him develop techniques for dealing with these difficulties a further series of simple games has been devised. By observing how the child copes with them the teacher may learn something of his specific problems.

Repetition of the same choice

In this game the child is given a dish of mixed red and blue beads, all of the same size, and a tray, rack or set of rods on which the beads may be placed one at a time.

It is possible, if the child has some comprehension of simple instructions and of colour names, for him to do the task correctly if the teacher says "Put the blue beads on the rods." The child learns nothing from this since he has obeyed the instruction mechanically, like a sheepdog obeying a whistle. If, on the other hand, the teacher says simply "You do it" and then demonstrates the rule by allowing only the blue beads to remain on the rods, removing the red beads and returning them to the child's dish, the child is given the opportunity to formulate the rule of the game for himself. Once he has made the inference that only blue beads are acceptable he can modify his actions accordingly.

This process of inferring the rule is to some extent a visual analogy of the young normal child's learning of auditory-vocal word labels. In this latter situation too, he eventually picks up the rules by observing what is acceptable. Therefore this second method of presentation may further the learning processes underlying language. The game also gives the opportunity of helping the child to learn the left to right rule. The teacher can point to the first on the left and then the next in sequence until the child has acquired the automatic habit.

If the child learns the game easily, the rule can be changed so that red instead of blue beads are acceptable. In this way it will be possible to see how quickly he can change his "set".

A series of choices, each between two items

The previous game asked little more of the child than that he should continue to match items to his first choice. The next game requires that he should make a series of choices, each between two items.

The teacher has a number of red cubes and yellow cubes and the child is given cylindrical beads of the same colours. The teacher places red or yellow cubes, one at a time, in random order in front of the child. The child should then place a cylinder of the same colour on top of the cube presented by the teacher. This game requires the child to accept the presence and collaboration of another person, which is an additional problem for some children.

The next game, which also requires a series of binary choices, is harder to perform. The material consists of a tray of blue and yellow 5 cm cubes. The structuring apparatus is a strip of card with blue and yellow 5 cm squares stuck on it in a row but in random order of colour. The child is to start at the first square on the left, then work along the squares in order, one at a time, to the right, pointing to each square in turn and placing a matching cube on it.

Some children find this game very difficult. Even when they point to the next square they may still select the cube appropriate to the previous one. Children who verbalise may not find that saying the words helps them in the visuo-motor task. They may say "blue" but still select a yellow cube.

The nature of the material shows that a choice has to be made and some children find this very disturbing. Some are distracted by irrelevant auditory and visual stimuli in the environment. They need to listen and look for a moment and can then bring their attention back to the task. Others may rock themselves to and fro in an effort to deal with the problem. Sometimes such children find continual decision making intolerable. In this situation the task should be limited to matching very few items, perhaps only two or three, depending on how much the child can tolerate. It needs delicate judgement to avoid, on the one hand, pushing the child too far and, on the other, allowing him to refuse the task altogether and thus fail to learn a necessary skill. The best approach is to start from what the child can do, however limited, and then gradually to extend the scope of the tasks in steps which are small enough for him to surmount with some effort but without distress.

Sorting tasks

To exercise choice, it is necessary to observe that there are alternatives from which to choose. A game of sorting may help to show whether a child can scan a display and make this kind of observation. All that is needed are items that differ on one variable only, such as colour, shape, or size, plus a box or tray with two compartments or two threading sticks. The child is allowed to notice for himself that the items can be sorted into two kinds and put into the containers.

The child should be allowed to work as he pleases; for example, when he has grasped the idea of the task he may prefer to pick up several items at once and then place them into the appropriate container. He should finish the task without correction. If he gets it right he can try with other materials, which are sorted on different variables. If he fails, he can be gently encouraged to try again, this time dealing with one item at a time. If he still fails then the materials should be packed up cheerfully, without comment and the child given a chance to try another day. The important thing is not that the child should solve the problem the first time it is presented but that he should discover the rules for himself. It may then be possible for him to apply the basic rules of sorting to any collection of objects.

Up to this point all the games have involved visuo-motor abilities and have demanded the formation of concepts, but the use of symbols (labels) for the concepts has not been necessary. A child must have the concept of colour differences in order to sort by colour, but he can do this without knowing the colour names or identifying them by any other kind of symbol. The games to be described from now on require the child to use symbols to represent objects or concepts.

Memory

By simplifying and structuring the visuo-motor tasks the child can be helped to deal with objects according to their similarities and differences, but it is difficult to know how far it is possible to improve long- or short-term memory. However, one can devise simple tests of memory in order to decide how far teaching can progress and these tasks may also help the child to use his memory more efficiently.

In the context of developing language, the most important aspect of memory is the ability to retrieve a wide range of relevant associations. Good storage of items is of little help if, as in autistic children, the associations to any input are rigidly limited and stereotyped.

The series of games already described will have revealed some facts about the child's ability to memorise and recall visually presented material. They can easily be adapted to test memory for verbal input. For example, the child can be given blue beads and yellow beads and a one-hole posting box. He can be asked to post the blue beads and then, when this is finished, to start again but this time to post the yellow ones. He has to remember one instruction, then forget this one and remember something different.

Another test of memory is the recall of items in a visuo-spatial sequence. The child is shown a series of pictures, then one is covered and the child asked to name or otherwise indicate the hidden item. This task can be varied by covering pictures in different positions in the sequence.

If the child succeeds in these simple tests of memory he can be asked to remember four items that he has just seen, felt and named, which is a more difficult task.

An even harder task involves memory for the auditory-vocal associations of items in a spatial sequence. Three different objects are hidden, one under each of three cups in a row. The child is told the names of the objects under all the cups and then asked to name the object under one of them. He can also be asked to remember under which cup another of the objects was said to be hidden.

Each of the memory tasks can be presented in at least two different ways to both test and, it is hoped, to extend the child's ability to switch from the recall of one type of association to another.

During the course of the day, in group work, in individual sessions, at meal times, bed time, or in any other situation, formal or informal, opportunities of helping the child to recall associations present themselves and should be used. When attempts are made to engage him in conversation an autistic child usually brings out his automatic stereotyped phrases. He should be encouraged to think again and make a different comment, perhaps in answer to a rephrasing of the question. He should not be badgered or rushed, but given time to adjust his thoughts so that he can produce a more spontaneous, less stereotyped answer. Providing the child is allowed to respond at his own pace, he can be given these exercises in short-term memory in brief sessions frequently throughout the day.

Widening the scope of the programme

When the child has accepted the teacher as part of his environment, has shown himself willing to work, is able to pay attention to visually presented tasks, can make a choice, has grasped that objects or concepts can be represented by symbols, holds information in his memory and can recall items as required, he then needs further opportunities to develop strategies for dealing with all kinds of situations where rules have to be deduced and applied in a flexible way.

The games played by the child should gradually increase in difficulty so that he moves from solving tasks by trial and error to dealing with little problems which can be solved only if he sees an underlying pattern or concept and appreciates simple analogies. Games of classifying can progress from simple sorting on colour to those which involve much more complex concepts such as animals versus plants; or the association of ideas such as cup and saucer, or sausage and frying pan. Structuring apparatus may be used in the early stages to suggest ways of sorting, until the child can scan and see a rule for working without such aids.

As well as grouping objects by using concepts, it is possible to abstract the separate features which characterise objects. A child can be shown a yellow cylinder and asked to "describe" it by selecting, from the materials given him, a patch of yellow colour and a circle (the latter being the shape of the cylinder in cross section). He can also be asked to find an article when the teacher "describes" it by presenting some of its separate features.

Games which involve the child in working to rules and taking turns with other people (adults and children), such as variations on ludo and picture lotto, are valuable for developing co-operation. Arranging each set of games so that the same materials are used in different ways can be done all through the series to encourage flexibility of approach.

A child with a severe language problem cannot be expected to give concentrated attention for long periods. He needs tasks which can be performed in a short space of time but which require him to think. Their completion brings the immediate reward of a successful outcome of effort geared to the child's level of development. It is best not to present a long series of exercises all based on the same principle, but to vary the kinds of tasks so that the child has to attend and think afresh about each one.

Visual analogies of language

At this stage, the games aim to develop the flexible use of symbols by means of visual analogies of language. The simpler exercises at this level involve the use of arbitrary symbols for objects or concepts such as the colour red to symbolise "warm" or a cross to mean "yellow". These symbols can be used in one game only, or they may be continued through a series of games. For example, when the child has the idea that a cross (X) is being used as a label for yellow, he can be shown an X followed by an uncoloured picture of an object such as a car. This means that he has to find a yellow car. The arbitrary symbols may be displayed for the child to refer to, or, in a more difficult version, he may have to recall them from memory.

When a child finds a yellow car in response to the X and the drawing of a car, as described above, he has in effect "read" the information presented. The game can also be played so that the child observes the yellow car and then arranges the pictures to describe it, which is analogous to the process of writing. The correct order of the "words" can be emphasised in these exercises.

The last game to be described here is the most complex and demonstrates most clearly the learning processes necessary for the development of useful language as distinct from a vocabulary of labels.

The language model uses four miniature toy animals; a sheep, a pig, a hen and a cow and five small, square section, coloured rods, such as those available in the Cuisinaire apparatus, one each of red, green, yellow, pink and brown.

The child is asked to associate the red rod with the sheep and green with the pig. The two animals are placed on the table handy for the child. In front of the child are arranged the red rod, placed horizontally and the brown rod standing upright to the right of it. The child is invited to do something about the red rod. He places the sheep by it. The brown rod is then "walked" with large, slow, deliberate steps to the right. A slight gesture, pointing to the child and then to the sheep, indicates that he is to do something about it. He is not told what to do. The brown rod again begins to walk, and the child should reason that he is to do the same with the sheep. As soon as he begins to make the sheep walk, the brown rod is returned to its position, standing upright to the right of the red rod and the child is congratulated.

A new arrangement of rods is made: the green rod lying horizontally on the table and the brown rod standing to the right. The child should infer that the pig is to walk and makes it do so. If the child touches the brown rod, he is told that that belongs to the teacher: the pig is his.

The sheep and hen are now put beside the child and another arrangement of rods is made. The green rod is laid horizontally and on its right, the brown rod is also laid in the horizontal position. The child is asked to watch carefully. The tutor picks up the brown rod and clappers it quickly along to the right, making a "running" noise, then replaces it as before to the right of the green rod. The child who has already learnt to associate the pig with the green rod should now make the pig run. Other arrangements of the rods are made and the child makes the animals walk or run as appropriate.

When the child has grasped the general idea, the yellow rod should be placed in a horizontal position, like the rods representing the sheep and the pig. He should infer that this represents the hen which can also be made to walk or run in response to the positions of the brown rod.

Next, the cow is put with the other animals and the pink rod is laid horizontally. While the child is giving close attention, the brown rod is stood to the right and made to fall over backwards. This is done again, with deliberation, and left lying down, but at right angles to the horizontal position of the rods representing the animals. The child is to deduce that the pink rod represents the cow and the brown rod lying down means "fall".

The child now has 4 "word-labels" (nouns); red for sheep, green for pig, yellow for hen, pink for cow. He also has 3 verbs, brown rod standing upright for walk, brown rod lying horizontally for run, and brown rod lying vertically for fall.

The child may be exercised in several ways:

1. "Read"—the teacher makes an arrangement of rods and the child moves the animals.
2. "Observe and write"—the teacher makes the animals move and the child places the rods appropriately.
3. "Write something"—the child arranges the rods and the teacher reads the arrangement and moves the animals.
4. "Do something"—the child moves the animals and the teacher writes what the animal did.

The whole exercise has required the child to associate two word-labels with animals and deduce the association of a third and fourth; associate three "verbs" with their actions; classify "nouns" as coloured horizontal rods and "verbs" as indicated by the position of the brown rod; make observations about word order (word-label on the left and verb to the right of it). It has asked him to use short-term memory and to scan, internally, his memories of association of label and object, verb and action.

Aims and Uses of the Programme

All this does not pretend to be a method of teaching language. It attempts only to alert the attention of the children and foster the learning of skills needed for the development of language. A list may be made of matters on which the child's attention is focussed, such as the attributes of things, association of perceptions in different modalities, similarities and differences, association of ideas, patterns and categories, simple analogies, but these are means to the end that the children should become generally more alert intellectually.

The programme should take its place as one part of the general plan of teaching. After working for a period of time which varies for each child, a change may be seen. The child becomes more alert, more ready to be involved, busier, more aware of the teacher as a person, making deliberate efforts to gain approval. When this happens there is often a spurt in progress in other aspects of learning and development, such as drawing and writing. Executive speech may improve together with the ability to comprehend and use symbols. The child who benefits in this way is more observant and watchful and begins to go forward on his own. The use of the series of games can be terminated at any point if it becomes obvious that the child's language development has progressed sufficiently to make their continuation unnecessary. They should also be terminated if it is clear that the child can make no further progress.

The methods of working described here are, in many ways, different from those used in operant conditioning. Both approaches are structured in the sense that the teacher decides what the child should be doing, but the essence of the series of games is that the child is allowed to find the rules for himself, as the normal child seems to do when acquiring language. Most operant programmes, on the other hand, try to build up skills such as language by the direct teaching of every tiny step in performance.

Both approaches have their place, and the art of teaching handicapped children is to know when to choose one and when the other.

These games have been used with pre-school children with severe language problems, some of whom were autistic. The latter were clearly less able to create ideas spontaneously and to use associations freely. Much work remains to be done on the eventual results of using this approach for children with different syndromes of impairments. In the meantime, it is useful for assessing in detail the level any child has reached in his ability to form concepts and use symbols. It may also, if started early enough, help a little towards overcoming the severe handicaps characteristic of early childhood autism.

CHAPTER 9

TOWARDS REDUCING BEHAVIOR PROBLEMS IN AUTISTIC CHILDREN

ERIC SCHOPLER

The special behavior problems of autistic children can be distinguished from their special learning difficulties, recognizing that this distinction is more apparent than real. The term "behavioral problem" is often used for referring to the autistic child's problems with other people, especially adults like parents and teachers. These behavior problems, however, have the same basis in the child's perceptual deficits, his language impairment and handicap of understanding, as his special problems of learning. In this chapter a brief historical perspective will be presented to point up some of the myth beliefs which have added to the difficulties of understanding and managing autistic children. This will be followed by a description of the children and the Program from which both the clinical and research data were taken; the conceptual framework for the Program; the problem hierarchy; parent counseling problems; and the potential outcome of treatment.

Historical Perspective

Strange and mysterious children have appeared throughout known history. Often their reported life history began midway through childhood. Their origins sometimes were a matter of spooky rumor and sometimes wild theoretical speculation. Some have been referred to as feral children, suckled and reared by wolves or other wild animals. More recently feral children have been redefined as

221

autistic. The best known of the wolf reared group were probably Romulus and Remus. Legend has it that they were cast into the Tiber River, somehow retrieved and reared by wolves, until they could rejoin the human community in order to found Rome. Many other such cases have been recorded. The purposes of this chapter, however, may best be served by confining the discussion to the case of Kamala (Gesell, 1941).

The Reverend J. A. L. Singh discovered Kamala and her sister Amala on 8 October 1929, in Midnapore, India. The Rev Singh had come to Midnapore "fired with a zeal" to find aborigines. According to his statement, Midnapore was not in the jurisdiction of his parish. But, perhaps because the natives had been terrified by ghosts, perhaps because of divine inspiration, he sought out the parish of Midnapore. After investigating the ghosts, he reported to his parishioners that these were not ghosts at all, but children reared by wolves, found in a wolf den and then transferred by the Rev Singh to his orphanage. Amala died after only 1 year at the orphanage. Singh's diary was confined to Kamala.

This diary was translated into English by Dr Zingg of the University of Denver and studied by Dr Gesell of Yale University. In Dr Gesell's (1941) report, there was no question about the child's wolf foster parentage. Instead he reconstructed from his imagination how the now well-known Gesell norms manifested themselves in the wolf's den. An even more jarring suspension of rationality may be found on page 72 where Gesell described the 17-year old Kamala with the language and social behavior of a 3-year old child. Nevertheless, he considered her as normal... "that Kamala was born a normal infant"... and that there were... "clinical indications of her essential normality." The clinical indications cited by Gesell revolve around Kamala's successful adjustment to the wolf den, an adjustment which in fact had been constructed purely from Gesell's imagination.

Kamala, or rather Rev Singh's diary of her, also drew the attention of the eminent psychologist, Bettelheim (1959). He believed that she was not likely raised by wolves at all. Instead, he presented clinical examples that Kamala, like other feral children, behaved very much like autistic children at his school. He argued that the so-called feral children were actually autistic children who had been neglected and emotionally deprived by their mothers. He concluded that he had succeeded in demonstrating that there were no feral children—only feral mothers.

In this case authorities on theology, child development, and psychoanalysis each found their own favorite and unsubstantiated theory in the same child. Singh claimed that the frightening "ghost child" was the foster daughter of a wolf. Gesell interpreted her symptoms of retardation or mental deficiency as "normal" reponses to a wolf den; and Bettelheim had the revelation that the nonexisting, feral children were actually autistic, with "feral mothers." Kamala's place in the history of autism is significant, not because of the theories certain widely published experts claimed about her and her origin, but rather because these same theories have had confused and misguided implications for the treatment of autistic children (Schopler, 1973). When the atmosphere of professional guidance has included myths and incompatible interpretations, there is little wonder that both parental and professional efforts to manage the distorted behavior of autistic children have often resulted only in bizarre behavior.

Clinical-Research Context

Most of the clinical and research data referred to below came from a group of autistic children and their parents studied in our Developmental Therapy Program for the past 8 years (Schopler and Reichler, 1971a). The children were between the ages of 4 and 10. They were diagnosed on a rating system described in Reichler and Schopler (1971) based on the Creak (1964) criteria. The behaviors of autistic children are described in Chapter 2 and in L. Wing (1975a). Parents were described in greater detail elsewhere (Schopler, 1973). As a group they fell within normal limits according to all indicators with the exception that they had a handicapped child.

In our Treatment Program, parents functioned as cotherapists (Schopler and Reichler, 1971b). That is, they collaborated with the staff, both in efforts to understand the children and also in working out optimum special education approaches and behavior management techniques. The staff recognized that diagnostic indicators were mainly behavioral and that these behaviors were sufficiently broad to use the terms "psychotic" and "autistic" interchangeably. From .he most current reviews on the status of autism (Rutter, 1968; Ornitz, 1973) three propositions can be derived regarding causation. (1) For individual children, the specific causes are usually unknown. (2) There is no single underlying cause to account for the autistic condition. Instead the condition is multiply determined. (3) Most likely the primary causes involve some form of brain abnormality, manifesting itself by impairment of appropriate perception and understanding. The resulting variability in behavioral symptoms depends in large part on the child's age, the time of onset, and the severity of the impairment.

The above propositions have replaced the traditional, psychoanalytically derived emphasis on parental feelings, attitudes, and personalities as the primary cause of autism. The propositions are consistent with current research and clinical observations. Accordingly, it was no great discovery to see that parents were reacting with perplexity and concern to their unusual children rather than the other way around. Therefore, when parents became cotherapists or collaborators with the professional staff, effective methods of special education and behavioral management related to the specific needs of the children could be developed quite rapidly.

Therapy sessions take place through the use of a one-way observation room. The frequency of the sessions, each lasting an hour, ranges from twice a week to once every 6 weeks. The professional staff developed a diagnostic profile of each child's various developmental levels in different skills and learning modalities. The special education approaches based on this evaluation and also on parents' observations are demonstrated to parents as they observe through the one-way mirror. A home program is written out and used by parents in daily sessions with their child.

This Program, known as Division TEACCH, in the Department of Psychiatry of the University of North Carolina School of Medicine, has been adopted on a state wide basis in North Carolina. It includes three Centers, covering the Eastern, Central, and Western parts of the state. In these Centers, both educational and behavioral interventions are worked out individually for each child and family. Also attached to the Centers are special education classrooms located in the public school system. One of the Centers' main goals, in collaboration with the parents, is to work out an individualised educational experience for the child, integrated between home and school. Having briefly described the program context in which the children's behavior was observed and managed with their families, some aspects of the theoretical and conceptual framework guiding the Program will be discussed next.

Theoretical framework and concepts

Parents of autistic children, and some other parents too, have suffered unnecessary doubts and self-criticism because of the theories and myths erroneously applied to child rearing. Two converging myths were already discussed in the introduction. These included the belief that the maturational and developmental sequences in the human infant had an immutably powerful tendency towards normal development. Even the severest developmental deviations were interpreted as normal reactions to environmental stress (Gesell, 1941). Equally off the deep end were the psychoanalytic theories which enabled Bettelheim to formulate the causes of autism as due to parents stressing their children like concentration camp victims (Bettelheim, 1967) and to argue that the concept of feral children be replaced by "feral mothers" (Bettelheim, 1959). Since it was our clinical experience that many autistic children and their parents have actually been harmed by these beliefs, it was tempting to advocate that parents and staff adhere to no theoretical beliefs. Instead, these could be replaced by the empirical, scientific system brought from the animal laboratory to the operant conditioning of autistic children. The relatively simple stimulus-response theory held out the promise of shaping any desirable behavior if only the appropriate reinforcement contingencies could be found. To many behaviorists the face validity of this expectation seemed sufficient to justify ignoring those aspects of the child's life which did not appear to have a direct bearing on the specific behavior they were trying to modify.

The use of operant conditioning was reported by investigators working directly with autistic-like children since 1790 (Itard, 1801, 1807a,b,c). This kind of knowledge has been obfuscated by modern myths. Operant conditioning was rediscovered under the banner of science and research. However, the rigid animal research methodology advocated by many behaviorists did not seem to offer adequate answers to many appropriate questions parents asked about their autistic children. The failures and limitations of such a research technique applied to human families have been honestly acknowledged in the follow-up report of Lovaas (1973).

In our Developmental Therapy Program we have advocated a problem oriented approach. Rather than looking for a scientific or universal technique, we try to find the best available answer to the problems raised by families with autistic children and then use the most appropriate intervention available for their resolution. This empiricism is shaped by a developmental concept, applied in an interaction framework. The relativity of resolutions employed is formally acknowledged with both parents and staff, in order to tie interventions into the real world.

The *concept of development* is emphasised as a reminder that children, both normal and otherwise, change with age more rapidly than do adults. Children's adaptational skills and also the manifestations of their handicaps are formed, at least in part, by their age and developmental level. This may or even should appear obvious. However, numerous myths about the emotional development of children have served to confuse and mislead parents about simple developmental levels. For example, the myth of the Oedipus Complex has convinced some professionals and parents that the sexual impulses of a 5-year old boy have a greater bearing on his future than what he may learn in school. In a similar vein, many believe that the emotional and intellectual nuances of parental interactions during the first 2 years of their infant's life will determine the scope of his adjustment difficulties as an adult. There is no research evidence that the adult personality is significantly determined by experiences confined to the first 2 years. It is too often ignored that the infant is protected against subtleties of negative interpersonal exchanges by limitations in his perceptual and cognitive development.

It is especially important with autistic children to recognise that various behaviors and functions of the same child may be operating at different developmental levels. For example, a 5-year old autistic child may have gross motor skills normal for his age, but the language level of a 2-year old. The most appropriate adult responses can often best be approximated from the normal response to a particular developmental level. The 5-year old could be taught to use a tricycle, but this might be done using speech simple enough to be understood by a 2-year old. This is not to say that the behavior of autistic children is exactly like that of a younger normal child. It is, however, to say that one of the sound and humane bridges to the special understanding needed by autistic children is across their similarities and common needs with younger normal children.

The interaction model

Another popularisation of a now old fashioned point of view is the simplistic dichotomising of what was called the nature-nurture controversy. From this view came questions like, Is behavior caused genetically or environmentally? Is it organic or functional? These questions and the overly simple answers they imply are replaced by an interaction model. With this model it is assumed that the directions of a young child's development are based on the interactions with his parents. With the normal child, the parent tends to gear his expectations to his child's age and developmental level. Under such conditions the parent–child interaction tends to be reciprocal. By and large, the parent shapes his child's behavior around parental expectations. The child in turn has an effect on the parent's behavior. The extent to which biological factors determine the normal child's effect on his parents depends largely on his age and developmental levels. For instance, the human infant is born with a biologically determined set of reflexes and responses. These appear in regular developmental sequences, relatively unaffected by learned experience. Some of these responses, such as the smile, are basic to social development. Even when their smiles are still reflexive and not yet a social response, some infants smile a great deal while others smile less. The infant's smile can influence his mother's

involvement. Freedman (1966) found that infants who smile frequently tend to be fatter than infrequent smilers. With an autistic
infant who has biologically impaired reflexes and social responses,
the mother is negatively reinforced for her mothering efforts. The
interaction cycle is directed more by biological factors than it is
with the normal child. However, even with the normal child,
biological factors direct interactional patterns more frequently at the
early ages than they do later on.

In addition to his parents, the child's interaction matrix includes
many other persons and factors, depending on his age, sex, and the
social values he is reared with. An autistic child living on a busy city
street will become involved in different interaction sequences from
one living in the country. The number of siblings will affect the
distribution of family stresses and in turn the interactions with the
autistic child. In short, there are a great many factors, varying by
individual cases, which will define the interaction matrix for an
individual child and the particular behavior interfering with his
adaptation. Conceptually, the interaction model is more complex
than the stimulus-response model of the behaviorists. It does not
hold out the behaviorists' hope that for each specific behavior
problem, a scientifically established intervention can be found which
when carefully applied will produce the desired behavior. On the
other hand, it has the advantage of admitting a wider range of
factors when working out a particular problem. This may include the
acceptance of certain child behavior by the parent or teacher side of
the interaction, rather than searching unrealistically for better
techniques of behavior modification. The child's developmental
level is a key factor in deciding through which side of the interaction
to effect an improved adaptation. For example, if a 7-year old child's
language is at the level of an 18-month old, his optimum adaptational
potential may be better served when the adult accepts his language
impairment and spends teaching efforts on non-verbal self-help skills.

Relativity of behavior

From a behaviorist position it is natural to be searching for and
hoping to tap a "pivotal response" in the autistic child, an "interven-

ing variable," which when modified will improve a host of other functions. If you could teach the child normal eye contact, he might become related, learn to talk, and so on. The disappointment in not finding behavior leading to a "pivotal response" was eloquently documented by Lovaas (1973). The inclination to formulate a technique that will cure or help all autistic children is pursued by many professionals and many such techniques are found in the clinical marketplace, from megavitamins to electronic typewriters. All of them have reported some success, none of them for all autistic children. This lack of success in "curing" autistic children should surprise no one. The level of intelligence and degree and extent of impairment are not the same for all these children. Their individual differences are more impressive than their similarities. There is in fact no more basis for employing such a concept as the "pivotal response" than there is for claiming the possibility of an exclusive and totally successful rehabilitative technique. Many professionals have fallen into this trap. If they stumble on a technique that helps one child, they feel that they have not played their social role unless other autistic children can be made to fit their treatment techniques. This is precisely one of the reasons why we found parents of autistic children to be most effective as cotherapists with their own children. The parental social role enabled parents to obtain satisfaction from helping their own child. Unlike professionals, the successful techniques they found did not have to be applicable to a whole group of children before parents could experience success.

Conceptually we have found a most suitable fit between parents functioning as cotherapists and the relativity of the child's behavior. The autistic child's response repertoire, because of his handicap, is less variable or flexible than the normal child's, but the adaptational outcome of behavioral conflict is most fruitfully regarded as situation specific. A characteristic autistic behavior—say persistence in playing with jigsaw puzzles—may be adaptive during a free period at school and maladaptive during "show and tell" sessions. Other typical autistic behavior such as temper tantrums may be maladaptive in most social situations. Nevertheless the relationship between the behavior and the contexts in which it appears is worth emphasising in order to discover the most effective intervention. In the example of the jigsaw puzzle play, 2 adaptive solutions might be: (a) use puzzles during free period to help teach the child communication skills, and (b) change the child's curriculum so as to postpone or eliminate "show and tell". Even the more persistent behaviors need relatively different solutions. Temper tantrums in the home may be resolved by isolation; tantrums in the supermarket by making other plans for the child during shopping trips. Conceptually, the most useful emphasis appears to be on clearly defining adaptational problems for the child and his family and understanding the relative differences between the same behavior problems expressed in different circumstances. This is not to say that we should abandon the search for scientific generalisable solutions to these adaptation problems. Rather, it should be kept in mind that attempts to conceptualise the problems of autistic children as if they were a general entity—like the pseudo-scientific jargonese "self stim"—are inconsistent with optimum adaptation and often actually interfere with optimum adaptation which can be achieved by individualised, situation specific solutions.

Problem hierarchy

The relative aspects of autistic children's behavior problems do not mean that there are no priorities in planning behavior modification. Since the amount of time for special intervention is limited, priorities for modification need to be established in meaningful hierarchies. These should be assessed according to the survival values of the behavior involved rather than by research feasibility. Priorities may be represented by: (1) risks to the child's life, (2) risks to the child's living within the family, (3) risks to his access to special education, and (4) access to normal education.

First priority needs to be given to problems which risk the child's life. These could include running into a busy street, eating toxic substances, self-destructive behavior. Just a few possible solutions aimed at a child's inability to cope with the traffic hazards could include teaching him traffic signals, keeping him in the house when unattended, fencing in the back yard. Choice of the most appropriate intervention should be guided by the developmental level appropriate to the child. At higher levels, symbols tend to be the most efficient when they can be used. Teaching the child spoken, written, or visual signals for traffic dangers is simpler, cheaper, and more appropriate than building back-yard fences. On the other hand, in some circumstances, building a fence will be more appropriate than keeping him indoors or finding constant adult company for him outside the house. These decisions can only be made on an individual basis for each child and family.

In my experience direct threat to the child's survival is less common than threat to his survival within a viable family. Some few residential schools and homes are a satisfactory alternative to the autistic child in his own family and some children are better off in institutions. Some good residential care units, such as small family-like homes, are being developed, but they are still rare. Until such units become established, the majority of autistic children are better off in their own homes than elsewhere. Behavior problems threatening the child's family existence tend to be the most serious threat to his optimum adaptation. The range of behaviors which may threaten his family life is quite wide. These include temper tantrums, messy eating habits, special food preferences, poor toileting habits such as urinating in the heat vents, and an inability to stay out of siblings' property. Only the life style the family is trying to build or maintain can define these adaptational problems. The autistic child's survival is often best assured if adaptation can be made with only minimum imposition or change demanded from his family's life style.

A third order of survival may be represented by the child's ability to participate in a special education program. The requirements for his survival there depend in part on the nature of the program. Generally the child needs the ability to get along with and tolerate other children, to use the toilet, and to show responsiveness to the teacher. The child's chances for success and survival in a special school are enhanced when communication between school and home is relatively open and the efforts to socialise and teach the child in both places are integrated. All too often the relationship between parent and teacher develops so that no agreement is reached regarding the child's behavior problems. The teacher is convinced that the child's most disruptive behaviors originate in the home and the parents suspect that the teacher is unable to handle their child. In most instances a joint effort between home and school to gain more control over the child's unacceptable behavior is the most effective.

A fourth level of adaptation is represented by the range of behavior problems that may jeopardise an autistic child's participation in a normal classroom. The majority of autistic children have sufficiently severe language and cognitive impairments to make normal competition with their age peers impossible. The children who are given a trial in normal school usually have shown only mild signs of autism, considerable scatter in learning skills, and relatively specific learning disabilities. Because they have some peak skills, it is easy to over-expect from these children (Schopler and Reichler, 1972). Low threshold for frustration, quick temper, and negativistic behaviors often characterise these children. Realistic assessment and understanding of the child's development and learning disability are essential for planning the most appropriate program of behavior modification.

Problems of parent counseling

So far I have discussed some historical perspective with emphasis on how some past beliefs and theories have had an adverse effect on the behavior management of autistic children. I have also discussed how an interaction framework, and concepts of development and of the relativity of behavior have been useful in our Program for autistic children and their parents. These concepts also apply to counseling problems with parents. That is, these problems are defined by the interaction between the autistic child, his parents, and the professional resources available to parents in their community.

For the sake of this discussion, counseling problems with parents may be separated into those that are general and those that are specific. General problems are those that cut across different behaviors with the same child. They may involve, for example, a parent's frustration over the child's picky eating, hand flapping, and lack of verbal responsiveness. Such general problems have often been superficially traced to parental attitudes such as discouragement, disappointment, and anger. These problems are regarded as general because they are not necessarily resolved when scientific behavior modification techniques are used on each of the child's specific behaviors. Even when such techniques show signs of being successful, the effects do not always last nor do they generalise to other situations (Lovaas, 1973). On the other hand, specific counseling problems are those relating to particular interactions with the child. They are relatively easily understood by another interested person. They are the actual problems of living with an autistically handicapped child, undistorted by excessive social and emotional pressures. These two aspects of parent counseling overlap. They are, however, worth trying to separate because they tend to respond best to different kinds of intervention. In our experience, the general counseling problems are often unresponsive to, or even aggravated by, specific professional techniques. They are most elusive to define. We have been able to identify the following three basic aspects of general counseling problems with parents. They include (1) parental confusion, (2) erroneous expectations, and (3) conflicting social roles of parent and professional. While these three seem especially important, they are not suggested as all-inclusive.

Parental confusion

When a parent first learns that his child is showing developmental peculiarities which are later considered autistic, the seeds are already sown for parental confusion, which can readily grow to hopeless exasperation. Myth-beliefs about child rearing, causes of deviant development and how to overcome them have all been pre-established in both popular and professional thinking. Some of these have already been described in the first part of this chapter. They include the idea that a child's development deviates from the normal range mainly in response to environmental extremes (Bettelheim, 1967) or in response to improper conditioning procedures (Ferster, 1961). The parent of a child with developmental disability is often obliged to discover what sort of extreme he has supposedly inflicted on his child and whether this stress was transmitted because of the parents' personality pathology (Kanner, 1949) or through faulty communication (Meyers and Goldfarb, 1961) due to marital discord. The psychoanalytically derived interpretation of autism as social withdrawal from an unfavorable emotional climate in the family has had widespread clinical acceptance, as has the belief that long-term psychoanalytic therapy can resolve the emotional disturbance, revealing a normal child. These are some of the simplified beliefs with too much popular acceptance in the recent past. It is perhaps less well known that these same beliefs are also still held by many professionals. The ideas underlying parental confusion already present in the mass culture before the autistic child was born are shared by the parents and readily supported by professionals (Schopler, 1971).

Hand in hand with this confusing myth system comes the lack of access parents have to results of diagnostic evaluations. Frequently we have come across families who have taken their child to several diagnostic centers, only to have their concern and confusion increased with each additional evaluation. When we obtained the results of these evaluations and also tried to discover the source of parental confusion, the records were often stamped "Confidential". This stamp meant confidential from parents. There are, of course, many possible explanations for this practice. We have been able to identify three most probable ones. (1) The evaluation was written up as a psychoanalytic interpretation of family personalities and how their interactions have produced the autistic child. Professionals sense that such interpretations would be "resisted" by the families, or to put it more simply, would be experienced as insulting. There may also be a semi-conscious awareness that such an evaluation was focused on inappropriate history information, leading to an inability to answer the main questions parents have regarding their child: what is wrong and what can we do about it? (2) A second reason is that some indications of brain damage were found in the child. These indications may be based on soft signs or other uncertainties. The "confidentiality" is an attempt to protect parents from the shock and discouragement of knowing uncertain and unpleasant possibilities. This kind of shielding has a predictable effect of increasing parental dread and confusion. (3) A third reason for the confidentiality has to do with protecting professional status. For example, IQ scores were often regarded as top secret. It was overlooked that IQ scores are foremost scores on a test performance. Insofar as the child's test performance actually related to his behavior in other life areas, it was usually no secret from parents anyhow (Schopler and Reichler, 1972). We have found that a frank sharing of both professional knowledge and ignorance was appreciated by most parents. It enabled them to react, think, and feel more rationally about their child.

Confusion reduction is brought about through corrective interaction between parents and professionals. Parents need to persist in requesting frank information and professionals to be clear and consistent in providing it. For example, in our Program, records and charts are not kept secret from parents. IQ scores are not kept as classified information. How they are derived, their limits and use are briefly explained. In a similar fashion the limitations of neurological tests, still largely based on the neurological assessment of adults, are reviewed. The absence of diagnostic precision is acknowledged, including the fact that because a child may be considered autistic or psychotic does not mean that he may not also be brain damaged and retarded. We do not withhold from parents our clinical impressions regarding a child with the kind of language impairment characterising most autistic children. Even when there are no hard signs of brain abnormality from a neurological evaluation, we admit to parents that we have not yet been able to uncover clinical evidence demonstrating such language impairment to be the result of defective child rearing practice. Our experience has been that parents' shock at unpleasant information and lack of clear knowledge was never as great as the confusion resulting from professional attempts to protect them from both.

Erroneous expectations

We have been discussing the confusion and perplexity in managing their autistic child's behavior which arises when parents are given no, or misleading, information concerning diagnosis. Related to this source of mismanagement but different from it is the uncertainty as to the behavior which can reasonably be expected from their child. In both our clinical and research investigations we have found that parents are quite accurate at estimating their own child's level of functioning. In one study (Schopler and Reichler, 1972) we asked parents to estimate their child's developmental levels in the areas of sociability, cognition, language, self-help, motor coordination, and overall development. Parents were asked to make these estimates during the initial diagnostic interview, before any psychological testing was done. These estimates were made in years and months and then compared with the mental ages obtained from subsequent test results. Parental estimates were found to reach significantly high correlations with test results. Parents were able to differentiate higher and lower levels at which their child was functioning in different areas. However, we noted that parents had greater difficulty knowing what to do and what to expect from this understanding. They were uncertain about its meaning for the child's future in both the short and long term—that is, his potential to achieve relative independence in his own life. Too much uncertainty as to what to expect from the child in the present is unsettling and crippling to effective interaction with the child. Absence of any realistic long-range expectations adds anxiety about the future to the present daily uncertainties.

The inappropriate and erroneous myth beliefs noted in the introductory paragraphs of this chapter make a substantial contribution to distorting parental expectations. For example, there was an hour-long television program in October, 1973, about an 8-year old autistic boy living in Chicago. He was the photogenic, eighth child out of nine in a white middle-class family headed by two stable and reasonable parents. The film was narrated in part by Dr Bruno Bettelheim, the established proponent of the claim that autism is a social withdrawal from emotionally damaging experience. The narration of this program proceeded in measured tone to remind the viewer that there are opposing theories on the cause of autism, but that in fact the causes are unknown. Following on the heels of this declaration came the psychologist's analysis that when Terry was 6 months old his mother was also looking after another infant. This resulted in significant sibling rivalry and emotional problems for

Terry. The incident was given as the undoubted cause of Terry's autism. It is ironic and characteristic that Terry's parents were the only ones in this film expressing skepticism about this pronouncement.

In order to make social withdrawal a causal explanation for autism, the clinician must first ignore current research on the subject (Rutter, 1968) and secondly violate common sense. Not only does this theory of "social withdrawal" mislead parents about the current knowledge of autism, it also suggests that the condition can be reversed through vague emotional therapeutic experience. Parents become unsure about trying to have the child conform to their style of life. If they try to structure socially desirable behavior their child may "withdraw further into his own shell." This kind of concern usually obscures and misrepresents the child's special educational or vocational rehabilitation needs.

Other considerations mitigate against the formulation of realistic expectations for an autistic child both by parents and professionals. All sorts of treatments, at widely ranging costs, from megavitamin therapy to residential treatment, are covered in the press. These are usually held out as effective. They are usually difficult to evaluate. When the child's special educational needs are obvious, a class is not always available in a particular community. Sometimes a special education program is funded this year, but not for next year. It may have an age limit which excludes the child. When he reaches adolescence a needed sheltered workshop may not be available, or the child may not have received the appropriate education and training to make use of the existing facility. Other examples of limited resources can be cited. What they add up to is this: When the special educational provisions needed for an autistic child are unavailable, it is impossible to have clear and rational expectations for the child's future.

In our Program we have found that we could help parents avoid irrational expectations by sharing with them both the results of their child's intelligence testing and the probabilities derived from current research. Rather than hiding assessment attempts behind the mysterious term "untestable", we have found substantial clinical support for Alpern's (1967) finding that even uncooperative autistic children will respond to testing when easier or lower developmental test items are used. If a child responds to an easier item, lack of cooperation or "untestability" can no longer be the main explanation for his poor test performance. We share with parents not only the test results but also the statistical probabilities for improvement (Gittelman and Birch, 1967). Autistic children in an IQ range under 50 tend to remain stable over time, while children with IQ's upward from 50 tend to be more variable over time, depending upon their education and experience. This kind of information, when elaborated with accurate observation of the child's individual learning peculiarities and rate of learning, forms a valuable basis for realistic expectations. Parents can be shown how to observe and record the way their child learns, how many repetitions are needed to insure integration of a new skill or concept.

Another general obstacle to the counseling of parents concerning appropriate management may be found in the conflicting social roles of parent and professional.

Conflicting social roles of parent and professional

Professionals are sometimes referred to as "the authorities", especially in England. The definitions of authority in the dictionary refer to the power to make statements, state opinions, and select citations and precedents for a particular expert decision. To be an authority the emphasis is on special information and knowledge, and access to the research and information of other authorities. To fulfill this social role, it is necessary to have expert knowledge of a field, an exclusiveness that is sometimes defined by special terminology and jargon. Because of lengthy educational preparation, apprenticeship, and professional certification, it has become part of the professional's social role to consider these preparations both necessary and sufficient for attaining authority status. To have the professional role evaluated, to be held accountable to anyone other than professional peers, is usually not part of the authority self-concept. In fact the disinclination of authorities to take responsibility for their professional activities reached some kind of zenith in the physical sciences. From this area of human endeavor came the concept of "basic research". In the past some scientists have argued that their search for basic truth was not to be marred with responsibility for the use of their discoveries and inventions, apparently oblivious to the narrow use of, for example, atomic bombs. How far an authority must go to protect his social role varies according to the area of specialisation. The professional role seems to work best when it pertains to clearly defined activities such as dentistry and library science. There are other areas of activity where different roles overlap, which in time evokes struggles of territoriality and influence. The process of child rearing may well be the foremost example of such a battleground.

The parent role is generally defined as meaning responsibility for child rearing. Responsibility means to be morally, legally, and mentally accountable. Not too many generations ago the division between parental responsibility and parental authority was negligible. Today, with the increasing population proliferation, the increasing division of labor, and specialised bureaus, the split between parental authority and responsibility has often reached painful and ludicrous proportions. In the case of autistic children the level of confusion and myth-beliefs held by professionals has been high. This has been due to the unhappy combination of not having better knowledge available at the same time as the maintenance of the professional role demanded more specialised knowledge. In our Program there is no denying the maintenance functions of any professional role. However, if these get out of proportion, the effects are often socially unproductive or harmful. The lack of congruity between professional and parental roles, and also between authority and responsibility appear to be further major sources of parental disability in rearing autistic children.

Both parents and professionals have contributed to the creation of the incongruity between parental responsibility and professional authority. Parents wanted and needed someone to search for causes or to make authoritative statements about causes. Professionals wanted and needed to fulfill this role. The trouble was that many causal hypotheses had been developed and also many different kinds of treatments. Most of the etiological theories had some plausibility and most of the treatments seemed successful at least with some children. It is of interest that since infantile autism was first published as a diagnostic entity (Kanner, 1943) the least plausible theory of causation—parental psychopathology and mismanagement—has had the most sustained support. It is the least plausible from the point of view of empirical clinical research and observation. It is perhaps the most plausible from the point of view of social role needs. The social role demands of parents a sense of responsibility for and a natural inclination to help and sustain their own child. Parental uncertainty and self-questioning are predictable responses to the autistic child's obscure developmental peculiarities. The professional role, on the other hand, demands authoritative responses to questions of probable causes and treatment of choice. When the answers to these questions are unknown and the absence of professional consensus is known, then the hypothesis of parental guilt and its treatment consequences seem to be the most suitable for sustaining both parent and professional social roles.

Rather than dividing the two roles by authority and responsibility, they could both be defined as having authority-responsibility components, but in different circumstances. Parents have the strongest motivation for rearing their child effectively and within the range of their own life styles. In fact they have the greatest potential for being the primary experts on their own child, for understanding the child's learning levels, and forming realistic expectations for his future. In addition to recognition of their authority over their child, they also are entitled to share the responsibility for his care. Such sharing of social responsibility has been widely established for handicaps like blindness, old age, and retardation, but has not in the past been extended to parents of autistic children.

The role of the professional worker in this field also needs to be redefined. Instead of, by tradition, reigning supreme in his chosen domain, he in his turn, should share responsibility with the parents. His authority should be used for developing and appropriately using services such as special schools, sheltered workshops and other necessary provisions. He should be responsible for helping families with handicapped children and ensuring that they have access to the services they need. Since the professional is supported by the fees or taxes paid by the parents, his accountability to them cannot be denied.

Some examples of how these roles can be modified will be cited from our Developmental Therapy Program. (1) The professional or therapist demonstrates special education approaches and behavior modification techniques to the parent, observing through a one-way mirror. This prevents giving advice on management procedures which cannot be carried out in practice. (2) Rather than using as therapists specialised professionals who have both expertise and commitment to their speciality and area of expertise, we have used non-specialised therapists. They are free to develop commitment to the rational help and support of the family with the handicapped child, rather than to their own special discipline. (3) The criteria for successful interventions are not established in a behavioral laboratory. Instead, interventions are judged by how effective they are within the child's family and living context. If a behaviorist publishes "research proof" that a child's tantruming is extinguished by isolating him and if the use of this technique does not work in a given family, we do not attempt to control the child's environment for scientific conformity with the behavioral lab. Instead of assuming the parents' home environment to be ineffective, we consider that the "scientific" behavior-shaping technique may be ineffective and search for a method to fit the child within the life style of his family.

Parental guidance for specific problems

In the preceding sections the emphasis was on the social attitudes that undermine general parental ability to manage the autistic child. Some possible solutions to these obstacles to general management were suggested. Even if reasonable social support and collaboration between parents and professionals are achieved, still remaining will be the special needs and rights of a handicapped child. There would, no doubt, be a reduction in extremes of parental guilt, disappointment, sense of failure, the attending unrealistic pressures on the child, and his bizarre responses. But even then, the special needs arising from the child's handicaps will still require special effort and consideration at home and in the community.

The position taken in this discussion is that there are not many specific problem-solving techniques available to professionals at this time. Even though there are procedures for managing behavior with systematic rewards and punishments, it is not usually the scientific method which helps parents. Most of them have raised other children successfully, using the operant procedures of parents long predating the psychologist's discovery of behavioral principles. In our experience, parents of autistic children have tried a great many different interventions with their child long before they sought professional guidance. Some parental efforts are ingenious, some seem unsympathetic to the child, and others appear desperate. In most such cases we have found that parents have attempted a "reasonable intervention" (one we would agree with) but not for very long and not with very much confidence or success. After we decide to try the reasonable intervention again and support the parents by taking the responsibility with them for repeating the method, the outcome is often quite successful. It would be possible to write up a glossary of effective interventions, describing the behavior problem, explaining why or by whom the request for management originated, followed by how it was carried out. No doubt such a glossary would be helpful to parents and others caring for such children. However, it would not answer the specific management questions raised by the interactions with specific autistic children. To maximise the child's adaptation within the family, in our experience individualised solutions offer the best chance of success. These solutions can be derived from asking the following kinds of questions: Can the child be taught responses to solve the management issue? Can some changes be made in the child's environment? Can the parents tolerate or accept behavior that cannot readily be modified? The solutions implied by each of these questions have attending costs and risks to be shared between parents and professionals. Individualised solutions are best made in terms of long-range treatment aims.

Treatment Aims and Severity of Impairment

Management crises of autistic children frequently result from poor fit between treatment aims for the child and the severity of his handicap. Some of these crises come in the form of school expulsion, requests to medicate a disturbing child, increasing negativism, or self-destructive behavior. Whenever we had such a crisis in our Program, it invariably also involved conflicting or inappropriate treatment aims for the child by responsible adults. These crises usually differ from each other according to the individual personality differences of the people involved and their situational peculiarities. To some extent, however, discrepancies between treatment aims and impairments are also shaped by the lag between the establishment of research knowledge, and its dissemination to and acceptance by both professionals and parents. In the discussion of erroneous expectations, page 235, I have already alluded to the probabilities for improvement as based on IQ figures and the longitudinal stability of the lower IQ range (Gittelman and Birch, 1967). Gittelman's findings have been discounted by some because they appear to be inconsistent with current distrust for the validity of intelligence testing and IQ scores. There is little question that IQ scores have been misinterpreted and misused in the past. McCall *et al.* (1973) gave data for the Fels Longitudinal Study which showed that normal middle class children changed an average of 28·5 IQ points between $2\frac{1}{2}$ and 17 years of age, some changing more than 40 points. However, even within this normal sample there was less variation over time for children with lower scores than for those with higher scores. The decrease in longitudinal variability of IQ becomes even greater when retarded children are retested. The difference in IQ stability between retarded and normal children is in part due to test construction. Single test items contribute more to score change on the high end of the test than on the low test items. More important still is the wider response range and ability to learn from testing to retesting. These are greater for the normal than for the retarded child. The reservations for predicting retest IQ with normal children simply do not apply equally to the retarded.

A second and perhaps even more important piece of information for balancing treatment aims with severity of impairment comes from several follow-up studies of autistic children. DeMyer *et al.* (1973) found that 89 per cent of the autistic children in their follow-up study were severely or moderately retarded, a somewhat higher rate than the 68 per cent in that group found by Mittler (1966). These IQ levels remained stable over the 10-year follow-up period.

There is no follow-up research to my knowledge which does not uphold the absence of change in this group of children.

These findings clearly indicate that treatment aims for autistic children have much in common with those for retarded children, especially as the autistic symptoms diminished over time. Treatment aims will differ with every individual. The levels of adaptation to be anticipated according to the degree of retardation have been projected by Baroff (1974). The following descriptive schema applies to individuals 18 years or older whose retardation is mild, moderate, or severe.

Mild mental retardation refers to an IQ range of 50 to 70 with a mental age from 8 to 11 years. Most retarded individuals fall into this category and live in the community. Their self-help skills are generally good; their language tends to be functional. They are capable of social relationships, though these are tinged with dependency. Academically they are considered educable and average achievement is third-grade level. Vocationally they are capable of unskilled employment on a marginally competitive basis. They may get married, become parents, maintain an independent adjustment, but may need assistance during stress. Autistic children in this category tend to have the most variable IQ scores. They include children with special peak skills which sometimes can be developed into means for earning a livelihood. For example, several autistic children with musical peak skills have become piano tuners. However, because of the severity of their language impairment few autistic children achieve this level of functioning. Most of them are in the subsequent two categories.

Moderate mental retardation covers an IQ range of 30 to 49, with a mental age range of 5 to 8 years. This group includes about 15 per cent of all retarded individuals and 75 per cent of them live in the community. They tend to have almost complete self-help skills. Language is usually functional but intelligibility may be impaired. They are able to form some relationships with peers and adults. Academically they are usually considered trainable but do not acquire functional academic skills. Vocationally they are capable of some degree of productive work but only in a sheltered work setting. They usually do not marry and are not capable of the degree of self-management necessary for independent living.

Severe mental retardation refers to the IQ range of less than 30 and a mental age less than 5 years. This includes only 5 per cent of all who are retarded. Some are maintained in the community but most are in institutional settings. Self-help skills are either absent or only partial. Language is almost non-existent. Social skills are confined to minimal interactions. Vocationally they are generally not capable of performing productive work even in a sheltered workshop. They can benefit from so-called activity center programs. They will always need more or less complete supervision as adults.

The above three categories are not absolute. However, they do represent a developmental framework which cannot be ignored without undue suffering. Autistic children in the third group of severely handicapped need special education and training in order to attain the treatment aims possible for their group, just like the children with moderate and mild handicaps. However, their rate of learning will be slower and their achievements at a lower level than the other two groups.

Autistic children at all developmental levels require structure (Schopler *et al.*, 1971) and active teaching in order to maximise their potential. The aims of teaching and treatment should be geared to the limitations represented by each of the three levels of retarded development described above. Professional advice is needed to plan the specific steps of skill development in each child's program and also to do so within reasonable long-range expectations. When parents can collaborate with professionals in defining realistically the short- and long-term aims of education for their child, the interaction between child, parent, and community can proceed without undue stress and without socially exacerbated management problems. In this way a humane life can be planned for the child, while at the same time, meeting the needs of both parents and community.

CHAPTER 10

THE SEVERELY RETARDED AUTISTIC CHILD

JANET CARR

The Significance of Intelligence in Autistic Children

Many studies of autistic children do not differentiate between children of different levels of intelligence. In earlier writings, the view generally held was either that all autistic children are of good intelligence or that intelligence test results are too unreliable in these children to be meaningful (Kanner and Lesser, 1958; Anthony, 1958b—both papers discussed by Lockyer and Rutter, 1969). Recently, however, the significance of intelligence level has been recognised, especially in view of the high proportion of autistic children who have been found to be severely retarded. Rutter and Lockyer (1967) found that, in a group of 63 autistic children, 10 could not be tested and 51 per cent of the remaining 53 children had IQ's of 50 or below. Examination of Vineland scores suggested that untestable children could be assumed to have IQ's below 50; if these were included then 59 per cent of the total group of 63 had IQ's below 50. Chess (1971) found that of children with congenital rubella who were diagnosed as autistic, 50 per cent had IQ's below 50. Lotter (1967b) found 56 per cent of autistic 8–10 year olds in Middlesex were severely retarded, with IQ's below 50. (The age-specific prevalence of severe mental retardation among the total population of children aged 9 to 11 years on the Isle of Wight was found by Rutter et al. (1970) to be approximately 3 per 1000).

Some studies have found results of intelligence tests to be an important factor in predicting the future development of autistic children. Lockyer and Rutter (1969) found that IQ at 5 years, even if derived from a small number of tests or from incomplete testing, was significantly correlated with IQ on tests carried out between 5 and 15 years later, and that initial IQ was similar to IQ at follow-up (that is, not consistently higher or lower). Children whose initial IQ's had been below 60 or who were untestable were more likely to show a poor or very poor adjustment, being severely handicapped and limited in independence at follow-up (Rutter *et al.* 1967). Absence of speech at 5 years has been thought to be strongly predictive of later failure to develop speech but this too has been found to be related to IQ; of 22 children with IQ's below 60 and without useful speech at 5 years, only 2 were speaking at follow-up, while of 10 without speech at 5 years but with IQ's of 60 or more, 5 were speaking at follow-up (Rutter *et al.*, 1967).

Intelligence level also appears to be related to the development of fits in later life; of the 10 children developing fits in the follow-up period 8 had initial IQ's below 60 (Rutter *et al.*, 1967). In a later study (Rutter *et al.*, 1971), of the 27 children with IQ's below 50 or untestable, 17 (nearly two-thirds) developed fits at some time, and 4 more showed evidence of possible brain disorder. In contrast, of the 12 children with performance IQ's in adolescence of at least 80, only 4 (one-third) showed evidence of probable brain damage. The authors comment, "these findings strongly suggest that most, if not all, autistic children with severe 'intellectual retardation' develop their disorder as a result of brain dysfunction."

In general, low IQ, even when assessed as early as 5 years, appears to carry a poor prognosis. On the other hand the *behaviour* of the children did not appear to be much affected by IQ. Rutter and Lockyer (1967) found that if they divided their group of autistic children into those with IQ's below 60 and of 60 and above, there was no difference in the frequency of behaviour problems such as social aloofness, echolalia, ritualistic and compulsive phenomena. Only stereotyped repetitive movements and self injury were more frequent in the more retarded children. Wing (1971) also compared children with IQ's above or below 60 and found no difference in the behaviour of the children as babies (poor sleep, lack of interest, lack of responsiveness, etc.) nor (1969) in the symptoms shown by older children. However, it has been noted that, in the brighter children, routines and rituals tend to be more complicated in form than in those of lower general intelligence (Wolff and Chess, 1964).

DeMyer and her colleagues also distinguish between autistic children of different levels of ability. A large number of the children they studied had IQ's below 50. It is of interest to note that, even among those who were severely retarded, there were some who had one or a few specific non-verbal skills which they could perform at or near their chronological age level, while others had a uniformly low profile of perceptuomotor skills. The differences between the groups are discussed in detail in Chapter 6.

Mittler *et al.* (1966) compared three groups of children, designated Psychotic (N = 27) Borderline Psychotic (N = 21) and Subnormal (N = 25), all of whom had been discharged from Smith Hospital between 1951 and 1963. Forty per cent of the Psychotic group were untestable at admission, as against 5 per cent of the Borderline and 14 per cent of the Subnormal group. Mean IQ on admission of the Psychotic group was 49·7, that of the Subnormal group 47·4, while the Borderline group tended to be less severely handicapped, with a significantly higher mean IQ of 61·3. When followed up, on average 8 years later, all of the 10 children in the Psychotic group who could be tested on both occasions showed IQ gains, with a mean increase of 24 IQ points, compared with an increase of about 3 points in the other two groups. It is suggested (Rutter, 1966) that this unusually large increase may be due to the fact that the initial test for this group was the Binet, "a test likely to underestimate the score of children handicapped in their language function" while the second test was the Wechsler which is less disadvantageous to autistic children; so the increase may have been more apparent than real. In the Psychotic group, IQ on admission was clearly related to educational outcome: no child originally untestable or of IQ less than 50 later attended school (including schools for the ESN) whereas all but 1 child originally found to have an IQ over 50 did so (Mann–Whitney U test, P = ·01). In the Borderline and Subnormal groups the association between IQ and educational outcome, although in the same direction as in the Psychotic group, was less clear cut and failed to reach significance. Hence in this study too, IQ was shown to have particular predictive significance for psychotic children.

Lotter (1966) found that a period of apparently normal early development followed by a setback was not predictive of a higher intelligence level later; of 9 "setback" children, 7 (78 per cent) were later found to have IQ's below 55, compared with 14 (64 per cent) of the 22 "gradual onset" children. Fifty six per cent (9 out of 16) of the total group with average milestones and 81 per cent (13 out of 16) of those with delayed milestones were later found to have IQ's below 55, but this difference is not statistically significant. In this study an autistic child had a greater than 1 in 2 chance of being severely mentally retarded even where his early development appeared normal although this chance was increased if his early development was retarded. Early developmental retardation combined with "complicating factors" (such as fits, EEG abnormalities, deafness due to rubella, severe early illness, signs of brain damage) was predictive of later low IQ; 10 out of 13 children with early retardation who later scored below IQ 55 showed these complicating factors, but none of the children with later IQ's above 55 and only 1 of those with later IQ's below 55 but without early developmental retardation did so (Lotter, 1967a,b). So children showing both early developmental retardation and complicating factors had a high probability of being severely mentally retarded but absence of the complicating factors did not necessarily predict a high IQ in those without early developmental retardation. IQ was also strongly associated with the development of speech. Speech was rated from 1—"speech freely and adequately used"—to 4—"Mute" and all the 10 children with IQ's of over 55 fell into categories 1 and 2, compared with only 3 of the 22 low IQ children.

Gittelman and Birch (1967) followed the progress of 97 children who were or had been at a school for children diagnosed as "childhood schizophrenics". Eighty eight of these had been tested, and 56 retested at intervals ranging from 9 months to 10 years, with a mean interval of 3 years 6 months. Comparing the children of normal and borderline intelligence (IQ 70 or above) with the retarded group (IQ 69 or below) the latter group was found to have been identified earlier; 98 per cent were first seen at the age of 5 or younger, compared with 59 per cent of the non-retarded group. The retarded children were less likely to have been speaking in sentences by the age of 5; this was achieved by 7 per cent of the retarded compared with 72 per cent of the non-retarded group. Dividing the children into those initially scoring over 50 and those scoring 50 or below, the mean IQ of the higher group showed no significant change on retesting (going from 81·6 to 82·7) while that of the severely retarded group showed a significant decrease (from 41·6 to 32·9). IQ was also found to be related to ratings of neurological deficit in the children; those rated as having moderate or severe dysfunction had a significantly lower mean IQ (51·2), compared with those rated as having mild or no signs (mean IQ 88·9). Seventy-five per cent of the severely and moderately affected group showed a decrease in IQ on retesting compared with only 13 per cent of the mildly affected group. In the follow-up study IQ was found to be significantly related to outcome; not only were the retarded children more likely to be in residential placement but only a quarter of the children with initial IQ's of 50 or less were judged to be improved on follow-up, compared with nearly two-thirds of those with initial IQ's over 50. So in this study the retarded children had come to notice earlier; were less likely to have developed speech by 5 years; were more likely to show signs of neurological involvement and decrease in IQ on retesting; and on follow-up were more likely to be in residential placement and to be judged unimproved.

Kolvin *et al.* (1971e) like Gittelman and Birch, also found intelligence to be related to age of onset of psychotic illness. Early onset was defined as before 3 years and late onset as after 5 years. Taking IQ 70 as the cut-off point, 78 per cent of the early group but only 16·6 per cent of the late group had IQ's below 70.

Another study (Bartak and Rutter, 1971) found IQ to be a good prognostic indicator of reading improvement. Of 50 children followed up over a 20-month period, 22 had made progress in reading. Their mean Merrill–Palmer IQ was 68·6, while 20 children who had not made progress in reading had a mean Merrill–Palmer IQ of 49·0, a difference significant at the 1 per cent level. None of those untestable or with an IQ of 43 or less on the Merrill–Palmer had improved in reading, whereas 65 per cent of those scoring 44 or more had done so (significant at the ·01 per cent level). Presumably this cut-off point, of IQ 44, was chosen to fit the available data. If the more conventional cut-off point of 50 had been chosen, the figures for reading improvement appear to be 24 per cent and 50 per cent respectively with the difference just failing to reach significance at the 5 per cent level. In an earlier study (Lockyer and Rutter, 1969) no child with an IQ of 50 or less had learnt to read while 5 such children in the later study had done so. It is pointed out (Bartak and Rutter, 1971) that the children in the later study had received special schooling, and it is interesting that this had had an effect not only on the brighter children but also on a number of those scoring at the severely retarded level.

The findings from these studies can be summarized as follows. Between a half and two-thirds of all autistic children are found to be severely retarded with IQ's below 50 (Lotter, 1966; Rutter and Lockyer, 1967; Chess, 1971) and the more retarded children tend to be identified earlier (Gittelman and Birch, 1967; Kolvin *et al.*, 1971e). Severely retarded children are more likely to develop fits in later life (Rutter *et al.*, 1967) and to show signs of neurological involvement (Gittelman and Birch, 1967). IQ in the group of autistic children as a whole seems to remain remarkably stable (Lockyer and Rutter, 1967; Gittelman and Birch, 1967). One study found a large increase in IQ (Mittler *et al.*, 1966) but this may have been due in part to the test used and to selection of cases. In general, there is a slight tendency to lower retest IQ's in those children who initially had low scores (Lockyer and Rutter, 1967; Gittelman and Birch, 1967). The prognosis for the severely retarded group is considerably poorer than for the less retarded, in social outcome (Mittler *et al.*, 1966; Gittelman and Birch, 1967; Rutter *et al.*, 1967) speech development (Lotter, 1966; Gittelman and Birch, 1967; Rutter *et al.*, 1967) and in educational progress (Bartak and Rutter, 1971). Behavioural characteristics, however, seem very similar in the severely retarded and in the non-retarded group (Wing, 1969, 1971); only stereotyped repetitive movements and self-injury were more frequently found in the more retarded children (Rutter and Lockyer, 1967).

From these studies it is clear that prognosis varies with IQ; "IQ's of less than 50 suggest a clear and unambiguous poor prognosis for normal development. IQ's over 50 indicate a greater variability in prognosis" (Schopler and Reichler, 1971a). It should be noted that on the whole this variability relates largely to the course of the illness and to the social outcome, and not to changes in IQ; even in those autistic children who improve considerably, IQ remains little changed (Rutter, 1966). There are occasional exceptions to this rule, such as the case quoted by Schopler and Reichler (1971a) in which the child's IQ rose from 57 to 101 following treatment. It was presumably cases such as this which led to the early idea that the autistic condition suppressed the level of the functioning intelligence in autistic children, and a belief in their latent intelligence that "has prevented even experienced psychologists from committing themselves about a psychotic child's intellectual potential" (Kolvin, 1971b).

Problems of the Severely Retarded Autistic Child

Certain problem behaviours, although not peculiar to them, are typically found in severely retarded children who show items of autistic behaviour and these raise considerable difficulties of management.

Self injury

Self injury is found in autistic children of all levels of ability (as well as in other severely retarded children) but occurs significantly more often in those with an IQ below 60 (Rutter and Lockyer, 1967). The injury may consist of self biting, especially of the hand or arm; elbow or leg banging; hair pulling or rubbing; face scratching; self slapping, especially face slapping; chin banging; window breaking, leading to cuts; and head banging. The injury may be caused by the child himself inflicting damage on his body, as when he bites his own hand, or by the child damaging himself on something in his environment, as when he bangs his head or elbow on a hard surface. Biting, especially of the hand or wrist, and head banging have been found to be by far the commonest forms of self injury in autistic children (Rutter and Lockyer, 1967).

When the child is restrained or protected to prevent the self injury he will often show considerable ingenuity in finding other ways to damage himself. One 5-year old banged his forehead and was fitted with a helmet to protect it; he then banged the back of his head, but when that was protected went successively on to his chin, cheek bones, nose and eyes. Other children whose hands are strapped to the side of the cot to prevent hand or wrist biting, will bite their upper arms. Typically the restraints are effective only as long as they are in use, and as soon as they are removed the children return to their self injurious behaviour. There is no evidence that the habits die out with compulsory disuse.

Self injury may cause damage to the child in differing degree, ranging from bruises from slapping and callouses from biting to open wounds and haematomas that may be life endangering. In addition, self injury, especially in its more severe forms, is extremely alarming for the parents or staff caring for the child. This may result not only in a lowering of staff morale, particularly where there are conflicts as to how the behaviour should be handled, but also sometimes in a reluctance to place demands on the child to learn or to take part in activities if there is the danger that this will lead to an increase in the self injury. Thus the child's normal activities may be reduced both by his preoccupation with the self injurious behaviour (as in self stimulation, discussed below) and by the reluctance of those caring for him to insist on his participation in constructive pursuits.

The reasons for children injuring themselves deliberately are not clear but there are two explanations, not necessarily mutually exclusive, that seem feasible. The first is that the self injurious activity acts as a stimulus that is in some way pleasurable to the child, and hence that it is related to other self stimulatory activities such as rocking, flapping, etc. This explanation is supported by the observation that self injury seems to be shown more frequently in institutionalised children who, being under-occupied, tend to lack other stimulation. The fact that the more retarded children, who are also less accessible to environmental stimulation than those with somewhat higher intelligence, have a higher rate of self injury (Rutter and Lockyer, 1967) also supports this view. The other explanation is that the behaviour is attention seeking. (The behaviour is undoubtedly attention *getting*—it is hard not to pay attention to a child who is tearing his face or hammering his head.) However, studies by Lovaas and Simmons (1969) and by Lovaas *et al.* (1965) suggest that, while self injurious behaviour may be increased by attention which is contingent upon the behaviour, it is not decreased by ignoring the behaviour. Another study (Bucher and Lovaas, 1968) found that when a child was left unattended without restraints his head banging was extinguished, but not before he had hit himself over ten thousand times. Withdrawal of attention contingent upon the self injurious behaviour has been found eventually to decrease the behaviour but not to eliminate it entirely (Tate and Baroff, 1966; Jenkins, 1973).

Extinction by non-reinforcement (usually by withdrawing attention) would in many ways be the preferred method of treatment of self injury but presents several difficulties—the lack of total extinction, the practical difficulty experienced by people in ignoring the behaviour, and the ethical impossibility of ignoring behaviour which is dangerous to the child's life or health. Consequently treatments involving aversive stimuli such as shouting, slapping, shaking, or electric shock of sufficient strength to give an unpleasant, though very brief, sensation but not to cause any injury, have been used. Studies of the use of aversive treatment have been well reviewed recently (Gardner, 1969; Smolev, 1971) and only a summary of the findings will be given here. Briefly, the use of electric shock and other aversive treatment markedly decreased the rate of self injurious responses in all the studies reported. Many studies reported the combination of positive reinforcement of desirable behaviour with aversive treatment of the undesirable behaviour, thus making it uncertain which aspect was the more important in the child's progress; however it was clear that in many subjects the initial rate of self injury was so high that little positively reinforceable behaviour could occur. Suppression of the undesirable behaviours was essential to allow the desirable behaviours to occur. Contrary to expectation the children were not apparently cowed, terrified or made miserable by aversive stimuli. Many studies report that the children appeared happier and more responsive to many aspects of their environment than they had been previously.

The follow-up studies of treatment by aversive stimuli that have been reported are comparatively short; most are in terms of days (20 to 94 days) and only 2 (Hamilton *et al.*, 1967; Hamilton and Standahl, 1967) reported studies which were followed up for as long as a year. Relapse is mentioned in 2 studies only (Blackwood, 1962; Banks and Locke, 1966) and no procedures to deal with this are described. In view of experience at Hilda Lewis House with a boy whose severe head banging, treated with shock, disappeared almost completely for 6 months, only to reappear in an exacerbated form after a physical illness, it would be interesting to know whether longer follow-up would have shown similar results in some other studies. Nevertheless, where the self injurious behaviour is dangerous to the child's own life or health, the overwhelming weight of the published literature suggests that aversive treatment is the most effective method at present available.

In practice, when using aversive stimuli, there are many problems which have to be anticipated and dealt with.

Some people, especially those who choose to enter the caring professions, feel deeply that a handicapped person, especially a child, should not be punished for behaviour for which he is not responsible. They may interpret aversive operant techniques as a "punishment" in the sense of moral retribution, instead of simply as an effective method of preventing the child from harming himself. A few go to the other extreme and believe that disturbed behaviour is the sign of a spoilt child. They may have punitive attitudes which would allow them to use aversive techniques inappropriately and too often.

For obvious reasons the more extreme forms of aversive conditioning, such as electric shock, can be employed only when the behaviour to be extinguished poses a danger to life or of severe injury. The staff concerned should have ample opportunity for explanation and discussion, not only of the techniques but also of their personal feelings on the issue. It is necessary for everyone to understand that the child is not being "blamed" for his behaviour but that experience has shown that, used properly, aversive stimulation can reduce or eliminate self injury. Members of staff who feel unable to participate should not be pressed to do so. It is likely that the method can succeed only where there is a sufficient level of agreement among all concerned to ensure absolutely consistent action at all times.

No treatment of this kind can be used without the permission of the child's parents. They, too, need explanation and the opportunity for discussion, not once only but many times throughout the period when the programme is being carried out.

In order to achieve complete consistency of approach from everyone involved, one person, usually the psychologist who has devised the programme, must be in complete charge of the day-to-day details. However, the team will work most effectively if the members can discuss freely with each other and exchange observations and ideas.

There is always criticism of operant methods especially from people who feel that all problems can be solved by giving sufficient love and attention. Those who have been faced with the prospect of allowing a child to die or sustain severe, permanent harm from the results of his own self injury which years of love and attention have failed to eliminate, know that sometimes one is forced to choose the lesser of two evils. When this happens, the responsible attitude is to use the aversive techniques with the maximum of professional skill and knowledge to ensure, as far as possible, that they will be successful.

Where the behaviour is not dangerous to life or health either extinction procedures may be used, or the reinforcement of incompatible responses. Here the child is reinforced for behaviour which, so long as the child is engaging in it, makes it impossible for him simultaneously to injure himself. An example of this may be seen in the treatment devised for a partially blind child who persistently poked her fingers into the sides of her eyes or under her eyeballs, forcing them out of their sockets. A tape recording was made of strange and interesting sounds, which the child enjoyed*. She was given two switches which had to be continually pressed, one with each hand, to work the tape recorder and produce the enjoyable

*The tape recordings and the other pieces of apparatus were all constructed by Dr H. Campbell, Neurophysiological Unit, Institute of Psychiatry.

noises. However, with the remarkable ingenuity that these severely retarded children often display when it is a question of getting something they want, she soon learnt that she could press the switch with her elbow and get the sound she enjoyed while still having her hand free to poke her eyes. A new pair of switches was made that could be pressed only with the finger tips; now if she wanted to hear the sound she could not poke her eyes. In this way a response (switch pressing) had been identified which was reinforced (by the sounds) and which was incompatible with the eye poking, thus weakening the strength of the eye poking behaviour.

Stereotyped movements and self stimulation

Stereotyped, repetitive movements were, with self injury, the behavioural categories which Rutter and Lockyer (1967) found to occur more frequently in the more retarded autistic children. Rocking and hand flapping, especially movements of the hand that alter the light falling on the child's face, are perhaps the most common, but twiddling, flicking and flapping of objects are also seen. Jumping and spinning, described in children of higher level (Wing, 1969) are less frequently seen, possibly because of poorly developed motor skills; although one severely retarded boy, who was fascinated by things turning (for example the turning globe which precedes some television programmes) would sometimes turn himself rather slowly in small circles.

Such stereotyped and self stimulatory behaviours present a problem primarily because they make the child less accessible to the teaching of more adaptive behaviours; they engage all the child's attention, so that he is unlikely to take notice of possible alternative pursuits and they are often highly reinforcing and more attractive to him than are the alternatives. One school of thought maintains that in order to teach more desirable behaviours and skills, these stereotyped activities must be interrupted and eliminated, even if this involves aversive stimulation (Lovaas, 1973). However, providing that the activity is not self injuring, it may in some cases be put to more positive effect by using it as a reinforcer for a desired behaviour. One boy, who constantly twiddled a plastic cup on his thumb, learnt to surrender it when he was being taught a simple manipulative task. He was reinforced for completing the task by being allowed to have the cup back and to twiddle it for a short period. The ultimate aim of such a programme would be that the new more interesting behaviours would themselves acquire reinforcing properties and, becoming preferred, would eventually replace the stereotyped behaviours.

The other major problem that stereotypies present, apart from self injury discussed previously, is that they make the child appear odd and peculiar to the outside world. This may be a particular problem for parents, who wish their child to be accepted by the general public and find the bizarre behaviour yet another barrier to acceptance. This in itself would make the attempt to get rid of the behaviour worthwhile, even if there were no other reason to do so.

Lack of response to verbal and gestural stimuli

A primary characteristic of the autistic child is his difficulty in using and comprehending language and this is seen in an even more pronounced form in those who are severely subnormal. Speech is usually absent but if the child has any words they are likely to be echolalic and not used in a functional, useful way. Comprehension of speech is also extremely restricted; if present at all it may be limited to a response when the child hears his own name and to a narrow range of commands—"give it to me", "stand up", "sit on the chair". Even when the child is thought to comprehend a set of instructions, his response to them may be quite variable. For example, one 13-year old boy consistently obeyed when told to "sit down"; but with other commands with which he was thought to be equally familiar, such as "give me the cup" and "take off your shoes", on some occasions he responded correctly but on others his behaviour appeared to be random.

Similarly the children tend not to use or respond to gestural signals. The result is that the children can be controlled only by physical guidance or constraint; they may have to be held and led from one place to another because neither speech nor gesture is useful in conveying to them what they should do.

Lack of ability to communicate with others

It is extremely hard for the severely retarded autistic child to convey his needs apart from those that can be satisfied by pulling an adult to a desired object. He cannot easily let people know when he is bored, puzzled, or alarmed, and any signal that he appears to make may be open to a variety of interpretations. In particular, it is hard for the child to convey when he is in pain or not feeling well. As a result the adults around him may be constantly on the alert for signs of physical illness, the more watchful because these may be so non-specific. Any deterioration in the child's mood, any regression to earlier, less desirable behaviour patterns, increase in aggression or violent behaviour may make the concerned adults wonder whether he is ill. The situation is further complicated by the fact that minor illnesses and infections, especially among children in institutions, are in any case fairly frequent occurrences. No one wants to overlook a cast iron, genuine physical illness which might be producing or exacerbating disturbed behaviour and so parents and staff make every effort to pick up, in the absence of communication from the child, the slightest clue that they think may indicate that he is unwell. Any child who goes off his food is a natural suspect for the sick list; vomiting may be self induced but always raises the possibility of illness. One child was thought to hold his ears as a sign that he was unwell—not only with ear ache but with more distant afflictions such as constipation. With minor illnesses occurring at a high rate among retarded children the prediction that these signs indicate illness will be fairly frequently confirmed.

Problems arise if "illness in the child" comes to equal "diminution in discipline and demands on him", and if the sick child is given more latitude, treated more permissively, allowed to get away with more bad behaviour, and not expected to perform to the standards normally demanded of him, all in contrast to the situation when he is thought to be well. When deterioration in the child's behaviour is taken as a sign of illness, the permissive treatment may lead to further regression. One little boy, who had had haematomas both of the scalp and of the cerebrum due to head banging, and had suffered a right-sided weakness of neurological origin, after a period of considerable progress, once more became withdrawn, passive, floppy, resistant, and his head banging recurred. It was impossible for the adults in charge of him not to think immediately that he must be ill and, although he had no temperature, every cough, every sign of drowsiness was noted with concern. As he had had several similar episodes previously, and as one consistent finding was that the less that was asked of him the less he would do and the more withdrawn and negative he became, losing skills that he had already mastered, it was determined on this occasion that a certain level of participation would continue to be demanded of him. This plan was carried out and, in spite of the fears of the staff, no convincing signs of physical illness were manifested. This is just one example of the situation where the child's inability to communicate leads to an increase in anxiety about his physical condition which, though sometimes justified, may have a bad effect on his psychological treatment.

When a lack of any communication system poses such formidable problems as it does with these severely retarded children it becomes a matter of urgency to try to discover a method by which they may be enabled to communicate. Speech is of course the eventual goal, and programmes of speech training for autistic children have been described (Lovaas, 1966; Risley and Wolf, 1967). It has been suggested that a non-communicating child may need to learn non-verbal imitation first, in order to facilitate verbal imitation (Schopler and Reichler, 1971a), although Yule, Berger and Howlin (1972) point out that there is no experimental evidence to show that training in imitation is a necessary precursor to training in comprehension and expression. Bricker and Bricker (1973) nevertheless found that imitative sign training facilitated receptive language development in severely retarded children.

This leads on to the question as to whether severely retarded autistic children may be taught a manual sign language, such as the Paget–Gorman system. Since this involves the child in imitation of hand movements, and since autistic children have a particular difficulty in copying any body movements (DeMyer, 1971) this may seem a formidable or even a hopeless task. However, at Hilda Lewis House one autistic girl was taught a certain amount of sign language, and this appeared to facilitate speech. A deaf and autistic boy is at present being taught some of the Paget–Gorman signs, which he appears to learn very quickly when the subject matter (that is, food) is interesting to him. With both children it has been possible to teach them to use and to respond to sign language, on request, in a teaching situation. The big problem is to convey to them that this may be useful and that communication has a practical value to them so that they will use it spontaneously. It is likely that the same difficulty will be found in speech programmes. Nevertheless it seems that for severely retarded autistic children the use of sign language, both as a communication system in itself and as a facilitator of speech, would repay further research.

Resistance to learning new skills

As part of the resistance to change characteristic of autistic children (Rutter and Lockyer, 1967; Kolvin, 1971b), resistance to learning new skills is frequently found. Children with extremely limited skills and behaviours vigorously resist efforts to introduce them to different and, to the normal child, more interesting activities, preferring to be left alone to rock, rub, twiddle or twirl. Since his reaction may take the form of violent tantrums the child may make it difficult for his teachers to continue their efforts to interest him in new activities. The most useful approach to this problem seems to be that of operant conditioning; that is, prompting the child's response to the new situation and rewarding its completion. For example a hyper-active 9-year old boy who refused to take part in school activities, preferring to run around the classroom or twirl on one foot, was made to sit down and complete an inset board. As he would not do this spontaneously, the trainer guided his hand to pick up and place the pieces by holding her hand over his. At first he resisted violently, attempting to bite or scratch the trainer, but as he began to realise what was wanted of him and to realise that each successful placement was followed by a small piece of biscuit, he became compliant, stopped attacking the trainer, and began to need less prompting and to do more of the task on his own.

One problem of this approach may be the difficulty of finding adequate reinforcers for the individual child; the primary one of food is reinforcing to most autistic children but may not be powerful enough to overcome their resistance. Sometimes this can be solved by using the child's regular meals, given bite by bite, as a reinforcer. In other cases food is not reinforcing at all, while social attention and praise too often are not sufficiently strong initially, so that it may be necessary to search for other forms of reinforcement. Tickling or music have been found useful, while one boy learnt a range of new skills when rewarded by a few seconds of an electric toothbrush in his mouth. Some children appear to be strongly reinforced by reactions of annoyance or anger from adults, or of distress from other children. Since they gain reinforcement of this sort as a reaction to their undesirable behaviours—for instance spitting at adults or attacking other children—these may be difficult to control.

Whatever method is chosen to teach the child, it is most important that the teacher should have the determination and the stamina to persist with it; to go on despite the tantrums, the upsets and the set-backs. Persistence and a refusal to be discouraged on the part of the teacher are among the most important factors in teaching the children new behaviours. One boy, already described in this chapter, was wedded to his "twiddler", which he insisted on having on his thumb whenever he was indoors, even at mealtimes, when it hampered his ability to feed himself. It was decided that he should learn to eat properly without his twiddler and his mother agreed to remove it from him during meals. This provoked screams of ear-splitting intensity, the more distressing to the mother because her house was a terraced one and she was afraid of the neighbours' reactions. The programme was instituted on a Tuesday evening, and, in the mother's words; "I decided I would keep it up to the weekend and then phone you if he was still carrying on, but on Thursday evening he suddenly stopped and now he quite accepts that his twiddler is taken away before his meals." This mother's truly heroic persistence paid off.

In other instances, where such a direct confrontation is undesirable, it may be possible to alter the child's environment by subtle stages so that he acquires a new skill without realizing that he has done so. At an earlier stage of his development the boy described above refused to drink from a cup and would drink only by sips out of a spoon. After attempts to train him to use a cup had failed, it was decided to change his spoon gradually into a cup.* The spoon was made a little bigger, then, when he was using that well, a little deeper; then the handle was made shorter, and then curved. The boy accepted each new spoon with equanimity, apparently never noticing that it was different from the previous one. Gradually the spoon became more and more like a cup. A tricky point was reached when it was too big to be dipped into the cup of milk as he usually did to get his drink. The nurse instead poured in a few drops, and this moment passed without calamity. At last the "spoon" handle was fixed onto an ordinary plastic cup and almost at once it broke off. The boy was then given a standard plastic cup which he picked up and drank from without any more ado.

Mood fluctuations

Complicating the handling of the children is what seems to be a tendency for them to have swings of mood or of behaviour patterns. There are times, lasting weeks or even months, when a child seems to be making good progress, learning new and useful skills, when behaviour problems seem to be lessening and staff congratulate themselves that the treatment being currently applied is apparently appropriate. Then come times when all the progress is lost, the child regresses in both learning and behaviour and again becomes a problem to manage. When these downwards swings occur there is an understandable wish to discover the reason. Illness may be invoked, and any cough, cold, dental or abdominal disturbance may be suspected as being the cause of the trouble. Staff at a school or institution may look to see whether there has been any trouble at home, and parents may look to staff changes at school or institution. Alterations in the child's routine, a holiday, a new school bus driver, or even changes in the weather may be thought to be responsible. It

---

*All the structural changes of spoon into cup were carried out by Mrs Sheena Wickens, the head occupational therapist at Hilda Lewis House. A plastic substance which could be moulded into shape and then set hard was used.

is not difficult to find some factor or event which coincides reasonably closely with the child's altered behaviour and which may be thought to explain it.

Needless to say each of the factors described above *could* be responsible for a change in the child's behaviour. The difficulty lies in ascertaining that any one has been responsible for any one particular change, while it is impossible to return to or reproduce exactly the former conditions of the child's environment. As these mood swings recur over time with a number of children it begins to seem possible that they are, at least in part, endogenously caused and that the external events that are blamed are, again at least in part, coincidental rather than causal. Systematic data to confirm or refute this hypothesis are lacking at present but research in this area would be of great interest as well as helpful in planning programmes of management. In the meantime it seems reasonable to suppose that both successes and failures in treatment methods may in some cases be confounded by purely random factors.

Treatment Settings

The treatment of the children may take place in any of a number of settings—either in long-term residence, in residence for a limited period, with the child as a weekly boarder or as a day patient, or the child may be seen and treated entirely at home (in which case the treatment may be carried out by a professional therapist or by the child's own family).

In the past, long-term care was advocated, for autistic as well as for retarded children, because it was thought that it was best for the child to be taught and handled by experts. More recently, there has been a less inflated idea of what the institution is likely to achieve for the child and long-term care is more likely to be resorted to for the sake of the family who can no longer cope with a very abnormal and difficult child. This will continue to be an important reason for a child to go into a residential unit, but whether this will be of the greatest benefit to the child is more debatable. Attendance as a weekly boarder relieves the family of the major part of the care of the child but ensures that they keep in contact with him—though families may sometimes feel that the week-end, a time of relaxation for most families, is a time of extra strain for them and they may need an occasional week-end without him. Attendance as a day patient provides a normal pattern for the child—like other children going to school, he leaves home in the morning and returns in the late afternoon—though it carries the same possible drawbacks for the family as does weekly boarding, and is more suitable for less severely disturbed children.

Treatment at home, carried out mainly by the child's parents or other members of his family, may be the most effective for those children whose families can tolerate their presence in the home. Howlin *et al.* (1973) discuss the disadvantages of hospital based treatment: children who make progress while they are in hospital often regress when they go home; parents who previously handled their child well may be less able to do so after a long period of separation; problems occurring at home may not occur, and therefore may not be available for treatment, in the hospital setting. (This last problem has also been experienced in Hilda Lewis House.) Since the ultimate aim is usually for the child to live at home the preferred techniques are those that will enable this to be achieved most efficiently. Further, where the parents themselves can act as the child's therapists, every step in his progress can be a source of satisfaction to them; they have the pleasure of knowing that it is they and not some outside agent who are responsible for the improvement in their child. This may be a source of considerable comfort to parents who have previously felt distressed, guilty and helpless in the face of their child's condition.

Howlin *et al.* give an outline of the way in which treatment at home is undertaken, with initial assessments, functional analyses, base line measures, selection of the problem to be tackled—often first a practical problem of management which is causing difficulties to the family—and teaching the techniques of behaviour modification to the parents. In addition they stress the importance of counselling for the families where this becomes necessary; the difficulty the parents experience in generalising their skills to deal with new problems; and the necessity for caution in assuming that changes once made will be permanent. Nevertheless they clearly feel that, in spite of the difficulties, this home based treatment method is the one to be preferred and in this conclusion the present writer warmly concurs.

Educational Setting

There are schools for the severely retarded child, and there are also a few schools which specialise in teaching autistic children. In which of these does the severely retarded autistic child properly belong? In practice the question is usually settled by the fact that there are not enough schools for autistic children to provide sufficient places even for those of higher intelligence. The majority of the severely retarded autistic children are admitted to the schools for the ESN (severe) or (special care), where their particular problems may cause great difficulty for the staff and the other children. Suggestions for improving services are discussed in Chapter 12.

The Aims of Education and Management

The severity of the handicaps of the children discussed in this chapter and their extremely poor prognosis raise important questions concerning the ethics of treatment, not only of autistic but also of all severely retarded children. What is the point of expending so much time, effort and money on children who will achieve so little? When resources such as money, buildings, equipment and teachers are in short supply should they not be devoted to those who could make better use of them—the physically handicapped, the maladjusted, the culturally deprived children? The first answer must be in moral rather than scientific terms; these children are human beings and are entitled to the greatest possible opportunity of developing their full potential.* Indeed it may be said that since the children's potential is so limited it is the more important that they should realise it to the full.

*That there are whole populations in the world to whom such an opportunity is denied makes it no less a basic human right.

On a more practical level, in spite of their resistance to learning new ways of behaviour, any useful skills, any adaptive behaviour patterns that they can learn, any maladaptive behaviours that can be extinguished, are likely to benefit the children by creating a more positive social climate for them. Whether they live in the community or whether they live in an institution, the people around them—parents, friends, training centre staff, nurses, whoever they may be—are likely in general to react more warmly to children and adults who have the higher levels of skill and less behavioural disturbance. This in turn is likely to generate a happier and more enriching life for the children.

In some cases the acquisition of certain skills may result in crucial changes of attitude on the part of caretakers. A child who learns to obey simple commands—"come here", "sit down"—becomes more human in the eyes of those dealing with him, compared with how he appeared when he could be controlled only by physical handling. The staff become more interested in him as a person and this alters all their interchanges with him. Some skills, such as toilet training, may be vital if the child is to be acceptable in social situations outside his own home or an institution. One severely retarded boy was taught to dress himself and this enabled him to be accepted on a high-grade ward run on progressive lines instead of being placed in a much more restrictive setting in the institution to which he was admitted.

The acquisition of skills by the child is especially important for his parents. In the first place, these may lessen the burden of caring for him. Equally important perhaps is the emotional satisfaction they may gain from seeing their child make progress, especially if they themselves have been involved in his teaching and have contributed to that progress.

It should be said, however, that not all parents agree that the children should be stimulated to develop their potential to the utmost. These parents are not unfeeling, nor unintelligent. Usually they have arrived at their position after years of struggling with the child, trying hard to help him, to control him, to provide some sort of normal life for the rest of the family, and they are exhausted. One such family, of a 10-year old, partially deaf, hyper-active, aggressive, destructive boy, had given up the attempt to stimulate and interest him, as these attempts had led to disaster for the family. If they took him on a coach outing his screaming ruined the day for the whole family. Expeditions of this kind would be followed by several days of tantrums and disturbed behaviour. They dared not take him for walks in unfamiliar places as he would not rest until he had explored them minutely and the parents felt that they had not the time for this. Any new experience "lightened his mind", as the father put it. The family's one wish was that the boy should remain calm, contained, unstimulated, perhaps not realising his maximum capacity, but manageable. In a situation of this kind it seems reasonable to suggest that the family should not be asked to continue to take the responsibility for, and bear the consequences of, training and stimulating the child; at this point the task should be passed to others.

Of all the sub-groups of autistic children, those who are severely mentally retarded are the most vulnerable to changes in the environment. Even though a well planned programme of management and teaching produces good results in one situation, it cannot be assumed that the child himself has changed in any way that is permanent. The lack of inner language, which is most profound in the severely retarded autistic child, prevents the building up of a repertoire of behaviour under the child's own control. In effect, it is the adults around the child who must learn how to manage him since he cannot learn how to manage himself. Even basic skills which have been acquired as a result of patient teaching can sometimes be lost if their performance is not encouraged and rewarded. The provision of an appropriate environment is therefore crucial if the child is to behave well and realise his potential abilities.

Fortunately there is a tendency for improvement with increasing age. Although the cognitive and language handicaps remain, it appears to be rare to find the severe secondary behaviour disturbances in adults after about 25 to 30 years of age (Bone *et al.*, 1972; Corbett and Radford, to be published). By this time, however, if no special help is given, the autistic adolescent or adult with a past history of difficult, aggressive behaviour is likely to have been placed in an institution and to have lost contact with his family because they found regular visiting too distressing. An ideal service would include sufficient residential provision of a high enough quality to give the parents and families a genuine choice between home and institutional care. The parents who wished to remain in contact should be given every help and encouragement, but the feelings of those who prefer not to visit should, equally, be respected.

CHAPTER 11

MEDICAL MANAGEMENT

JOHN CORBETT

When parents begin to realise that their child is handicapped, their first reaction is to hope for a medical cure. Many attempts have been made to find such a simple solution to the problem of early childhood autism, but so far without success. However, medical care sometimes plays a valuable part in alleviating secondary behaviour problems and treating associated conditions such as epilepsy. General health care is also important and presents some special problems in autistic children and adults.

In this chapter, medical assessment, physical treatments, and the role of the doctor will be discussed.

Medical Assessment

The provision of diagnostic and assessment services is discussed in Chapter 12. The detailed assessment of impairments, behaviour problems and skills in children with autism and related conditions needs to be carried out by a team whose members have special experience in the field of language and communication problems. Owing to the comparative rarity of these conditions such teams would in general have to be based on a region rather than a local area. Initially, most children will be seen by a general practitioner or community physician and referred to a paediatrician or child psychiatrist who may be working at a local assessment centre for handicapped children or child psychiatric clinic. The Sheldon report (DHSS 1968) recommended that assessment centres should be

271

provided as part of the child health services at district general hospitals but with regional reference centres.

Time is needed to observe the child's behaviour, to assess his responses to various learning situations, and to decide if there are any medical treatments which might alleviate some of the problems. This can best be done on a daily basis either by attendance at a day hospital or by peripatetic assessment in a day educational or nursery unit catering for handicapped children. Admission to hospital as an in-patient is very rarely desirable at this stage. Any drastic change in the environment of a young autistic child may lead to deterioration in behaviour which could interfere with the assessment process and which would increase the pressure on the family when the child returned home.

Medical examination and special tests

It is not usually possible to carry out a full medical examination when an autistic child is seen for the first time, but a careful history taken from the parents and observation of the child will show if the diagnostic features described in Chapter 2 are present.

During the course of several visits it may be possible to make a limited but routine examination for any associated physical abnormalities. Tests can be carried out on the blood (which should be possible on one sample) in order to exclude chromosomal abnormalities, and on the urine and blood to detect inborn errors of metabolism such as aminonacidurias, and rare but important storage diseases.

An EEG is often indicated but, as it may be difficult to do without sedation in young children, it may be left until the child is able to co-operate, unless there is any clinical evidence of epilepsy.

Apart from epilepsy, associated conditions which can be diagnosed and treated are rare. This means that a decision as to how to proceed must be made by carefully weighing the clinical necessity for special physical investigations against any distress that may be caused to the child. In centres where a number of autistic children are seen, the technicians responsible for carrying out these tests should be sufficiently experienced to minimise any distress to the child.

Investigation of hearing

One of the major problems facing the clinician in the early diagnosis of autism is the exclusion of deafness as a cause for the delay in language development. Detailed questioning of the parents and very careful observation of the child's response to sound-making toys of various frequencies, or free field audiometry, may be sufficient to show whether or not the child can hear normally, although sometimes the observations may have to be repeated on several occasions in order to give a conclusive result.

In some cases, particularly where there is a combination of hearing impairment and autism, more specialised tests will be required. It is usually difficult to gain the child's co-operation sufficiently to carry out conventional pure tone audiometry, although it may be possible to condition a child to respond reliably to the tones that he can hear. Bricker *et al.* (1968) described the construction and use of apparatus which automatically dispenses suitable reinforcers of small size and which can be used to train children to make operant responses. For some children, more objective tests such as evoked response audiometry under light anaesthesia (Davis, 1968; Suzuki and Tayuchi, 1968) cochleography (Aaran *et al.*, 1969; Beagley, 1973) or crossed acoustic reflex audiometry (Yoshie and Okudairn, 1969; Doueck, 1973) may be necessary. These latter tests which record cortical evoked responses or potentials directly from the auditory nerve and from the vestigial muscle behind the ear respectively merely give an indication of the passage of nerve impulses from the ear to various levels in the central nervous system and do not provide information about the child's ability to use the sound he perceives in language development. They are, however, valuable in being entirely independent of the child's ability to co-operate and a positive result will serve to exclude any need for amplification of sound for the child. It is very important that this decision be made on the basis of such accurate audiometric assessment since injudicious use of a hearing aid may be very distressing to the autistic child and result in increased behaviour disturbance. Among the techniques mentioned, crossed acoustic reflex audiometry holds out most promise as this is a simple screening device which requires only the placement of two electrodes behind the ears. This can be done without discomfort and without sedation of the child, but is at present still in the experimental stage and requires further evaluation before it can be recommended for routine clinical use in the autistic child.

Medical Treatments

Treatment of behaviour disorders

The behaviour problems which may occur in autistic children such as hyperkinesis, restlessness, temper tantrum, destructiveness, aggression, self injury and disturbance of sleep are particularly distressing to parents and siblings. Some autistic children are extremely anxious and fearful to a degree which seriously interferes with everyday activities. A variety of physical treatments, especially the psychotropic drugs, have been tried in order to alleviate these problems. Unfortunately very few adequately controlled studies of their effectiveness have been carried out. Most of the studies which have been done are characterised by heterogeneity of the samples of children studied; poverty of clinical data; lack of control of other relevant variables such as methods of managing the children's behaviour applied during the course of the trial; the use of rating scales that have not been adequately tested for reliability and validity and failure to use objective measures such as level of activity. The possible effects of the physical measures, especially medication, upon the children's learning abilities are often ignored although these are obviously of importance. Very few studies have been designed to follow up the long-term effects of the treatments used (Corbett, 1972a).

Despite the paucity of good research in this field, certain points have emerged from clinical experience which will be discussed in this section.

Psychotropic drugs

Useful reviews of the present state of knowledge of the use of drugs in behavioural disorders in children have been published by Sprague and Werry (1971) and Freeman (1970). In this short account, it is possible only to highlight some of the special problems encountered when prescribing drugs for autistic children.

In general, it should be emphasised that the results of treating behaviour disturbances with drugs alone tend to be very disappointing in the long term although there may be an initial response. The first choice of treatment for behaviour problems is appropriate behaviour management based on the principles of learning theory. In some cases, however, the behaviour problems are so severe that it is difficult to control the child sufficiently to initiate a programme. In other cases, aggression or self mutilation have reached such dangerous proportions that drugs have to be tried. If drugs are to be given it is important to combine them with a plan of behavioural management involving a careful structuring of all aspects of the child's environment. The period of initial response (whether it is caused by a temporary change in attitude on the part of parents or staff or whether it is a genuine pharmacological effect) provides the opportunity to put the planned programme into effect (Brady, 1971). With good behaviour management it may be possible to reduce and eventually to withdraw medication altogether. Variability of response between different people makes systematic evaluation of drug therapy difficult, although trials using the principles of evaluation described by Shapiro (1966) for the single case study may be helpful in deciding where a particular drug is effective in an individual case.

The barbiturates. On the whole, barbiturates are ineffective in the control of over-active and aggressive behaviour in autism and, as with other forms of brain damage in children, they may in fact paradoxically increase over-activity and irritability. This particularly applies to the use of phenobarbitone and also primidone in the treatment of epilepsy in such children.

Amphetamines and methylphenidate. Amphetamines and methylphenidate, which may have a paradoxically beneficial effect in controlling over-activity in the non-autistic hyperkinetic, particularly the epileptic, child, are said to be ineffective in autistic children (Fish, 1968).

The major tranquillisers. The phenothiazines such as chloropromazine, thioridazine and pericyazine are probably most effective in autistic children in the management of over-activity and also of anxiety. One report suggests that thioridazine is particularly useful in the treatment of stereotyped behaviour, such as rocking, in the retarded autistic child (Davis *et al.*, 1969), but it is also true that this is the only drug which has been systematically evaluated in this condition. It is generally found that autistic children require larger doses of these and other drugs than the normal child. Inadequate doses may exacerbate the behavioural symptoms and make the child more irritable, while large doses are more prone to produce side effects such as sedation, impairment of learning, tremor, rigidity and extra-pyramidal side effects (McAndrew *et al.*, 1972). The last may be partially controlled by concomitant administration of anti-parkinsonian agents such as orphenadrine. Other side effects such as jaundice, blood dyscrasias and photo-sensitivity (which last occurs particularly with chlorpromazine) seem to be based more on individual sensitivity and are thus less predictable. Photo-sensitivity may be avoided by the use of thioridazine or pericyazine instead of chlorpromazine. Pericyazine, which can be given in a larger dose towards the latter part of the day when the child is ready for bed, may also be tried if chlorpromazine or thioridazine have too great a sedative effect.

Piperazine derivatives such as trifluoperazine and perphenazine are less sedative in their action and may be particularly effective in the more anxious autistic child where attempts to stop ritualistic behaviour result in temper outbursts and distress. Although, on the whole, freer from side effects, these drugs are particularly prone to produce acute dystonia and, in the relatively large doses which are usually required, concomitant administration of anti-parkinsonian agents is usually necessary. It is always desirable to start with a small dose and gradually increase until the optimum level is reached.

There is often difficulty over administration of medication to an autistic child, and in this case, the use of the butyrophenone derivative, haloperidol, is particularly helpful as this can be given as a colourless, odourless, concentrate administered in the form of drops each containing 0·1 mg. Haloperidol is less sedative than the phenothiazines but more so than the piperazine derivatives. Like the latter it is particularly prone to cause dystonic side effects in a dose of over 3 mgs a day, but these can be prevented by anti-parkinsonian drugs. In adults, haloperidol may cause depressive symptoms. Occasionally a child receiving this drug becomes irritable and miserable. If this happens the drug should be withdrawn.

The minor tranquillisers. Minor tranquillisers such as chlordiazepoxide and diazepam are relatively ineffective in dealing with over-activity or behavioural disturbance in children but may be helpful in an autistic child who is particularly anxious.

Anti-depressants. Anti-depressants are rarely indicated in the treatment of behaviour disturbance in autistic children unless there is clear-cut evidence of a super-added depressive illness (Campbell *et al.*, 1971).

Lithium. A recent controlled study of lithium in autistic children (Campbell *et al.*, 1972) suggests that, while it is generally ineffective in the autistic child, there may occasionally be an unpredictable beneficial response which will justify its use, particularly if there is a periodic quality to the child's behaviour disturbance suggestive of a cyclical mood change, which cannot be explained in any other way.

Night sedatives. The control of sleep disturbance may be difficult in the young autistic child and night sedation on its own is often ineffective. Careful structuring of the child's sleeping situation, the preparation for bed, appropriate lighting of the bedroom, control of temperature and extraneous sounds may be particularly important. Medication may be helpful as an adjuvant if given in appropriate doses and here chloral or a mixture of chloral and one of the phenothiazines may be most effective. If these fail, nitrazepam can be tried. In the older child a short or medium acting barbiturate, such as nembutal or butobarbitone, may be effective if given in adequate doses.

Large doses of vitamins

Rimland (1971b) has suggested that the behaviour of autistic children can be improved by giving mega-doses of vitamins. He has initiated a therapeutic trial but so far no results are available. There does not seem any *a priori* reason why this type of treatment should be successful.

Electro-convulsive treatment (ECT)

Lauretta Bender (1947) and Bender and Keeler (1952) used ECT in a large series of children whom they labelled "schizophrenic". The exact nature of the children's handicaps were not specified in any detail. It seems likely that the series was markedly heterogeneous, but perhaps contained some autistic children. The authors claimed that there was some post-shock improvement in behaviour, but, in another paper, Bender (1955) noted that although there may be a temporary improvement, ECT does not produce any lasting effect in "schizophrenic" children.

Kanner and Eisenberg (1955) described one classically autistic child who, when seen at 4 years of age, appeared to have a comparatively good prognosis. He was given ECT at 5 years (*not* prescribed by Kanner or any of his colleagues) and the child's condition deteriorated immediately after this. At the age of 11 years he was in a state hospital, completely socially withdrawn and inaccessible.

The weight of the evidence suggests that early childhood autism is a disorder of development resulting from organic causes, so there is no theoretical or practical justification for using ECT in the treatment of autistic children or adults.

Management of epilepsy

Epilepsy is one of the commonest of the conditions associated with early childhood autism, although it may not be manifested until adolescence and early adult life (see Chapter 2). Some autistic children and adults have only a few fits with long intervals between which do not require any drug treatment. If the fits occur sufficiently frequently to require medication, the treatment given should follow the same lines as in non-autistic epileptic children. The autistic child usually has difficulty in describing his symptoms, so electro-encephalographic (EEG) assessment and control of dosage by regular estimation of blood drug levels are particularly important.

Anti-convulsants are rarely indicated for the treatment of over-active or aggressive behaviour in autistic children unless there is clear-cut evidence that this behaviour is associated with seizures, supported by the finding of characteristic epileptic discharges on the EEG. There is some suggestion that in these circumstances pheny-toin and particularly sulthiame may be the most effective drugs, particularly where the epileptic discharges are localised to the region of the temporal lobe.

The problems of adolescence

Puberty occurs in autistic children at the same age and in the same way as in normal children. Because of the basic lack of imagination most autistic adolescent boys and girls have no idea of the wider implications of the physical changes they are experiencing and often accept them in a surprisingly matter-of-fact way. The problems that arise are mostly due to the social naivety and lack of reticence which continue from childhood into adult life.

Inappropriate sexual behaviour

Parents are often worried about the sexual development of their handicapped children. On the whole, interest in adult sexual experi-ence is conspicuous by its absence. The difficulties that are much more likely to occur are masturbation in public, a childish curiosity about other people's bodies, and a startling lack of awareness that, in most company, it is necessary to be fully clothed. It is unfortunate that, after social withdrawal in early childhood, undiscriminating sociability and a desire for physical affection on a childish level may develop in an autistic adolescent at an age when they are inappro-priate and produce social disapproval.

These problems should be dealt with in the same way as other socially unacceptable behaviour; that is by the use of appropriate behaviour management. Parents and others who look after hand-icapped children sometimes worry that the discouragement of sexual expression will cause a severe neurosis in addition to the existing handicaps. There is no evidence to confirm this fear. As long as the problems are handled consistently, with common sense and without undue emotion, no harm will be done and the adolescent will benefit from the fact that his social life does not have to be restricted. It is, of course, important for parents and others to understand that masturbation is a normal activity and that there is no need to interfere as long as it occurs in privacy.

A few severely handicapped autistic adolescent boys show socially embarrassing behaviour with sexual connotations such as exposing themselves or persistent touching of other people. Excessive sexual and aggressive drives can be reduced in males by the use of hormones or other recently developed drugs (see, for example, Deberdt, 1971; Cooper *et al.*, 1972). The problem with an autistic adolescent is to decide if the behaviour is primarily sexual in origin and therefore possibly amenable to this kind of drug treatment, or if it is just one manifestation of a general behaviour problem arising from social naivety.

Autistic adolescents who have made good progress may achieve sufficient independence to go out by themselves. At this stage, some of them have a simple, open, friendliness towards others which causes concern in case they become passively involved in heterosexual or homosexual contacts. Parents need to lay down certain rules of conduct, expressed in simple terms and repeated over and over again, but there is no absolute guarantee that such problems will not occur. The risks have to be weighed carefully against the advantage to be gained from allowing some independence, and a decision taken for each individual adolescent. As a result of their innocence, social naivety and inability to use non-verbal communication, young autistic adults have little idea how to give the conventionally accepted signals of sexual invitation and this in itself affords a certain amount of protection against sexual exploitation.

Problems of menstruation

Most autistic girls who have achieved a reasonable level in other self-care skills will be able to learn to cope with the practical problems of menstruation, given some supervision. Programmes to teach this step by step can be devised as for any of the other problems of self care. Once a pattern has been established, the typical resistance to change and insistence on routines confers a considerable advantage in maintaining good standards of hygiene. Premenstrual tension and dysmenorrhoea can occur in autistic as in other adolescent girls. While the fact of menstruation may be accepted without question, the severe pain of spasmodic dysmenorrhoea is especially distressing and frightening to an autistic girl, since it cannot be explained in any way which she can appreciate. Sedatives and analgesics together with smooth muscle relaxants such as Edrisal may help. If they are not effective then the hormone tablets used as contraceptives can be tried. These are given on the usual plan of one tablet daily for 21 days with a break of 7 days. On this regime, pain during menstruation is often reduced even if not prevented altogether. There is the added advantage, especially for the autistic girl, that the periods are completely regular and predictable.

There are now three types of oral contraceptives available, which contain respectively a moderate dose, a low dose and an ultra-low dose of oestrogen. The low dose pills have proved effective in reducing spasmodic dysmenorrhoea, for example Minovlar, Norinyl-1 or Minilyn. The risk of thrombosis, which in any case is negligible, is even less on the low dose of oestrogen. Furthermore, these pills tend to halve the amount of blood lost during the menstrual period. The effect of the ultra-low dose of oestrogen on dysmenorrhoea is not yet known.

It is also possible to use a progestational substance such as Duphaston which does not interfere with ovulation but does reduce dysmenorrhoea. These pills are also taken for 21 days, starting on the fifth day of the cycle, as for the oral contraceptives.

Dilatation of the cervix is sometimes an effective treatment for painful menstruation. If spasmodic dysmenorrhoea is severe and intractable, the operation of pre-sacral neurectomy may be indicated. This involves a laparotomy in order to cut the parasympathetic nerve supply to the pelvis. It has no long-term side-effects and usually gives relief for 3 to 5 years.

Research work is being carried out in this field. There is every likelihood that new non-hormonal preparations will become available with a specific action on the contractions of the uterus which are the cause of the cramp-like pain of spasmodic dysmenorrhoea.

Parents may ask about the possibility of suppressing menstruation altogether, either because of dysmenorrhoea that does not respond to other treatment or, more often, because the degree of handicap and behaviour disturbance gives rise to severe practical problems of management. If, for example, a girl tends to destroy clothing, including sanitary protection, unless constantly supervised, it is obvious that menstruation, when it occurs, is an added burden to everyone concerned.

It is technically possible to prevent menstruation by the daily administration of appropriate hormones. In Sweden, Lydecken (1972) has used the synthetic hormone preparation Lynestrenol (alpha-methyl-lynestrenol) in a fairly high dose (5 mg daily) given throughout the menstrual cycle. In 130 institutionalised retarded girls treated for periods of up to 3 years very few side effects were noted, and there were no cases of thrombosis. The author felt that there were beneficial effects on behaviour and that the numbers of seizures were reduced in women who were epileptic.

Despite this favourable report some caution is necessary. The main problem is that of breakthrough bleeding occurring at irregular intervals, which may begin after a few weeks of taking the pills continuously and could be more troublesome than the regularly occurring menstrual period. The long-term effects of continuous administration of contraceptive hormones in human beings are unknown since there has been no opportunity for observing them. The problems of menstruations, both the amount of bleeding and the pain, are usually reduced by the low oestrogen dose pills mentioned previously. It may be helpful to suppress menstruation for one or two cycles at intervals, especially when its occurrence would cause special difficulties such as on a holiday away from home. This compromise does not produce the problems associated with longer term suppression. It is also possible to use the same hormone preparations, with medical supervision, to lengthen the menstrual cycle, reducing the number of periods to perhaps three or four per year.

Sometimes parents who have to cope with a severely handicapped adolescent who cannot care for herself and who has frequent, heavy and perhaps painful periods ask about the possibility of hysterectomy. Quite apart from the physical dangers of such a major operation, it is likely to produce considerable psychological disturbance in an autistic person who cannot understand what is happening. This alone might well produce exacerbation of behaviour problems but, in addition, there is the danger of long-term side effects due to hormonal changes following disturbance of the pelvic organs. These also may have marked adverse effects on behaviour and general progress. From every point of view, therefore, this operation is contra-indicated as a means of dealing with unwanted menstruation.

General physical care

Marked fluctuations in the behaviour disturbances shown by autistic children may occur, especially in those who have the most severe problems in understanding and using language. Often, no cause of any kind can be identified for these fluctuations, but their occurrence suggests interesting possibilities for research into the possible physical, psychological or social causes.

Sometimes, however, exacerbations in behaviour disturbance may be due to physical ill-health or pain. Autistic children often cannot explain their distress or indicate the site of any physical symptoms. The sudden onset of screaming, temper outbursts, increased restlessness and other disturbed behaviour may indicate such physical ailments as toothache, earache or abdominal pain. If any unexpected changes in behaviour occur, the possibility of a physical illness should be considered. A careful physical examination is necessary to exclude such a cause, and may have to be repeated even if nothing positive could be found on the first occasion, since pain often precedes detectable localizing signs. The problems of management which may arise from unexplained cyclical changes in behaviour are discussed in Chapter 10.

Eccentric diets are not uncommon in autism. These may last for a short time only, but if they continue for weeks or months and if the food taken is severely restricted, signs of nutritional deficiencies may occur and will have to be treated. A method of managing severe feeding problems, using learning theory principles, on an in-patient basis, has been described by Clancy *et al.* (1969b).

If an autistic child has to have a surgical operation, the possibility of marked resistance to the effects of sedatives and hypnotics should be borne in mind when planning pre-medication and anaesthesia. Sometimes the children are extremely confused and disturbed during the stage of recovery from an anaesthetic and may need extra sedation to prevent damage to stitches, blood drips or other apparatus.

The whole business of being admitted to hospital and undergoing examinations and surgical procedures is distressing to any child but especially so to the routine-bound autistic child. It is therefore most important to arrange for the parents or other familiar people to visit frequently and especially for someone the child knows to be present before the child is anaesthetized, and when he recovers, to give physical comfort and reassurance. Most autistic children have some favourite object which they should be allowed to have with them in hospital. This should not be mislaid or lost while the child is under the anaesthetic. These objects, trivial as they may seem to other people, are a vital link with the world for an autistic child. It may be desirable to wean him from these objects as he matures, but he needs them when he is ill and away from his own familiar environment.

Dental care

Regular dental care is of particular importance in handicapped children where food fads, the necessity of using carbohydrate foods as reinforcers in behaviour modification programmes and difficulties in training the child to clean his teeth may all predispose to dental decay, while the use of anti-convulsants such as phenytoin may lead to gum hypertrophy and gingivitis. As with all other forms of medical intervention, dental care requires time, patience and an unhurried approach by staff experienced in dealing with handicapped children. A dental service for handicapped children in which such facilities may be provided has been described by Pool (1972). A comprehensive review of the dental problems of handicapped children was given by Diner (1971).

The Role of the Doctor

The doctor's role in the care of autistic children and adults is a limited one. Medical skills are of primary importance in diagnosis, differential diagnosis, precise assessment of each child's handicaps and control of medication, but, in day-to-day management and education, teachers and psychologists, in partnership with the parents, have the major parts to play. Even in the subnormality hospitals, where doctors may be nominally responsible for the running of the institution, most of their work is administrative rather than strictly medical.

This does not mean that the doctor's contribution is negligible. His role in caring for the autistic child is to help to minimise the child's handicaps and in this way to facilitate the efforts of the other people who are concerned. He can also give support and reassurance by being ready with expert advice when, as sometimes happens, parents or professional staff are worried in case a child's behaviour problems are due to an intercurrent physical illness. In this situation, unless the doubt can be satisfactorily resolved, staff may become hesitant and unconfident in their handling of the child, leading to exacerbation of the difficult behaviour (see Chapter 10).

Autistic children tend to be unco-operative with strangers but much easier with people whom they know well. It is therefore a great advantage if the family doctor (and dentist as well) can get to know the child before any medical examinations or treatments become necessary. Regular contact in health as well as in illness allows the child to develop trust and confidence in the doctor. Also, if the doctor is familiar with the child's usual pattern of behaviour, it will be easier for him to evaluate the changes which may occur during physical illness.

Some doctors tend not to diagnose early childhood autism if they can avoid doing so, because they work in areas where there are few or no services for this condition. To make the diagnosis and then to say that no help is available would, they feel, upset the parents to no purpose.

This attitude, understandable though it may be, will never solve any problems. In some poorly served areas there is a vicious circle in which doctors do not diagnose autism because there are no services and local authorities provide no services because they know of no children with the diagnosis. The constructive approach is for the doctor to make the correct diagnosis and carefully assess the child's needs. He can then inform the relevant authorities, making practical suggestions as to how to help the child and the family, thus giving them the facts which are a necessary basis for action.

As with all childhood conditions which produce chronic, life long handicaps, team work between the various caring professions and the parents is essential. Doctors can make their full contribution only if they are willing to work as a member of a team on an equal basis with the other members.

Grateful acknowledgements are due to John R. Newton MD, MRCOG., Senior Lecturer and Consultant Obstetrician, Kings College Hospital, London, for his advice on the management of the medical problems of adolescence.

CHAPTER 12

PROVISION OF SERVICES

JOHN K. WING and LORNA WING

One of the features of a complex industrial culture is that society, in the shape of the local, regional or national government authorities, has to take over some of the functions that, in less developed countries, are left to the family or local community. These functions include education, vocational training and the care of the sick and handicapped. The extent of statutory responsibility varies in different countries but, even where the prevailing climate of opinion opposes the concept of the welfare state, there are still many services that are provided by government agencies.

Some people feel that it is uneconomic to spend money on caring for those who are chronically handicapped and unable to fend for themselves. The logical end point of this argument is that the weak should be left to die, as in some primitive cultures. In our society that solution is ethically unacceptable. Parents have the duty to look after their children, however handicapped. If they cannot do so it is tempting for society to provide the minimum assistance, such as large institutions run as cheaply as possible, as a convenient way of disposing of those who cannot help themselves. This was the attitude that led to the Poor Law workhouse system.

The argument in favour of this kind of solution is that the realities of life dictate that the strong should survive while the weakest go to the wall. Those taking this view forget that compassion for others is just as real a part of human life as are ruthlessness and aggression. The development of complex modern societies has depended as much upon co-operation as competition.

Concern for those in need arises partly from intuitive sympathy and partly from a distinctively human ability to think about the past,

287

plan for the future and to compare one's own lot with that of others. This exercise leads to the realisation that no one is immune from life's misfortunes. Even the strongest and healthiest may, at any time, through illness or accident, join the ranks of the handicapped. Even the most careful planner may be prevented from securing his own and his family's future through some unforseen circumstance entirely outside his control. The provision of social services can, therefore, be seen as enlightened self interest. It is also in the interest of society in general since, without support and help from outside, a handicapped person may be such a burden that other members of his family are prevented from making their full contribution to society.

Public interest in the welfare of the handicapped tends to be sporadic, not because of lack of feeling, but because at any one time most people are not personally involved, although few escape some kind of involvement during the course of a whole lifetime. Concern is aroused whenever there is a special campaign or when some abuse is exposed. Nevertheless, it is possible for low standards to exist in some services for a long time.

In recent years there has been a marked increase in the amount of publicity given to the problems of all kinds of handicapped people and this has been accompanied by greater general awareness and feeling that adequate services ought to be provided. Perhaps as a result of this process, a new attitude, diametrically opposed to the hard line mentioned above, has emerged. People adopting this new attitude, in its extreme form, wish to make the lives of handicapped children and adults as normal as possible by providing all services within the community and, as far as possible, doing away with any segregation.

The idea of "normalisation" is a humane and laudable one, but, in pursuing this aim, it is just as easy to ignore the specific needs of some handicapped people as it is if the opposite course of institutionalisation is adopted. The most reasonable compromise is to try to provide a wide variety of services, some within the normal community, some in specialised sheltered communities and some half way between so that the best solution can be found for each individual person. Standards should be maintained at a high level in all types of provision so that handicapped people can be helped to minimise their disabilities, utilise the skills they do possess and obtain some enjoyment from life.

Voluntary bodies and, in some countries, commercial firms have an important role in setting up services, but it would be impossible for them to organise and maintain comprehensive provision for everyone in need of help. Statutory authorities have to take the major responsibility if there are not to be large gaps in the network. A partnership between the state and the voluntary agencies can be particularly successful and this will be discussed later in this chapter.

Services for Autistic Children and Adults

Problems in providing services

Early childhood autism and similar conditions almost always lead to life-long handicap and a need for sheltered accommodation and occupation. Any plan for services must take the long-term nature of the impairments into account.

As well as the general problems encountered when planning services for any group of chronically handicapped people, there are some which are specific to autism and related disorders. To begin with, these conditions cannot be neatly fitted into existing administrative categories of mental retardation, or mental or physical illness. As emphasised in previous chapters, autistic behaviour can occur in association with any level of intelligence, the specific impairments range from very mild to very severe, and additional physical or mental handicaps may be present.

The organisational dilemmas presented by these variations in the degree of handicap are exacerbated by the fact that early childhood autism is not a common condition. Specialised services for autistic people have to draw from large populations if they are to be viable, so it is usually administratively easier to try to fit autistic children and adults into existing services for other types of handicaps, whether or not this is best for the individual concerned.

Unfortunately, mixing with other handicaps frequently produces problems, because the severe impairments affecting comprehension and use of all types of communication found in autism have a profound effect upon all aspects of functioning. The usual methods of child rearing and teaching and the usual rules governing the way in which adults relate to each other have to be quite drastically modified when dealing with an autistic child or adult. A child who has uncomplicated Down's syndrome and an IQ of 40, but who can communicate through a mixture of words, sounds and gestures can be managed on the same principles as those which work with young normal children. Caring for someone who is severely impaired in language, the most important of human abilities, needs specialised knowledge and experience of quite a different order.

The characteristic absence, or very poor development, of inner language means that the behaviour of autistic children and adults is dependant upon the immediate environment to a far greater extent than that of people, normal or retarded, who have at least some ability to think about recent events in the light of past experience and future aims. Even the most capable of autistic adults, having no inner resources to draw upon, is rarely able to cope with changes in his usual routine. The moderately or severely retarded autistic person has to have his programme carefully organised if he is to function anywhere near his potential. The techniques of behaviour modification are particularly appropriate if they are applied with sensitivity and with a knowledge of each individual's specific impairments.

Principles governing the provision of services

J. K. Wing (1972) listed under four headings the principles that are generally accepted in the U.K. as governing the local provision of health and social services for people with psychiatric conditions, including childhood autism and mental retardation.

The principles are, firstly, that the relevant authorities should accept responsibility for a whole geographical area and the services should be geographically accessible to everyone in that area. Secondly, the services should be comprehensive, varied in kind and adequate in number. Thirdly, the different kinds of services should be integrated, with good communication and easy transfer from one to another. Finally, the chief aim of the health and social services should be to "decrease or contain morbidity", first in the patient, secondly in the patient's immediate family and thirdly in the community at large. Wing defined "morbidity" as the combination of the primary biological or psychological impairments with the behavioural reactions that are secondary to these underlying impairments (see Chapter 2).

These principles are also relevant to education, although decreasing morbidity should be regarded as one of the aims of this service rather than its chief objective.

Wing also mentioned the social handicaps which arise from, for example, poverty, lack of education or inappropriate child rearing practices. These can occur independently of any biological or psychological impairment but, quite often, chronic illness and social handicap co-exist and each exacerbates the effects of the other. In a condition such as early childhood autism, additional social handicaps are most likely to occur because of the difficulty in providing appropriate management, education and occupational training.

One important implication of this analysis of principles is that the services should be concerned with impairments and handicaps and not solely with medical diagnosis. To illustrate this point, the example of Down's syndrome can be used. Most children with this condition are severely retarded but are sociable, develop imaginative play and are able to communicate effectively through gesture and facial expression even if their articulation is poor. A few have intelligence in the ESN range while, at the other end of the scale, a few are profoundly retarded and have elements of the autistic syndrome. Some have additional problems such as deafness, or congenital abnormalities of the heart. Those coming from large families may have the social disadvantages of poverty and an elderly, overworked mother in poor health herself. The service needs will depend upon the details of the child's impairments and handicaps, not upon the diagnosis of Down's syndrome alone.

The label "early childhood autism" covers a very wide range of children who differ in the severity of their primary impairments and secondary handicap and the number and severity of their associated problems. Therefore their service needs are equally varied, as will be emphasised in the rest of this chapter.

Calculations of service needs

The approximate prevalence rates which will be used to calculate the size of the service needs are based upon those found in a survey, in the former London Borough of Camberwell, of all children under 15 years of age who were attending any kind of special school or who were receiving remedial teaching or speech therapy (Wing, 1975). Camberwell had a total population of 162,600 in 1971.

One aim of this survey was to identify children with some or all of the elements of the autistic syndrome as described in Chapter 2. While those with the classic syndrome were reasonably easy to identify, it was much harder to define the borderlines. It was decided to accept all children in whom inner language was severely limited or absent, and who had at least some items of autistic behaviour. For example, 2 children with Down's syndrome, and 1 with untreated phenylketonuria were included because their behaviour fitted the criteria for inclusion. Children who were unable to walk without support were excluded. Many of these lacked inner language and showed autistic features but their physical and mental handicaps were so severe that these were the major determinants of their service needs, rather than the associated behaviour. Four children with severe visual or combined visual and auditory defects were also excluded, despite the presence of marked autistic behaviour, as their sensory defects posed additional special problems of teaching and management. In some areas units have been set up for children of this kind.

Lack of inner language was emphasised as an important criterion because, as discussed in Chapter 4, it has such a profound effect on general behaviour, social interaction and learning abilities that special teaching techniques are needed to help children with this severe impairment. Using this criterion gives a much wider group including more severely handicapped children than that covered by the classic descriptions of early childhood autism but it is appropriate when considering service needs. Whatever the scientific justification for separating the classic autistic syndrome from other rather similar conditions, there is no reason for doing this when planning services. The problem of teaching and management and the techniques used in solving them follow mainly from the language impairments regardless of their cause.

Although his screening procedure was not followed in detail, it was possible to select sub-groups from the Camberwell children which were roughly equivalent to Lotter's "nuclear" and "non-nuclear" autistic groups, described in Chapter 3 (Lotter, 1966). In Lotter's Middlesex survey the nuclear group (A) contained 2·0 children per 10,000 aged 8 to 10 and the non-nuclear group (B) 2·5 children. In Camberwell there were 2·0 children per 10,000 aged 5 to 15 years in group A and 2·8 in group B. (The total population of children aged 5 to 15 years in this area was approximately 27,000 in 1971.) Thus the rates for Camberwell are a little higher but of the same order as those in Middlesex.

Lotter found an additional group (C) of 3·3 children per 10,000 aged 8 to 10 who were not autistic but who had some behaviour similar to autistic children. In Camberwell there were 5·2 per 10,000 children who lacked inner language and who had some autistic behaviour. It is not possible to compare this group with Lotter's group C because he did not include an assessment of inner language as one of his criteria for the definition of autism.

In all, an age specific prevalence of 10·0 per 10,000 children aged 5 to 15 years with the problems mentioned above was found in Camberwell on one census day. The figures may be modified when the analysis is completed, but the differences will be small.

A plan for services

Many of the suggestions to be made below are in line with those proposed in the document *Better Services for the Mentally Handicapped* produced by the Department of Health and Social Security (1971). It is possible to utilise the existing and the projected retardation services for children and adults with autistic behaviour to quite a large extent, but certain modifications are necessary and some specialised provisions are required in order that the services should be flexible and comprehensive.

The headings under which the service needs will be described are summarised in Fig. 12.1.

Diagnostic services

Lotter (1966) showed that autistic children with associated physical disabilities tend to be diagnosed earliest, while those who are physically healthy with normal milestones are not recognised until their speech, behaviour difficulties, or learning problems bring them to notice.

Early detection of delay in cognitive, language and social skills is possible only if general practitioners, health visitors and welfare clinic doctors are as knowledgeable and experienced in these aspects of a baby's behaviour as they are concerning feeding and motor development. It is not possible to make a certain diagnosis of autism in the first one or two years of life but it is possible to note

A. *Structure of the services*
  1. Diagnosis
  2. Assessment
  3. Help for the family
    (a) Practical advice for parents on special aspects of child rearing
    (b) Practical help (domestic, financial, etc.)
    (c) Social work
    (d) Psychotherapy
  4. Education
    (a) Under 5 years of age
    (b) 5 to 16 years
    (c) 16 to 19 years.
  5. Employment (open and sheltered)
  6. Residential accommodation
  7. Specialist services (medical, dental, speech therapy, etc.)
  8. Leisure and recreation

B. *Related needs*
  9. Staff training
  10. Integration of different services
  11. Voluntary organisations.

Fig. 12.1. Children and adults with autism and related conditions. Summary of services needed

the early signs of problems affecting language development (Sheridan, 1969).

When it is suspected that a young child may have a delay in language development, or if he shows other evidence of abnormal behaviour, it should be possible to refer him to an assessment centre. The Department of Health and Social Security have recommended the setting up of comprehensive assessment centres staffed by multi-disciplinary teams to which children of any age and with any type of handicap may be referred (Chapter 11). The aim is for every area to have access to such a centre.

A service of this kind should be able to diagnose and assess children with autism and related handicaps. It is neither necessary nor practicable to set up separate centres for this purpose, provided that the staff of the comprehensive centres are well educated concerning the features of these conditions and the techniques of differential diagnosis. The advantage of such a centre is that it should have all the available expertise and equipment for psychiatric diagnosis, psychological testing and for investigation of vision and hearing, abnormalities of the central nervous system and associated physical disabilities. The assessment does not require that the child be taken into a residential setting if there are no other reasons for admission.

Assessment

After detection and diagnosis, the next step is more lengthy and difficult. It is to describe in detail the types of primary disability in each child, the extent of the secondary disabilities, and the social circumstances which are likely to affect outcome. This process takes months or even years and requires the combined knowledge and observation of doctors, psychologists, speech therapists, social workers, teachers and parents. Only the initial stages can be completed in the assessment centre. Subsequently the focus will shift to the home or to the school. A diagnostic label, be it childhood autism, psychosis, emotional disturbance or mental subnormality, is a useless impediment without this careful and progressive analysis of the problems experienced by the child and his family. The prescription of services can be made only on the basis of a detailed knowledge of visual, auditory and speech disabilities, behavioural disturbances, family attitudes and burdens, social, economic and domestic difficulties. A complete assessment requires the team approach with co-operation across the boundaries of professional and administrative hierarchies. This conception of the team is discussed in more detail in a later section of this chapter.

Help for the family

Practical advice for parents. One of the most important consequences of the autistic child's lack of inner language is that a pattern of skills and appropriate behaviour learnt, for example, at school tends not to be transferred to other situations unless the same methods of teaching and management are transferred as well. The improvements in functioning due to maturation are stable, but many aspects of behaviour, in the short term at least, are the direct results of conditioning and these are easily lost if the programme of behaviour management is discontinued (Bartak and Rutter, 1973; Lovaas *et al.*, 1973; Rutter and Bartak, 1973). It is therefore important to help parents to learn how to deal with behaviour problems and teach new skills so that improvements can occur at home as well as at school. The role that parents can play is discussed by Schopler in Chapter 9.

Expertise in behaviour management is being developed by psychologists who have the background knowledge derived from learning theory. Those who are most successful combine this theoretical knowledge with a detailed study of each individual's specific handicaps, an appreciation of his personality and emotional reactions, and a sound leavening of common sense about what can and cannot be done in the child's home or school. There is as yet no comprehensive provision of such help although workers in a few areas are giving this kind of service. Some of these are attached to universities and are working with families as part of a research project. Some are attached to mental retardation hospitals or children's psychiatric units, while others are local authority educational psychologists or else work for a voluntary body. At present this kind of counselling for parents of handicapped children depends upon the interest and initiative of individuals.

In order to make it a comprehensive service much careful planning will be needed. One possibility would be to involve the psychologists attached to the handicap assessment centres. This would not solve the need for similar help with some handicapped adults, unless the children's assessment centres were associated with centres for those adults who also need long-term supervision and care.

It is important for continuity that the same programme of management is carried out at school, at home, and in any residential centre to which a child may be admitted for short- or long-term care. The same psychologist should, ideally, be involved in all these situations but this will be possible only if a full range of services are provided on a community basis within each area.

Psychologists who work with families and with professional staff soon realise that, while some people acquire the skills of behaviour management quickly and easily, others are less able and a few fail completely. The reasons may be emotional feelings, learned attitudes concerning child care, or just lack of the speed and energy needed to act firmly and consistently all the time. Experience will teach when it is sensible to stop trying and to find some other, perhaps less ideal, but more practicable way of helping the family to cope. Rigid application of learning theory is as self-defeating in the end as the rigid application of any other theory or treatment method.

Practical help. The practical help required at home by families with an autistic child is much the same as for those with other types of mentally handicapped children. Domestic help, laundry facilities, help with transport if the child is difficult on buses and trains, and financial assistance, including the constant attendance allowance, may be needed. Many parents would be greatly helped if they could call on experienced people who could baby-sit for them occasionally to give them some relief from the constant care needed by a disturbed child. In some cases housing problems force parents to ask for residential care even when they would prefer to have the child at home, and rehousing may be the solution.

Social work. The social worker, in her work with families of handicapped people, has to provide information concerning all available services, rights and obligations, to act as an entrepreneur in obtaining these services for the handicapped person and his family and generally to be their champion and defender in all the struggles in which they will inevitably become involved throughout the handicapped person's whole life. In taking on these tasks the social worker will, in most cases, earn the friendship and trust of the family and will be able to discuss with them the less tangible emotional problems inherent in looking after a chronically dependent child or adult. This is especially likely to happen if the social worker has a real knowledge and understanding of the specific impairments found in the handicapping condition and the problems arising from them. If, however, the discussion of emotional problems is made the main focus of visits and the practical problems are relegated to second place, the social worker is likely to forfeit the respect of the family and to lose the chance of helping them.

Psychotherapy. The few relevant follow-up studies (Creak, 1963; Eisenberg, 1956, 1957a; Kanner, 1973) have provided no evidence that psycho-analytically oriented therapy for autistic children or their parents has produced any significant change in the children's primary impairments or secondary handicaps, although no properly controlled trials have been carried out.

Psychotherapy may be needed to help the parents because the disturbed behaviour of their child provokes ambivalent feelings and this, together with the inevitably prolonged period of dependence, may lead to profoundly disturbed relationships in the family, not only between mother and child and between siblings but also between the parents. Feelings of hostility and aggression towards a handicapped child may be difficult to deal with and result in guilt, anxiety and depression. Many parents are well able to deal with these problems (which are merely an exaggeration of problems familiar in all families even when there is no added stress) but some parents become overwhelmed by them.

As with social work, psychotherapy without help and advice on how to deal with the practical problems of rearing an autistic child (or one with any other handicap for that matter), is of little use and often produces resentment rather than co-operation. Even more resentment is engendered if the parents feel that the therapist believes their attitudes or child-rearing practices were the original cause of their child's handicaps. If, instead, parents are regarded as members of the therapeutic team (see Chapter 9) they are more likely, in the atmosphere of mutual trust and respect thus created, to be willing to discuss any emotional problems.

Education

Below the age of 5. The 1944 Education Act laid down that children who were ascertained as handicapped could receive education from the age of 2. Until 1971 severely mentally retarded children were excluded from education altogether but, as a result of the Education (Handicapped Children) Act of 1971, no child is now regarded as ineducable. The main problem in applying to autistic children the clause concerning education from the age of 2 is that they must be ascertained as handicapped with the consent of the parents. The diagnosis may not be made in the early years and parents may be reluctant to have their child officially labelled as handicapped at such an early age.

Attendance at a pre-school unit can be helpful for some autistic children and their families. The staff can begin the teaching of self-care skills, gradually introduce the child to the regular routine of a school day, and help him to become used to mixing with other children, so that he is well prepared by the time he reaches school age. A daily break from the care of the child can be a welcome relief for the mother and allow her to spend more time with other children in the family. Some play groups and nursery schools will accept autistic children. In a number of areas local authority day nurseries originally set up for normal children have units for children with any kind of handicap and some of these have coped very well with young autistic children. These latter units have the advantage of being open all the year round instead of keeping to school terms.

At this early age it is not usually necessary to separate autistic children from other children, whether handicapped or normal, nor to divide them according to level of ability. As long as the staff are understanding, willing to accept difficult behaviour and able to adopt appropriate methods of handling the problems, an autistic child can be included in the pre-school programme because most of the activities are practical rather than verbal.

In an area of 250,000 total population there are likely to be 16 children under the age of 5 with autistic behaviour who should be known to the services. Most of these are over the age of 2 and could benefit from attending a suitable pre-school service, so possibly 12 places would be needed (see Table 12.1).

School-age children. Education for handicapped children is a very wide concept covering far more than the usual school subjects. Teachers have to be as ready to tackle the problems of toilet training and managing aggressive or self-destructive behaviour as they are to teach reading and writing.

Education is necessary for severely and mildly retarded autistic children as well as for those in the normal range of intelligence. All these children need a carefully organised routine and teaching which is informed with the principles of learning theory, although the eventual aims of education are very different for the three groups mentioned. Autistic children with normal intelligence can learn academic skills and a few may eventually become independent. The mildly or moderately retarded autistic children are likely to be able to learn practical and domestic skills to a reasonable level and some reading and writing and number work for very simple practical purposes. They will need sheltered work and accommodation but can be usefully employed within these limits. For the severely retarded autistic children the aims are to improve self care and to capitalise on any other isolated skills that may be present. For all groups, increasing the child's own ability to control his behaviour is of great importance. Even the brightest autistic child may be precipitated into a temper tantrum if pushed too far by too many demands which he cannot meet and any training which helps to avoid this is of great value.

For children over 5 there are advantages to be gained from schools or all age units which specialise in teaching autistic children and those with related handicaps. Such schools or units can usually take children from under 5 to over 16 years of age and they cover the whole range of ability providing that there are not a disproportionate

Table 12.1
Children and adults with autism and related conditions. Numbers of places needed in the day and residential services for an area of 250,000 total population

I. Day provision

A. Children (under 16)

Nursery provision	Schools for normal, physically handicapped or ESN	Schools for autistic children	Schools for ESN (severe)	Units for ESN (special care)	Total
(mixed)	(mixed)	(specialised)	(mixed)	(specialised)	
12	3	4	6	21	46

B. Adults (16 and over)

Suitable open employment	Vocational training	Sheltered work	Adult training centres (mixed or specialised)	Adult special care units (mixed or specialised)	Total
	(mixed)	(mixed)			
6	2	16	26	90	140

Total children and adults 186

II. Residential provision

A. Children (under 16)

Hostels	Boarding schools		Units with high staff ratio and close supervision	Medical and nursing supervision	Total
(mixed)	(mixed or specialised)		(mixed or specialised)	(mixed or specialised)	
2	2		11	6	21

B. Adults (16 and over)

Hostels	Hostels for autism and related conditions	Sheltered communities	Units with high staff ratio and close supervision	Medical and nursing supervision	Total
(mixed)	(specialised)	(mixed or specialised)	(mixed or specialised)	(mixed or specialised)	
4	6	4	80	12	106

Total children and adults needing residential provision 127

N.B. The children and adults needing residential provision are included in the numbers needing day provision.

301

number who are severely retarded. The staff can acquire expertise and a successful school of this kind develops its own style and traditions into which new entrants fit with surprising rapidity.

Special classes (as distinct from special units covering the full school age range) attached to other kinds of schools have, in the authors' opinion, been less successful, with a few notable exceptions. They have to cope with a wide range of age and ability in one class. The older children who cannot move into the main school have to stay in the same class until some other placement is found for them. If there is only one qualified teacher she may feel very isolated. There is often a tendency for the unit to be ignored or rejected by the rest of the school unless the other staff are especially tolerant and interested. In the few cases where such classes have been successful, there has been active interest from the rest of the staff and the opportunity for supervised and guided mixing of the autistic and other children on social occasions such as meal times. Unsupervised mixing, for instance at playtime, is of dubious benefit since little or no social contact in fact takes place.

Placing autistic children in classes for normal or other handicapped children does work well with carefully selected children but often produces problems. These arise from the conflict between the special needs of the autistic child for organisation and for a predominantly non-verbal approach, and the needs of the other children for some freedom and the opportunity to converse and play imaginatively. It requires great skill to resolve these conflicting needs. The end result may be that the autistic child becomes disturbed or withdrawn and is excluded from the school, sometimes after he has lost the chance of admission to one of the few specialised units. Successful mixing seems to be most likely with two particular groups. Firstly some of the bright autistic children who are also quiet and well-behaved manage in normal schools, schools for various kinds of physical handicaps, or ESN schools, although they are vulnerable to teasing and find the going hard when exams approach. Secondly the quieter ones among the severely retarded autistic children may fit into a group in an ESN (severe) school that has a structured and organised approach. The one type of school into which autistic children rarely fit successfully is that for maladjusted children. The permissive atmosphere and the noisy acting-out behaviour is unsuitable for an autistic child. The mildly and moderately retarded autistic children and those of any level of ability whose behaviour is very disturbed are the hardest to mix with other children and are most likely to benefit from specialised provision.

The ideal system seems to be to have both specialised units and the possibility of admitting autistic children to other kinds of schools so that the best place can be found for each child. He may have different needs at different stages of his school career so transfer should be easy and informal.

A few of the existing specialised units arrange with nearby schools for children with other handicaps, or for normal children, to share certain activities under careful supervision, so that the autistic children are not isolated from those who can communicate. This is an excellent plan since it enables the staff to see if and when children are ready to move on to a more normal environment.

The disturbed, severely retarded child with autistic behaviour is a special problem which was thrust upon the unprepared teachers in ESN (severe) schools by the Education (Handicapped Children) Act 1971. Many schools have to put these children in their special care units where those with severe physical handicaps are also placed. If there is no physical separation of these two groups, the difficulties faced by the staff can be formidable. Special units designed for this type of child and attached to the ESN (severe) schools would solve many of these problems.

In an area of 250,000 total populations, there are likely to be a total of 34 children with autism or similar conditions (as defined in the Camberwell survey) aged 5 to 16 (see Table 12.1). Out of this total there are likely to be 4 children able to learn useful skills, including the usual school work, but who could function reasonably well only in a very structured and organised environment. They would need to attend a school specialising in autism and related conditions. Thus a school of 24 pupils would accept from an area of 2 million total population. The daily attenders would need transport and this might present a special problem in some scattered rural areas.

From the 31 remaining children, 3 might be able to attend a school for children with handicaps other than ESN (severe) or possibly a small school for normal children with understanding staff. A further 6 might be able to fit into the ordinary classes in an ESN (severe) school if the programme was carefully planned for them. Finally the largest group, 21 children, would need to be in an ESN (special care) unit, separated from the physically handicapped children, with sufficient trained staff, appropriate equipment and well designed accommodation to cope with the severe behavioural problems these children present.

At the moment, basing the calculation on the area of London which has been studied, 16 of the last group would be in residential care outside the local area. They would therefore not be attending local schools. If, however, future services are truly community based, then the local schools would presumably have to cope with these children.

Adolescents who might benefit from further education. Although physical development is usually normal, maturation of psychological functions is markedly delayed in autistic children. When they reach the usual school leaving age of 16 they are almost always too immature and naive to be able to work in open employment even if they have the necessary skills. The more able autistic adolescents would benefit from further education in a specialised unit where they could be taught how to cope with the demands of everyday life as well as continuing to learn academic and vocational subjects. They need to be shown how, for example, to travel on public transport, shop in small shops and supermarkets, use a telephone, change clothes regularly, do their personal laundry and cleaning and to cook adequate meals as well as eating in restaurants and cafeterias.

Education authorities are empowered to provide or pay fees for the education of handicapped children up to the age of 19. The 3 years from 17 to 19 would be used to prepare the brighter autistic adolescents for some degree of independence. In an area of 250,000 total population there might be 1 or 2 young people who could benefit from such provision (see Table 12.1). If those with other kinds of language problems were also included, a unit of this kind serving several local authority areas could be justified. The service would function most effectively if close contacts could be developed with sympathetic employers in the area served. Liaison with sheltered workshops would also be necessary for those young adults who could not manage open employment.

Employment

Now that the principle of education for all handicapped children has been accepted, at least in theory, the next major problem to be solved is that of employment for handicapped adults. Most autistic children and adults are poorly motivated to occupy themselves and need much supervision to keep them at the task in hand. Despite this apparent reluctance to engage in activity, experience shows that autistic behaviour, such as stereotyped movements and obsessional rituals, is much less in evidence when the child or adult is occupied. Furthermore, occupation which is within the capabilities of the person concerned seems to lead to a happier and more relaxed attitude with fewer temper tantrums or other behaviour disturbances.

Very few autistic adults are able to manage in open employment. The type of work which suits them is that which is organised around a regular routine, utilises their non-language dependent skills, does not involve them in too much contact with other people and does not need flexibility of thought nor the ability to adjust to changing demands. Autistic people are reliable once they have learnt a routine, but they are very vulnerable to any change and to teasing or bullying from work mates. Problems may also arise on the journey to and from work if, for example, buses are taken off before reaching their usual destination. An understanding employer is essential if an autistic adult is to settle into regular work.

The great majority need sheltered employment. Some could fit into sheltered workshops or factories if these were available. Many more need the less demanding environment provided by a day centre where production norms do not have to be met. In theory, adult training centres for the mentally retarded should be able to accept autistic people, especially since those who are only mildly or moderately retarded tend to have good visuo-spatial skills which are needed for the work usually available in the centres. The difficulty is that, as with autistic children, autistic adults and those with similar handicaps are different from people, whether normal or retarded, who are able to communicate and who have some inner language. The atmosphere in a good adult training centre is free and easy, there is a lot of chatter, laughter and noise and an amazing amount of social interaction. Supervision is unobtrusive and often a fair amount of choice of occupation is available. This setting, pleasant and appropriate as it is for the majority of retarded adults, can be bewildering and frightening for those who are autistic. When an autistic person does settle in a centre it is usually because the supervisor is especially understanding and gives extra attention and help. Sometimes success is achieved because it is possible to arrange for one volunteer or a member of staff to look after the autistic person until he can manage on his own. Some adult training centres are beginning to have special care units attached in which the most retarded autistic adults can be placed. As with the schools, there are problems in mixing the physically handicapped with those who are disturbed and aggressive in behaviour. There may be a place in the adult training centre system for units which specialise in autism and related conditions.

Calculations of prevalence rates for adults are much more approximate than for children and adolescents, because no epidemiological study has been done for those over the age of 16. Extrapolating from the rates for children, and allowing for some who lose their handicaps as they mature and for some increased mortality due to associated neurological conditions, in a hypothetical area of 250,000 people there would be perhaps 140 adults who, as children, would have fitted the criteria for inclusion in the Camberwell group. On the basis of a follow-up study done by Rutter and his colleagues (Rutter and Lockyer, 1967; Rutter *et al.*, 1967; Rutter, 1970a) and allowing for some additional improvement with time in the group who are beginning to make a good adjustment by the time of early adult life, 2 might be in a vocational training unit of the type mentioned above; 6 might be in regular paid employment; a further 16 might be able to work in sheltered conditions with other kinds of handicapped people; 26 would probably be able to attend an adult training centre especially if some trained staff were available; the remaining 90 would be severely retarded and would need the facilities of a special care unit (see Table 12.1).

There is no area of the country where such large numbers of autistic adults have been diagnosed, since it is only in the last one or two decades that the label has been used at all widely. The question arises as to the whereabouts of the unidentified adults. The follow-up study mentioned above and that by DeMyer *et al.* (1973) do not suggest either that the numbers of adults known are much smaller than would be predicted because many lose their handicaps in later life, nor that the increased mortality would be sufficient to account for the discrepancy.

From the case histories known to the present author it seems that, in the past, undiagnosed autistic children and adults have been classified under a variety of administrative categories. Some are chronic patients in mental hospitals, probably labelled as schizophrenic, and others are in subnormality hospitals. It is likely that some with useful skills whose behaviour is not troublesome are living at home with their parents. They may have attended special or small private schools but may be unknown to the mental health services. A few are probably living a quiet, routine existence in lodgings or hostels and are employed in an undemanding low-level occupation.

With increasing interest in the autistic syndrome and with better diagnostic facilities this picture is likely to change in the future. As the children who are known to the services now become adolescent and adult there will be a growing demand for appropriate services.

Residential accommodation

The provision of residential accommodation should be considered separately from the need for education and occupation. In an integrated community service, appropriate accommodation for those who could not live with their own families would be provided in the local area and the residents would attend the same schools, workshops and day centres as those who were at home.

If an autistic child has a united family and parents who want him to stay at home, then this is the ideal environment for him. The family should be given every support to help to care for the handicapped child. The majority of autistic children are able to live at home but there are some who cannot do so for a variety of reasons including behaviour disturbance too severe for the parents to manage, harmful effects upon the siblings, ill health of the parents, or separation due to divorce or death.

Some autistic adults continue to live at home, but, with increasing age, the number needing accommodation away from home steadily rises.

At the moment the majority of placements are in mental subnormality or psychiatric hospitals, mainly the former. In a survey of 176 adolescents aged over 15 carried out by the National Society for Autistic Children (1973), 83 (48 per cent) were in residential care of some kind, of whom 71 (39 per cent) were in long-stay hospitals. This sample, being taken from members of the NSAC, was biased in favour of the more able children as is shown by the fact that 16 (9 per cent) were in open employment. It is likely that an epidemiological survey would show an even higher percentage in subnormality or psychiatric hospitals.

The other types of permanent accommodation currently available, apart from that provided by some special boarding schools during the school term, are homes run by private individuals or voluntary bodies, a few hostels run by local authorities or voluntary bodies, and some sheltered communities, notably those run by the Steiner organisation or by Cottage and Rural Enterprises (CARE). None of these are specifically for autistic children or adults. Most were set up for mentally retarded people or for those with chronic psychiatric illnesses. It is difficult to find places for children or adults with early childhood autism or related conditions since the homes and hostels are not usually geared for people who need a lot of organisation and supervision and whose behaviour might be difficult when small changes in routine occur. Most of the present sheltered communities need to have residents who can do productive work. The severely retarded autistic adults cannot meet this requirement and the mildly or moderately retarded, though often with good visuo-spatial skills, need special training and supervision before they can become reliable workers.

Placement in a long-stay hospital, although the most usual solution, is often by no means ideal. People with severe problems in communication are especially vulnerable in a situation where there are many residents and few staff and become either withdrawn or disturbed unless they can be given special help.

As is the case for educational provision, the best solution seems to be a wide range of alternatives so that the appropriate place can be found for each individual.

If the recommendations of the D.H.S.S. document *Better Services for the Mentally Handicapped* (1971) are put into effect, local authority social service departments will provide hostels for mentally retarded and mentally ill children and adults within each local community. If the staff had adequate training, some autistic children and adults would be able to fit into this environment, which would have the advantage of allowing the maintenance of close contact with the family.

In some areas, especially in large conurbations, there could be hostels which specialised in accepting autistic people and those with similar handicaps. These could serve several adjacent boroughs and be associated with the local day centres. Hostels of this kind would help the group of autistic people who do not need the type of care provided by a hospital but cannot mix easily with those who have other kinds of handicaps.

Another possibility is the sheltered community. Some mixed communities could experiment with a small number of autistic adults, especially if one or two of the staff are given some special training. However there is also a place for a few communities specialising in autism and related problems. These can take people with a range of severity of handicap and can include some who are too severely impaired to be accepted anywhere else except in long-term hospitals. The National Society for Autistic Children is helping to support such a community opened in 1974.

Even if residential provision of the kinds outlined above were plentiful, there will always be a substantial number of children and adults who are too severely retarded and difficult in behaviour to fit in. The majority of the latter cannot live at home with their parents and they are usually admitted to long-term hospitals. Only a small number who are physically ill, or have frequent fits, or seriously injure themselves need actual medical and nursing care. The rest need close supervision and expert behaviour management. The children need to be looked after by people who are experienced in child care.

On the other hand, there is a real dilemma about placing disturbed and aggressive people in residential accommodation outside hospitals. The local authority hostels are not usually staffed and equipped to manage them. It might well prove difficult to staff community homes which specialised in such difficult cases.

It looks as if, in the near future at any rate, the hospital service will have to continue to care for this group, although voluntary bodies, hospitals and local authorities might experiment with different types of provision. The sheltered conditions provided by long-term hospitals are in many ways very suitable for people who are disturbed in behaviour and who have no compensating skills. Doctors and nurses have the philosophical attitudes necessary for the acceptance of distressing problems such as incontinence, aggression and self injury. The trouble is that the accepting attitude can go too far and can shut out the possibility of training in more appropriate behaviour.

Some hospitals are experimenting with special units for children and adults of this kind. If the staff can be given appropriate training and can work together with psychologists who are skilled in behaviour modification, this type of unit could be most successful and acceptable to the parents and relatives. Much work still needs to be done on the problem of maintaining staff morale and preventing swings of attitude between unrealistic optimism and total pessimism.

It is very helpful for families who have handicapped children or adults living at home to know that short-term residential care in a suitable environment can be provided in a special emergency, or so that the rest of the family can have a regular holiday and occasional weekends to themselves. If this kind of relief can be obtained easily, it is more likely that the child or adult will be able to remain at home. All types of residential units should therefore have enough places to give this service as well as long-term care. It should also be possible for older children and adults living at home to spend an occasional evening at the local hostel so that the family can have an evening out together.

In an area of 250,000 total population there are likely to be 2 children under 16 who need accommodation in a hostel for mixed handicaps, and 2 who need the closer supervision of a hostel or school boarding department specialising in autistic children. There would be 11 children with no medical or nursing problems but who need very close supervision and a high staff ratio and 6 who, because of severe aggressive or self-injurious behaviour, might need to be in a hospital unit. Thus out of a total of 50 children under 16, 21 would be in residential care of whom the majority would be in the older age groups (see Table 12.1).

For the adults in a hypothetical population of 250,000 people in which all autistic people were known to the services, 4 places might be needed in hostels for mixed handicaps, 6 in a specialised hostel, and 4 in a sheltered community. A further 80 would need residential care with a high staff ratio and close supervision and 12 would need medical and nursing care in a hospital. Therefore, out of 140 adults, 106 would be in some kind of residential provision. In particular almost all the severely retarded adults with autism or related conditions would be cared for in hospitals or special units (see Table 12.1). This is the case at present, but the provision of good day facilities, regular short-term care and support and counselling for the parents might change the situation to some extent, although it is difficult to predict how much. It is important that the enthusiasm for community care should not lead to unrealistic demands being placed on the families of severely handicapped people.

As noted above, extra places should be available in all types of units to allow for holiday and emergency care.

Specialist services

It may be necessary to admit autistic children or adults to a psychiatric or subnormality hospital unit for a short stay in order to deal with specific problems. These include acute feeding problems which can occur in young autistic children, severe disturbances in behaviour, especially self mutilation, or for the treatment of frequent epileptic fits, if these cannot be dealt with on an out-patient basis. At present, there are only a few psychiatric residential units for children in the whole of the country and this presents great problems since a child may have to be admitted to a hospital a long way from his own home.

One interesting model unit has been set up by the joint Bethlem and Maudsley hospitals (Corbett, 1972b). Hilda Lewis House has 25 beds for mentally retarded children, especially those with severe behaviour disturbances. It serves mainly one area of London and it accepts children on a day or residential basis for short, medium, or long periods. The idea of the unit is to back up the local community services by dealing with crises in behaviour which might otherwise lead to long-term care. Behaviour modification programmes are planned and the parents, teachers and other professional workers involved with each child are able to work with the Hilda Lewis staff so that they can continue with the same methods when the child goes home. Children with autistic behaviour are among those who have been admitted and the idea of such a service is particularly suitable for children of this kind.

Autistic adolescents and adults who have made good progress sometimes become unhappily aware that they are different from other people. The same group may, like anyone else, become depressed or anxious in response to sad events in life such as bereavement. In these situations, psychotherapy may be of value.

It is important for the therapist to understand the impairments found in autism, especially the characteristic literal and concrete approach to everything. This may make for difficulties if complex interpretations are given or if analogies and metaphors are used to explain symptoms.

There is little likelihood of effecting any radical improvement in the underlying impairments through psychotherapy or any other form of treatment. The main aim should be to help the autistic person to accept himself as he is by emphasising the skills he has and the contribution he can make to the community. Great patience is needed since such reassurance, given in the simplest possible terms, will probably have to be repeated many times and will be needed each time a stressful situation occurs.

Sometimes autistic adolescents and adults develop a clinically recognizable depressive illness. They may need treatment with anti-depressive drugs and possibly admission to a psychiatric hospital. The combination of the autistic syndrome with depression can present a most puzzling picture to those who are unfamiliar with this problem. A knowledge of the handicaps and limitations of autistic adults is necessary in planning a programme of treatment and rehabilitation. Long-term psychiatric and social work support in close co-operation with the parents is needed after discharge from in-patient or out-patient care.

Handicapped children and adults need general medical and dental care. In theory, they are able to obtain this on the National Health Service. In practice, problems of transport and of difficult behaviour during examination and treatment make parents reluctant to ask for help. Long waits in the waiting-room are a particular strain for an autistic child. Practical teaching about chronic conditions, including those affecting behaviour, given in the medical schools, might help future generations of family doctors and specialists to consider ways in which they could alleviate the difficulties met by families seeking treatment for a handicapped person.

Dental care is another special hazard. Most autistic children refuse to co-operate when they first see a dentist, but, with time and patience continued over many visits, they may eventually come to trust the person they know and allow some procedures to be carried out without general anaesthesia. Since dentists are paid for the treatment they give and not for the time they spend in getting to know the patient, it is not easy to find this approach to treatment on the National Health Service.

One London hospital set up an experimental unit for handicapped children. This was a well-equipped van which visited all special schools and units in the local boroughs at frequent intervals. The children got to know the dentist and much preventive care was possible as well as treatment of caries (Pool, 1972). This type of service is invaluable and could be put into operation everywhere.

Speech therapists are now trained to cope with all kinds of language problems and not just difficulties of articulation. They therefore can play an important part in the education of autistic children. One or two schools for children with autism or other language problems have speech therapists who are on the staff as teachers. Their special expertise is handed on to the other teaching staff while their own experience in the classroom ensures that their suggestions are appropriate for the school situation.

Autistic children have great difficulty in copying and learning skilled movements (see Chapter 6). This limits the extent and decreases the range of activities available to the children. Some physio-therapists and remedial gymnasts have taken a special interest in this field. Music therapists are also beginning to work with autistic children, capitalising on the almost universal fascination for music that they show in order to develop other skills and to improve social relationships.

Often speech therapists, physio-therapists and music therapists are in very short supply. Their skills may be best used in showing parents, teachers, nurses, and other staff how to carry on the work between occasional visits from the professional experts in these fields.

Occupational therapists are needed in various parts of the comprehensive service. If they have had experience with autistic people their skills would make them eminently suitable for running specialised day centres for adults both in the long-term care hospitals and in the units which give short-term care for specific problems. An occupational therapist, with her knowledge of practical crafts and her ingenuity in utilising available materials is especially well placed to help autistic children and adults whose skills are manual rather than verbal.

The important parts played by psychologists and by social workers have already been dealt with under other sections of this chapter.

Leisure and recreation

Leisure activities are difficult to organise for people with problems in communication (Dewey, 1973b). The social clubs for mentally retarded children and adults attract mainly those with Down's syndrome or the moderately retarded person who can converse even if only at a limited level. Plays, films, television and radio have limited or no appeal to those who do not have enough inner language to appreciate stories.

On the whole, the most acceptable pursuits are those involving physical activity such as swimming or horse riding, and those involving music. A few of the most able children and adults can learn to play musical instruments. A larger number learn to enjoy entertainments such as concerts, opera and musical shows. Circuses, cartoon films and slap-stick comedies may also be appreciated since the verbal content is minimal and the pleasure is in watching the action.

The most profoundly retarded autistic children and adults are too handicapped to take part in any kind of leisure pursuit. For the rest, there is a place for some special social clubs, perhaps associated with a school or day centre, which organise appropriate activities and have sufficient helpers to ensure that all the members can join in. These would have to draw people from a wide area to find sufficient members.

Staff training

The need for training in methods of working with autistic children and adults and others with severe language problems has been emphasised all through this chapter. A great deal is now known in this field and could be taught to those who are professionally involved.

Teachers would feel much more confident in their work with autistic children if they were given specialised training. In a recent survey carried out by the National Society for Autistic Children, teachers in special education were almost unanimous in their feeling that a special course was needed in this field. A course concentrating on autism alone would be far too narrow, but one which dealt with the whole range of impairments that can affect language development would be most appropriate. It would be of value to teachers in all kinds of special schools and in schools for normal children. The placing of autistic and similar children in non-specialist schools would be a much more realistic proposition if there were some members of the staff who understood the problems and could give helpful advice. Interest in post-graduate courses in this field for teachers is growing in some colleges and institutes of education and it is to be hoped that plans for these will soon be put into practice.

Training is also needed for social workers, supervisors of day centres and workshops, and for hostel staff. These all come under the social services departments of local authorities. The new plans for social work training and the possibility of specialising after the basic generic course should, if appropriate courses are organised within this framework, provide an opportunity for people who are interested to become expert in this field.

All the other specialists that have been mentioned, including doctors and nurses, need the opportunity to acquire the necessary skills if they are going to work with people with severe language problems. The undergraduate training should include an introduction to the field but more concentrated courses for those already qualified are needed. One suggestion that can be made is for training programmes which, for the first part at least, are multi-disciplinary and involve all the relevant professions, while the later parts could perhaps be more specialised. All possibilities have to be explored and tested in practice. The voluntary societies have a role here in stimulating interest in training and even in running experimental courses themselves, although the major part of training must, in the end, be provided by appropriate professional organisations.

Integration of services

A comprehensive plan for services for autistic children and adults involves workers from the education, health and social services department and frequently various voluntary bodies as well. At present the services which will accept people with this type of handicap are so scarce that placements are often made far away from the family and the local community. An integrated service does not therefore exist as yet.

If the community services suggested by the DHSS for mentally handicapped people are developed, then integration becomes a possibility. It can be achieved only if the various statutory and voluntary bodies involved develop the habit of working together and manage to solve the major problems of passing information from one department to another. Ideally, there should be teams containing members of all the relevant professions, perhaps based on the local assessment centre for handicapped children, but in close contact with the schools and other units in the area. Within one community these teams could be area based or else specialise in certain types of problems. Either way it should be possible for the handicapped children referred by the family doctors and welfare clinics to be seen eventually by people who have the appropriate special experience. For some of the rarer problems, referral to regional assessment centres might be necessary but the system should work smoothly with no awkward gaps.

The team's responsibility should not cease after the first diagnosis, assessment and placement. Supervision should continue so that help is available in any crisis and at the major changing points of life such as entering and leaving school. A complex network of professional relationships involving schools, hostels, workshops, day centres, hospitals and sheltered communities as well as the assessment centre, on an informal as well as a formal level, is necessary if the system is to work well. The need for assessment and supervision to continue into adult life was mentioned earlier. It is relevant to many other chronic handicaps as well as early childhood autism.

The organisation necessary for a smoothly working service of this kind, even on a purely local level, is formidable in its complexity. It is, however, a worthwhile goal and would ensure a high morale among the staff and peace of mind for the parents, as well as giving good care to the handicapped people themselves.

Voluntary organisations

Voluntary organisations working on behalf of handicapped children and adults carry out a variety of activities including education of the public, support for the parents and families, pressing for improvement in legal rights and services, and actually providing some specialised services.

The National Society for Autistic Children (which is also concerned with adults) has a partly parent and partly professional membership and undertakes all the above activities. In its first 10 years it concentrated on setting up specialised schools and it is now turning its attention to the needs of adolescents and adults.

A partnership between the state and a voluntary body, in which the latter sets up a school, a day centre, a sheltered community or other service and the former pays fees for people to attend, works very well. The voluntary organisation can experiment with new ideas whereas the statutory authorities have to be much more cautious. The latter can follow in the footsteps of the voluntary bodies if the experiments are successful and they can also learn from the failures.

The Role of the Parents

Although well planned services can do much to relieve the problems faced by families of handicapped children, the final responsibility must rest with the parents. A united and caring family is more important than any of the other factors which help such children to achieve their full potential. This is true for any handicapped child (not to mention normal children) but it has special relevance for children whose handicaps affect language and social communication. They have a special need for individual attention from adults who have a detailed understanding of their particular problems and their particular skills. Professional workers can give devoted care to the children in their charge, but the demands of a career and a variety of other factors make it highly unlikely that anyone other than a child's own parents can provide continuity over all the years of childhood and part of adult life as well.

Many parents, for very good reasons, are unable to look after their handicapped children, but a substantial number are both able and willing. These families should be encouraged and helped by the services. Ways should be found of making the best use of this "parent power" not only for the individual child but also in the organisation of the community services as a whole. The suspicious rivalry that sometimes seems to develop between parents and teachers or other professional workers is to be deplored as a sad waste of valuable energy.

It is to be hoped that the modern idea of encouraging consumer participation will produce constructive co-operation between everyone involved in services for the handicapped.

REFERENCES

(Abbreviations as in Index Medicus 1973)

Aaran, J. M., Portmann, C. C., Delauney, J., Perlerin, J., and Lenoir, J. (1969) The electrocochleogram: methods and results in children, *Rev. Laryngol. Otol. Rhinol. (Bord.)* **90**, 615.

Ainsworth, M. (1962) *Deprivation of Maternal Care*, Public Health Papers, No. 14, WHO, Geneva.

Allen, J., DeMyer, M. K., Norton, J. A., Pontius, W., and Yang, E. (1971) Intellectuality in parents of psychotic, subnormal and normal children, *J. Autism Child. Schizophrenia* **1**, 311.

Alpern, G. D. (1967) Measurement of "untestable" autistic children, *J. Abnorm. Psychol.* **72**, 478.

Anthony, E. J. (1958a) An aetiological approach to the diagnosis of psychosis in childhood, *Rev. Psychiatry Infant* **25**, 89.

Anthony, E. J. (1958b) An experimental approach to the psychopathology of childhood autism, *Br. J. Med. Psychol.* **31**, 211.

Anthony, E. J. (1962) Low-grade psychosis in childhood, *in* Richards, B. W. (eds.) *Proc. London Conf. Scientific Study Ment. Defic. Vol. 2*, May and Baker, Dagenham.

Argyle, M. (1972) Non-verbal communication in human social interaction, *in* Hinde, R. A. (ed.) *Non-Verbal Communication*, University Press, London.

Asperger, H. (1944) Die autistischen Psychopathen im Kindesalter, *Arch. Psychiatr. Nervenkr.* **117**, 76.

Asperger, H. (1960) *Autistisches Verhalten im Kindesalter in Jahrbuch für Jugendpsychiatrie und ihre Grundgebiete*, Hrsg v. W. Villinger, Stuttgart.

Attneave, F., and Benson, B. (1969) Spatial coding of tactual stimulation, *J. Exp. Psychol.* **81**, 216.

Banks, M., and Locke, B. J. (1966) Self injurious stereotypies and mild punishment with retarded subjects, *Working Paper No. 123*, Parsons Research Project, University of Kansas (cited by Gardner, 1969).

Baroff, G. S. (1974) *Mental Retardation: Nature, Cause, and Management*, Hemisphere, Washington, D.C.

Bartak, L., and Rutter, M. (1971) Educational treatment of autistic children, *in* Rutter, M. (ed.) *Infantile Autism: Concepts, Characteristics and Treatment*, Churchill, London.

Bartak, L., and Rutter, M. (1973) Special educational treatment of autistic children: a comparative study—1. Design of study and characteristics of units, *J. Child Psychol. Psychiatry* **14**, 161.

Bayley, N. (1969) *Bayley Scales of Infant Development*, Psychological Corporation, New York.

Beagley, H. A. (1973) Personal communication.

Beery, K. E. (1967) *Developmental Test of Visual-Motor Integration: Administration and Scoring Manual*, Follett Educational Corp., Chicago.

319

Bender, L. (1947) One hundred cases of childhood schizophrenia treated with electric shock, *Trans. Am. Neurol. Assoc.* **72**, 165.

Bender, L. (1955) The development of a schizophrenic child treated with electric convulsions at three years of age, *in* Caplan, G. (ed.) *Emotional Problems of Early Childhood*, Basic Books, New York.

Bender, L. (1956) Schizophrenia in childhood, *Am. J. Orthopsychiatry* **26**, 499.

Bender, L., and Keeler, W. R. (1952) The body image of schizophrenic children following electroshock therapy, *Am. J. Orthopsychiatry* **22**, 335.

Bergès, J., and Lézine, I. (1965) *The Imitation of Gestures*, trans. Parmelle, A. H. Clinics in Developmental Medicine No. 18, Heinemann, London.

Bettelheim, B. (1959) Feral children and autistic children, *Am. J. Sociol.* **64**, 455.

Bettelheim, B. (1967) *The Empty Fortress*, Collier-Macmillan, London.

Blackwood, R. O. (1962) *Operant Conditioning as a Method of Training the Mentally Retarded*, Unpublished Doctoral Dissertation, Ohio State University (cited by Gardner, 1969).

Bleuler, E. (1919) *Das Autistisch—Undisziplinierte Denken in der Mediziin und seine Überwindung*, Springer, Berlin.

Bleuler, E. (1950) *Dementia Praecox or the Group of Schizophrenias*, trans. Zinkin, J. International Universities Press, New York.

Bone, M., Spain, B., and Martin, F. (1972) *Plans and Provisions for the Mentally Handicapped*, National Institute for Social Work Training Series No. 23, Allen and Unwin, London.

Bonvallet, M., and Allen, M. B. (1963) Prolonged spontaneous and evoked activation following discrete bulbar lesions, *Electroencephalogr. Clin. Neurophysiol.* **15**, 969.

Böök, J. A., Nichtern, S., Gruenberg, E. (1963) Cytogenetical investigations in childhood schizophrenia, *Acta Psychiatr. Scand.* **39**, 309.

Bosch, G. (1962) *Der Frühkindliche Autismus*, Springer, Berlin.

Bosch, G. (1970) *Infantile Autism*, trans. Jordan, D. and I. Springer, Berlin.

Boullin, D. J., Coleman, M., and O'Brien, R. A. (1970) Abnormalities in platelet 5-hydroxytryptamine efflux in patients with infantile autism, *Nature*, **226**, 371.

Boullin, D. J., Coleman, M., O'Brien, R. A., and Rimland, B. (1971) Laboratory predictions of infantile autism based on 5-hydroxytryptamine efflux from blood platelets and their correlation with the Rimland E-2 score, *J. Autism Child. Schizophrenia* **1**, 63.

Bowlby, J. (1952) *Maternal Care and Mental Health*, W.H.O., Geneva.

Bradley, C. (1942) Biography of a schizophrenic child, *Nerv. Child* **1**, 141.

Brady, J. P. (1971) Drugs in behaviour therapy, *in* Masserman, J. M. (ed.) *Current Psychiatric Therapies*, Vol II, Grune and Stratton, New York.

Brask, B. H. (1970) A prevalence investigation of childhood psychosis, Paper given at *The 16th Scandinavian Congress of Psychiatry*.

Bricker, W. A., and Bricker, D. (1973) Behaviour modification programmes, *in* Mittler, P. (ed.) *Assessment for Learning in the Mentally Handicapped*, Churchill, London.

Bricker, D., Bricker, W. A., and Larsen, L. A. (1968) *Operant Audiometry for Difficult to Test Children*, Papers and Reports, Vol. 5, No. 19, Institute on Mental Retardation and Intellectual Development, Nashville, Tennessee.

Brown, R. (1965) *Social Psychology*, MacMillan, London.

Bryson, C. Q. (1972) Short-term memory and cross-model information processing in autistic children, *J. Learning Disabilities* **5**, 81.

Bucher, B., and Lovaas, O. I. (1968) Use of aversive stimulation in behaviour modification, *in* Jones, M. R. (ed.) *Miami Symposium on the Prediction of Behaviour, 1967: Aversive Stimulation*, University of Miami Press, Florida (cited by Gardner, 1969.)

Campbell, M., Fish, B., Korein, J., Shapiro, T., Collins, P., and Koh, C. (1972) Lithium and chlorpromazine. A controlled crossover study of hyperactive severely disturbed young children, *J. Autism Child. Schizophrenia* **2**, 234.

Campbell, M., Fish, B., Shapiro, T., and Floyd, A. (1971) Imipramine in pre-school autistic and schizophrenic children, *J. Autism Child. Schizophrenia* **3**, 267.

Chess, S. (1971) Autism in children with congenital rubella, *J. Autism Child. Schizophrenia* **1**, 33.

Churchill, D. W. (1971) Effects of success and failure in psychotic children, *Arch. Gen. Psychiatry* **25**, 208.

Churchill, D. W. (1972) The relationship of infantile autism and early childhood schizophrenia to developmental language disorders of childhood, *J. Autism Child. Schizophrenia* **2**, 182.

Clancy, H., Dugdale, A., and Rendle-Short, J. (1969a) The diagnosis of infantile autism, *Dev. Med. Child Neurol.* **11**, 432.

Clancy, H., Entsch, M., and Rendle-Short, J. (1969b) Infantile autism—the correction of feeding abnormalities, *Dev. Med. Child Neurol.* **11**, 569.

Clarke, A. D. B. (1972) Commentary on Koluchova's "Severe deprivation in twins: a case study," *J. Child Psychol. Psychiatry* **13**, 103.

Conrad, R. (1962) An association between memory errors due to acoustic masking of speech, *Nature*, **193**, 1313.

Cooper, A. J., Ismail, A. A. A., Phanjoo, A. L., and Love, D. L. (1972) Antiandrogen (cyproterone acetate) therapy in deviant hypersexuality, *Br. J. Psychiatry* **120**, 59.

Copeland, J., and Hodges, J. (1973) *For the Love of Ann*, Arrow Books, London.

Corbett, J. A. (1972a) Drug and behavioural treatment of mentally handicapped children, *Br. J. Hosp. Med.* **8**, 141.

Corbett, J. (1972b) Hilda Lewis House, *in* Wing, J. K., and Hailey, A. M. (eds.) *Evaluating a Community Psychiatric Service*, Oxford University Press, London.

Corbett, J., and Radford, M. (1975) Disturbed behaviour in severely mentally retarded adults (to be published).

Crawley, C. A. (1971) Infantile autism—an hypothesis, *J. Ir. Med. Assoc.* **64**, 335.

Creak, E. M. (Chairman) (1961) Schizophrenic syndrome in childhood: progress report of a working party (April, 1961), *Cerebral Palsy Bull.* **3**, 501.

Creak, E. M. (1963) Childhood psychosis. A review of 100 cases, *Br. J. Psychiatry* **109**, 84.

Creak, M. (1964) Schizophrenic syndrome in childhood: further progress report of a working party, *Dev. Med. Child Neurol.* **6**, 530.

Creak, M., and Ini, S. (1960) Families of psychotic children, *J. Child Psychol. Psychiatry* **1**, 156.

Crystal, D. (1970) Prosodic systems and language acquisition, *in* Leon, P. (ed.) *Prosodic Feature Analysis*, Didier, Paris.

Davis, H. (1968) Average evoked response audiometry in N. America, *Acta Otolaryngol. (Stockh.)* **65**, 79.

Davis, K. V., Sprague, R. L., and Werry, J. B. (1969) Stereotyped behaviour and activity level in severe retardates, *Am. J. Ment. Defic.* **73**, 721.

Deberdt, R. (1971) Benperidol (R4584) in the treatment of sexual offenders, *Acta. Psychiatr. Belg.* **71**, 396.

DeMyer, M. K. (1971) Perceptual limitations in autistic children and their relation to social and intellectual deficits, *in* Rutter, M. (ed.) *Infantile Autism: Concepts, Characteristics and Treatment,* Churchill, London.

DeMyer, M. K., Alpern, G. D., Barton, S., DeMyer, W. E., Churchill, D. W., Hingtgen, J. N., Bryson, C. Q., Pontius, W., and Kimberlin, C. (1972a) Imitation in autistic, early schizophrenic, and non-psychotic subnormal children, *J. Autism Child. Schizophrenia* **2**, 264.

DeMyer, M. K., Barton, S., Alpern, G. D., Kimberlin, C., Allen, J., Yang, E., and Steele, R. (1974) The measured intelligence of autistic children, *J. Autism Child. Schizophrenia* **4**, 42.

DeMyer, M. K., Barton, S., DeMyer, W. E., Norton, J. A., Allen, J., and Steele, R. (1973) Prognosis in autism: a follow-up study, *J. Autism Child. Schizophrenia* **3**, 199.

DeMyer, M. K., Barton, S., and Norton, J. A. (1972b) A comparison of adaptive, verbal, and motor profiles of psychotic and non-psychotic subnormal children, *J. Autism Child. Schizophrenia* **2**, 359.

DeMyer, M. K., Churchill, D. W., Pontius, W., and Gilkey, K. M. (1971a) A comparison of five diagnostic systems for childhood schizophrenia and infantile autism, *J. Autism Child. Schizophrenia* **1**, 175.

DeMyer, M. K., Norton, J. A., and Barton, S. (1971b) Social and adaptive behaviours of autistic children as measured in a structured psychiatric interview, *in* Churchill, D. W., Alpern, G. D., and DeMyer, M. K. (eds.) *Infantile Autism: Proceedings of the Indiana University Colloquium,* Charles C. Thomas, Springfield, Illinois.

DeMyer, M. K., Pontius, W., Norton, J. A., Barton, S., Allen, J., and Steele, R. (1972c) Parental practices and innate activity in normal, autistic, and brain-damaged infants, *J. Autism Child. Schizophrenia* **2**, 49.

DeMyer, M. K., Schwier, H., Bryson, C. Q., Solow, E., and Roeske, N. (1971c) Free fatty acid response to insulin and glucose stimulation in schizophrenic, autistic and emotionally disturbed children, *J. Autism Child. Schizophrenia* **1**, 436.

Department of Health and Social Security (1971) *Better Services for the Mentally Handicapped. Cmnd. 4683,* H.M.S.O., London.

Des Lauriers, A. M., and Carlson, C. F. (1969) *Your Child is Asleep,* Dorsey, Illinois.

Despert, J. L. (1951) Some considerations relating to the genesis of autistic behaviour in children, *Am. J. Orthopsychiatry* **21**, 335.

Despert, J. L. (1955) Differential diagnosis between obsessive-compulsive neurosis and schizophrenia in children, *in* Hoch, P., and Zubin, J. (eds.) *Psychopathology of Childhood,* Grune and Stratton, New York.

Dewey, M. A. (1973a) Vocational guidance for former autistic children, *Communication,* **4**, 67.

Dewey, M. A. (1973b) *Recreation for Autistic and Emotionally Disturbed Children,* U.S. Dept. of Health, Education and Welfare, Public Health Service, Rockville, Maryland.

Diner, H. (1971) Dentistry, *in* Wortis, J. (ed.) *Mental Retardation, Vol. III,* Grune and Stratton, New York.

Doehring, D. G. (1960) Visual spatial memory in aphasic children, *J. Speech Hear. Res.* **3**, 138.

Doueck, E. (1973) Crossed Acoustic Response, Paper read at *Third Symposium of the International Electric Response Audiometry Study Group*, Bordeaux.

Dunn, L. M. (1965) *Expanded Manual Peabody Picture Vocabulary Test*, American Guidance Service, Minneapolis.

Egan, D., Illingsworth, R. S., and MacKeith, R. C. (1969) *Developmental Screening 0–5 Years*, Clinics in Developmental Medicine No. 30, Heinemann, London.

Eisenberg, L. (1956) The autistic child in adolescence, *Am. J. Orthopsychiatry* **112**, 607.

Eisenberg, L. (1957a) The course of childhood schizophrenia, *Arch. Neurol. Psychiatry* **78**, 69.

Eisenberg, L. (1957b) Fathers of autistic children, *Am. J. Orthopsychiatry* **27**, 715.

Elgar, S., and Wing, L. (1969) *Teaching Autistic Children*, College of Special Education and N.S.A.C., London.

Everard, M. P. (ed.) (1975) *An Approach to Teaching Autistic Children*, Pergamon, Oxford.

Ferster, C. B. (1961) Positive reinforcement and behavioral deficits of autistic children, *Child. Dev.* **32**, 437.

Fish, B. (1968) Drug use in psychiatric disorders in children, *Am. J. Psychiatry* **124** (Suppl. 8), 31.

Fish, B. (1971) Contributions of developmental research to a theory of schizophrenia, *Except. Infant* **2**, 473.

Frankenburg, W. K., and Dodds, J. B. (1967) The Denver development screening test, test, *J. Pediatr.* **71**, 181.

Fraser, G. M., and Blockley, J. (1973) *The Language Disordered Child: A New Look at Theory and Treatment*, N.F.E.R., Windsor, Berks.

Freeman, D. G. (1966) The effects of kinesthetic stimulation on weight gain and on smiling in premature infants, Paper presented at the *Annual Meeting of the American Orthopsychiatric Association*, San Francisco.

Freeman, R. D. (1970) Psychopharmacology and the retarded child, *in* Menolascino, F. (ed.) *Psychiatric Approaches to Mental Retardation*, Basic Books, New York.

Frith, U. (1970a) Studies in pattern detection in normal and autistic children: reproduction and production of colour sequences, *J. Exp. Child Psychol.* **10**, 120.

Frith, U. (1970b) Studies in pattern perception in normal and autistic children: immediate recall of auditory sequences, *J. Abnorm. Psychol.* **76**, 413.

Frith, U., and Hermelin, B. (1969) The role of visual and motor cues for normal, subnormal and autistic children, *J. Child Psychol.* **10**, 153.

Gardner, W. I. (1969) Use of punishment procedures with the severely retarded: a review, *Am. J. Ment. Defic.* **74**, 86.

Gellner, L. (1959) *A Neurophysiological Concept of Mental Retardation and its Educational Implications*, J. D. Levinson Research Foundation, Chicago.

Geschwind, N. (1965) Disconnexion syndromes in animals and man. Part II, *Brain* **88**, 585.

Gesell, A. (1941) *Wolf Child and Human Child*, Harper and Row, New York.

Gesell, A., and Amatruda, C. S. (1965) *Normal and Abnormal Child Development, Clinical Methods and Pediatric Applications* (*second edition*), Harper and Row, New York.

Gesell, A. L., Halverson, M. M., and Amatruda, C. (1940) *The First Five Years of Life*, Harper and Row, New York.

Gesell, A., and Ilg, F. L. (1946) *The Child From Five to Ten*, Harper and Row, New York.

Gillies, Susan., Mittler, P., and Simon, G. B. (1963) Some characteristics of a group of psychotic children and their families, *Br. Psychol. Soc. Conference Proceedings*, Reading.

Gittelman, M., and Birch, H. G. (1967) Childhood schizophrenia: intellect, neurologic status, perinatal risk, prognosis, and family pathology, *Arch. Gen. Psychiatry* 17, 16.

Goldfarb, W. (1961) *Childhood Schizophrenia*, Harvard University Press, Cambridge, Mass.

Goldfarb, W. (1964) An investigation of childhood schizophrenia, *Arch. Gen. Psychiatry* 2, 620.

Goodwin, M. S., Cowen, M. A., and Goodwin, T. A. (1971) Malabsorption and cerebral dysfunction: a multivariate and comparative study of autistic children, *J. Autism Child. Schizophrenia* 1, 48.

Griffiths, P. (1972) *Developmental Aphasia: An Introduction*, Invalid Children's Aid Association, London.

Gruhle, H. W. (1929) *Psychologie der Schizophrenie*, Springer, Berlin.

Hamilton, J., and Standahl, J. (1967) Suppression of stereotyped screaming behaviour in a profoundly retarded institutionalised female, *Unpublished paper*, Gracewood State School, Georgia (cited by Gardner, 1969.)

Hamilton, H., Stephens, L., and Allen, P. (1967) Controlling aggressive and destructive behaviour in severely retarded institutionalised residents, *Am. J. Ment. Defic.* 71, 852.

Harlow, H. F. (1960) Primary affectional patterns in primates, *Am. J. Orthopsychiatry* 30, 676.

Harlow, H. F. (1961) The development of affectional patterns in infant monkeys, *in* Foss, B. M. (ed.) *Determinants of Infant Behaviour*, Methuen, London.

Haslam, J. (1809) *Observations on Madness and Melancholy*, Hayden, London.

Heeley, A. F., and Roberts, G. E. (1965) Tryptophan metabolism in psychotic children, *Dev. Med. Child Neurol.* 7, 46.

Hermelin, B. (1966) Psychological research, *in* Wing, J. K. (ed.) *Early Childhood Autism (First edition)*, Pergamon, Oxford.

Hermelin, B., and O'Connor, N. (1970) *Psychological Experiments with Autistic Children*, Pergamon, London.

Hermelin, B., and O'Connor, N. (1971) Spatial coding in normal, autistic and blind children, *Percep. Mot. Skills* 33, 127.

Himwich, H. E., Jenkins, R. L., Fujimore, M., Narasimhachari, N., and Ebersole, M. (1972) A biochemical study of early infantile autism, *J. Autism Child. Schizophrenia* 2, 114.

Hingtgen, J. N., and Churchill, D. W. (1969) Identification of perceptual limitations in mute autistic children, *Arch. Gen. Psychiatry* 21, 68.

Hirsh, I. J. (1967) Information processing in in-put channels for speech and language: the significance of serial order of stimuli, *in* Darley, F. D. (ed.) *Brain Mechanisms Underlying Speech and Language*, Grune and Stratton, New York.

Hirsh, I. J., Bilger, R. C., and Deatherage, B. (1956) The effects of auditory and visual backgrounds on apparent duration, *Am. J. Psychol.* 69, 561.

Howard, I. P., and Templeton, W. B. (1966) *Human Spatial Orientation*, Wiley, New York.

Howlin, P., Marchant, R., Rutter, M., Berger, M., Hersov, L., and Yule, W. (1973) A home-based approach to the treatment of autistic children, *J. Autism Child. Schizophrenia* **3**, 308.

Hutt, S. J., and Hutt, C. (eds.) (1970) *Behaviour Studies in Psychiatry*, Pergamon, Oxford.

Hutt, S. J., Hutt, C., Lee, D., and Ounsted, C. (1964) Arousal and childhood autism, *Nature* **204**, 908.

Hutt, S. J., Hutt, C., Lee, D., and Ounsted, C. (1965) A behavioural and electroencephalographic study of autistic children, *J. Psychiatr. Res.* **3**, 181.

Ingram, T. T. S. (1959) Specific developmental disorders of speech in childhood, *Brain* **82**, 450.

Ingram, T. T. S. (1969) Disorders of speech in childhood, *Br. J. Hosp. Med.* **2** 1608–1625.

Ingram, T. T. S. (1972) The classification of speech and language disorders in young children, in Rutter, M., and Martin, J. A. M. (eds.) *The Child with Delayed Speech*, Clinics in Developmental Medicine No. 43, Heinemann, London.

Inhelder, B., and Piaget, J. (1964) *The Early Growth of Logic in the Child: Classification and Seriation*, Routledge and Kegan Paul, London.

Itard, J. M. G. (1801, 1807a) Mémoire et rapport sur Victor de l'Aveyron, in Malson, L., *Les Enfants Sauvages*, Union Generale d'Editions, Paris, 1964.

Itard, J. M. G. (1801, 1807b) *The Wild Boy of Aveyron*, Eng. trans. of two reports by G. and M. Humphrey, 1932, Appleton-Century-Crofts, New York, 1962.

Itard, J. M. G. (1801, 1807c) *Of the First Developments of the Young Savage of Aveyron*, Eng. trans. 1802, and *Report on the Progress of Victor of Aveyron*, Eng. trans. by Joan White, NLB, London, 1972. (Published together with L. Malson, *Wolf Children.*)

Jenkins, J. (1973) Treatment of self-injurious behaviour, *Proc. R. Soc. Med.* **66**, 1141.

Jesperson, O. (1922) *Language—Its Development, Nature and Origin*, Henry Holt, New York.

Kallman, F. G., and Roth, B. (1956) Genetic aspects of pre-adolescent schizophrenia, *Am. J. Psychiatry* **112**, 599.

Kanner, L. (1943) Autistic disturbances of affective contact, *Nerv. Child* **2**, 217.

Kanner, L. (1946) Irrelevant and metaphorical language in early infantile autism, *Am. J. Psychiatry* **103**, 242.

Kanner, L. (1949) Problems of nosology and psychodynamics in early childhood autism, *Am. J. Orthopsychiatry* **19**, 416.

Kanner, L. (1954) To what extent is early childhood autism determined by constitutional inadequacies? *Proc. Assoc. Res. Nerv. Ment. Dis.* **33**, 378.

Kanner, L. (1959) Trends in child psychiatry, *J. Ment. Sci.* **105**, 581.

Kanner, L. (1968) Early infantile autism revisited, *Psychiatry Digest* **29**, 17.

Kanner, L. (1969) The children haven't read those books, *Acta Paedopsychiatr.* **36**, 2.

Kanner, L. (1973) *Childhood Psychosis: Initial Studies and New Insights*, Winston, Washington.

Kanner, L., and Eisenberg, L. (1955) Notes on the follow-up studies of autistic children, in Hoch, P. H., and Zubin, J. (eds.) *Psychopathology of Childhood*, Grune and Stratton, New York.

Kanner, L., and Eisenberg, L. (1956) Early infantile autism 1943–1955, *Am. J. Orthopsychiatry* **26**, 55.

Kanner, L., and Lesser, L. I. (1958) Early infantile autism, *Pediatr. Clin. North Am.* **5**, 711.

Keeler, W. R. (1958) Autistic patterns and defective communication in blind children with retrolental fibroplasia, *in* Hoch, P., and Zubin, J. (eds.) *Psychopathology of Communication*, Grune and Stratton, New York.

Kimura, D. (1964) Left-right differences in the perception of melodies, *Q. J. Exp. Psychol.* **16**, 355.

Knobloch, H., and Pasamanick, B. (1962) Etiologic factors in "early infantile autism" and "childhood schizophrenia", Paper given at *10th International Congress of Pediatrics*, Lisbon, Portugal.

Koegal, R. L., and Covert, A. (1972) The relationship of self stimulation and learning in autistic children, *J. Appl. Behav. Res.* **5**, 381.

Koegal, R., and Schreibman, L. (1974) The role of stimulus variables in teaching autistic children, *in* Lovaas, O. I. and Bucher, B. (eds.) *Readings in Behaviour Modification with Deviant Children*, in press.

Koluchova, J. (1972) Severe deprivation in twins: a case study, *J. Child Psychol. Psychiatry* **13**, 107.

Kolvin, I. (1971a) Diagnostic criteria and classification of childhood psychoses, *Br. J. Psychiatry* **118**, 381.

Kolvin, I. (1971b) Psychoses in childhood—a comparative study, *in* Rutter, M. (ed.) *Infantile Autism: Concepts, Characteristics and Treatment*, Churchill, London.

Kolvin, I., Ounsted, C., Humphrey, M., and McNay, A. (1971a) The phenomenology of childhood psychoses, *Br. J. Psychiatry* **118**, 385.

Kolvin, I., Ounsted, C., Richardson, L., and Garside, R. F. (1971b) The family and social background in childhood psychoses, *Br. J. Psychiatry* **118**, 396.

Kolvin, I., Garside, R. F., and Kidd, J. S. H. (1971c) Parental personality and attitude and childhood psychosis, *Br. J. Psychiatry* **118**, 403.

Kolvin, I., Ounsted, C., and Roth, M. (1971d) Cerebral dysfunction and childhood psychosis, *Br. J. Psychiatry* **118**, 407.

Kolvin, I., Humphrey, M., and McNay, A. (1971e) Cognitive factors in childhood psychoses, *Br. J. Psychiatry* **118**, 415.

Kozloff, U. A. (1973) *Reaching the Autistic Child: a Parent Training Program*, Research Press, Illinois.

Kretschmer, E. (1942) *Körperbau und Charakter*, p. 165, Springer, Berlin.

Laufer, M. W., and Gair, D. S. (1969) Childhood schizophrenia, *in* Bellak, L., and Loeb, L. (eds.) *The Schizophrenic Syndrome*, Grune and Stratton, New York.

Lenneberg, E. H. (1967) *Biological Foundations of Language*, Wiley, New York.

Levett, L. M. (1970) *A Method of Communication for Non-Speaking Severely Subnormal Children*, Spastics Society, London.

Lobascher, M. E., Kingerlee, P. E., and Gubbay, S. S. (1970) Childhood autism: an investigation of aetiological factors in twenty-five cases, *Br. J. Psychiatry* **117**, 525.

Lockyer, L., and Rutter, M. (1969) A five to fifteen-year follow-up study of infantile psychosis: III Psychological aspects, *Br. J. Psychiatry* **115**, 865.

Lotter, V. (1966) Epidemiology of autistic conditions in young children: I Prevalence, *Soc. Psychiatry* **1**, 124.

Lotter, V. (1967a) Epidemiology of autistic conditions in young children: II Some characteristics of the parents and children, *Soc. Psychiatry* **1**, 163.

Lotter, V. (1967b) *The Prevalence of the Autistic Syndrome in Children*, Ph.D. Thesis, University of London.

Lovaas, O. I. (1966) A programme for the establishment of speech in echolalic children, *in* Wing, J. K. (ed.) *Early Childhood Autism*, Pergamon, Oxford.

Lovaas, O. I. (1973) *Discussion at Behaviour Modification Workshop*, University College of North Wales, Bangor.

Lovaas, O. I., Berbereich, J. P., Perloff, B. F., and Schaeffer, B. (1966) Acquisition of imitative speech by schizophrenic children, *Science* **151**, 705.

Lovaas, O. I., Freitag, G., Gold, V. J., and Kassorla, I. C. (1965) Experimental studies in childhood schizophrenia: analysis of self-destructive behaviour, *J. Exp. Child Psychol.* **2**, 67.

Lovaas, I., and Koegal, R. L. (1973) Behaviour therapy with autistic children, *in Behaviour Modification*, 72nd Year Book of the National Society for the Study of Education, University of Chicago Press, Chicago.

Lovaas, O. I., Koegal, R., Simmons, J. Q., and Long, J. S. (1973) Some generalization and follow-up measures on autistic children in behaviour therapy, *J. Appl. Behav. Anal.* **6**, 131.

Lovaas, O. I., and Simmons, J. Q. (1969) Manipulation of self-destruction in three retarded children, *J. Appl. Behav. Anal.* **2**, 143.

Lowe, A. D., and Campbell, R. A. (1965) Temporal discrimination in aphasoid and normal children, *J. Speech Hear. Res.* **8**, 313.

Lydecken, K. (1972) Therapeutic amenorrhoea with lynestrenol in mental retardation, *Acta. Psychiatr. Scand.* Suppl. 229.

Lyons, J. (1972) Human language, *in* Hinde, R. A. (ed.) *Non-Verbal Communication*, University Press, Cambridge.

McAndrew, J. B., Case, Q., and Treffert, D. A. (1972) Effects of prolonged phenothiazine intake on psychotic and other hospitalized children, *J. Autism Child. Schizophrenia* **2**, 75.

McCall, R. B., Applebaum, M. I., and Hogarty, P. S. (1973) Developmental changes in mental performance, *Monogr. Soc. Res. Child Dev.* **38**, 1.

MacCulloch, M. J. and Sambrooks, J. E. (1972) Concepts of autism: a review, Paper presented at Burton Manor Symposium, *"Recent Developments in Psychiatry"*.

McCulloch, M. J., and Williams, L. (1971) On the nature of infantile autism. *Acta. Psychiatr. Scand.* **47**, 295.

McFie, J. (1961a) Intellectual impairment in children with localized post-infantile cerebral lesions, *J. Neurol. Neurosurg. Psychiatry* **24**, 361.

McFie, J. (1961b) The effects of hemispherectomy on intellectual functioning in cases of infantile hemiplegia, *J. Neurol. Neurosurg. Psychiatry* **24**, 246.

Mackay, D. M. (1972) Formal analysis of communicative processes, *in* Hinde, R. A. (ed.) *Non-Verbal Communication*, University Press, Cambridge.

McNeill, D. (1966) Developmental psycholinguistics, *in* Smith, F., and Miller, G. A. (eds.) *The Genesis of Language*, M.I.T. Cambridge, Mass.

Marteniuk, R. G., and Roy, E. A. (1972) The codability of kinesthetic location and distance information, *Acta Psychol.* **36**, 471.

Meyers, D. I., and Goldfarb, W. (1961) Studies of perplexity in mothers of schizophrenic children, *Am. J. Orthopsychiatry* **31**, 551.

Miller, G. A. (1967) *The Psychology of Communication: Seven Essays*, Penguin, Harmondsworth.

Minkowski, E. (1953) La Schizophrenie, Desclée de Brouwer, Paris.

Mittler, P., Gillies, S., and Jukes, E. (1966) Prognosis in psychotic children: report of a follow-up, *J. Ment. Defic. Res.* **10**, 73.

Montessori, M. (1912) *The Montessori Method*, Stokes, New York.

Morley, M. E. (1967) *The Development and Disorders of Speech in Childhood* (2nd ed.), Livingstone, Edinburgh.

Morton, J. (1970) A functional model of memory, *in* Norman, D. D. (ed.) *Models of Human Memory*, Academic Press, New York.

Mountcastle, V. B., and Powell, T. P. S. (1959) Central nervous mechanisms subserving position sense and kinesthesis, *Bull. Johns Hopkins Hosp.* **180**, 175.

National Society for Autistic Children (1973) *Nowhere To Go: a Report on the Plight of Autistic Adolescents*, N.S.A.C., London.

Neisser, U. (1967) *Cognitive Psychology*, Appleton-Century-Crofts, New York.

O'Connor, N. (1956) The evidence for the permanently disturbing effects of mother-child separation, *Acta Psychol.* **15**, 174.

O'Connor, N., and Hermelin, B. (1965) Visual analogies of verbal operations, *Lang. Speech* **8**, 197.

O'Connor, N., and Hermelin, B. (1967) The selective visual attention of psychotic children, *J. Child Psychol. Psychiatry* **8**, 167.

O'Connor, N., and Hermelin, B. (1972) Seeing and hearing and space and time, *Perception Psychophysics*, **11**, 46.

O'Connor, N., and Hermelin, B. (1973) The spatial or temporal organisation of short-term memory, *Q. J. Exp. Psychol.* **25**, 335.

O'Gorman, G. (1970) *The Nature of Childhood Autism*, Butterworths, London.

Ornitz, E. M. (1973) Childhood autism: a review of the clinical and experimental literature, *Calif. Med.* **118**, 29.

Ornitz, E. M., and Ritvo, E. R. (1968a) Perceptual inconstancy in early infantile autism, *Arch. Gen. Psychiatry* **18**, 76.

Ornitz, E. M., Ritvo, E. R. (1968b) Neurophysiologic mechanisms underlying perceptual inconstancy in autistic and schizophrenic children, *Arch. Gen. Psychiatry* **19**, 22.

Paivio, I. (1971) *Imagery and Verbal Processes*, Holt, Rinehart and Winston, Toronto.

Palmer, L. R. (1965) *Mycenaeans and Minoans*, (2nd ed.), Faber, London.

Park, C. C. (1968) *The Seige*, Colin Smythe, Gerrards Cross.

Phillips, E. E. (1957) Contributions to a learning theory account of childhood autism, *J. Psychol.* **43**, 117.

Pinneau, S. R. (1955) The infantile disorders of hospitalism and anaclitic depression, *Psychol. Bull.* **52**, 429.

Pitfield, M., and Oppenheim, A. N. (1964) Child rearing attitudes of mothers of psychotic children, *J. Child Psychol. Psychiatry* **5**, 51.

Pollack, M., and Woerner, M. G. (1966) Pre- and perinatal complications and "childhood schizophrenia": a comparison of five controlled studies, *J. Child Psychol. Psychiatry* **7**, 235.

Pool, D. (1972) An experimental dental service for handicapped children, *in* Wing, J. K., and Hailey, A. M. (eds.) *Evaluating a Community Psychiatric Service*, Oxford University Press, London.

Poppen, R., Stark, J., Eisenson, J., Forrest, T., and Wertheim, G. (1969) Visual sequencing performance of aphasic children, *J. Speech Hear. Res.* **12**, 288.

Popper, K. R. (1972) *Objective Knowledge: An Evolutionary Approach*, p. 24, Oxford University Press, London.

Potter, H. W. (1933) Schizophrenia in children, *Am. J. Psychiatry* **12**, 1253.

Prior, M., and Macmillan, M. B. (1973) Maintenance of sameness in children with Kanner's syndrome, *J. Autism Child. Schizophrenia* **3**, 154.

Pritchard, D. G. (1963) *Education of the Handicapped, 1760–1960,* Routledge, London.

Pronovost, W., Wakstein, M. P., and Wakstein, D. J. (1966) A longitudinal study of speech behaviour and language comprehension of fourteen children diagnosed as atypical or autistic, *Except. Child.* **33**, 19.

Rank, B. (1959) Adaptation of the psycho-analytic technique for the treatment of young children with atypical development, *Am. J. Orthopsychiatry* **19**, 130.

Reed, G. F. (1963) Elective mutism in children: a re-appraisal, *J. Child Psychol. Psychiatry* **4**, 99.

Reichler, R. J., and Schopler, E. (1971) Observations on the nature of human relatedness, *J. Autism Child. Schizophrenia* **1**, 283.

Ricks, D. M. (1972) *The Beginning of Verbal Communication in Normal and Autistic Children,* M.D. Thesis, London.

Ricks, D. M. (1975) Vocal communication in pre-verbal normal and autistic children, *in* O'Connor, N. (ed.) *Language, Cognitive Deficits and Retardation,* Butterworths, London.

Rimland, B. (1965) *Infantile Autism,* Methuen, London.

Rimland, B. (1968) On the objective diagnosis of infantile autism, *Acta Paedopsychiatr.* **35**, 146.

Rimland, B. (1971a) The differentiation of childhood psychoses; an analysis of checklists for 2,218 psychotic children, *J. Autism Child. Schizophrenia* **2**, 161.

Rimland, B. (1971b) High dosage levels of certain vitamins in the treatment of children with severe mental disorders, *in* Hawkins, D. R., and Pauling, L. (eds.) *Orthomolecular Psychiatry,* Freeman, San Francisco.

Risley, T., and Wolf, M. (1967) Establishing functional speech in echolalic children, *Behav. Res. Ther.* **5**, 73.

Ritvo, E. R., Cantwell, D., Johnson, E., Clements, M., Benbrook, F., Slagle, S., Kelley, P., and Ritz, M. (1971) Social class factors in autism, *J. Autism Child. Schizophrenia* **1**, 297.

Rowlands, P. (1972) *The Fugitive Mind,* Dent, London.

Rutt, C. N., and Offord, D. R. (1971) Pre-natal and perinatal complications in childhood schizophrenics and their siblings, *J. Nerv. Ment. Dis.* **152**, 324.

Rutter, M. (1965) Speech disorders in a series of autistic children, *in* Franklin, A. W. (ed.) *Children with Communication Problems,* Pitman, London.

Rutter, M. (1966) Behavioral and cognitive characteristics, *in* Wing, J. K. (ed.) *Early Childhood Autism* (*1st ed.*), Pergamon, Oxford.

Rutter, M. (1967) Psychotic disorders in early childhood, *in* Coppen, A. J. and Walk, A. (eds.) *Recent Developments in Schizophrenia, Br. J. Psychiatry* (Special Publication).

Rutter, M. (1968) Concepts of autism: a review of research, *J. Child Psychol. Psychiatry* **9**, 1.

Rutter, M. (1970a) Autistic children: infancy to adulthood, *Semin. Psychiatry* **2**, 435.

Rutter, M. (1970b) The assessment of language disorders in the young child, Paper given at *Spastics Society Study Group on Communication Disorders in Young Children; Assessment, Treatment and Care:* Alcuin College, York.

Rutter, M. (1972a) *Maternal Deprivation Reassessed,* Penguin, Harmondsworth.

Rutter, M. (1972b) Psychiatric causes of language retardation, *in* Rutter, M., and Martin, J. A. M. (eds.) *The Child with Delayed Speech,* Clinics in Developmental Medicine No. 43, Heinemann, London.

Rutter, M. (1972c) Clinical assessment of language disorders in the young child, *in* Rutter, M., and Martin, J. A. M. (eds.) *The Child with Delayed Speech*, Clinics in Developmental Medicine No. 43, Heinemann, London.

Rutter, M., and Bartak, L. (1973) Special educational treatment of autistic children: a comparative study—II. Follow-up findings and implications for services, *J. Child Psychol. Psychiatry* **14**, 241.

Rutter, M., Bartak, L., and Newman, S. (1971) Autism—a central disorder of cognition and language? *in* Rutter, M. (ed.) *Infantile Autism: Concepts, Characteristics and Treatment*, Churchill, London.

Rutter, M., and Bax, M. (1972) Normal development of speech and language, *in* Rutter, M., and Martin, J. A. M. (eds.) *The Child with Delayed Speech*, Clinics in Developmental Medicine, No. 43, Heinemann, London.

Rutter, M., Greenfield, D., and Lockyer, L. (1967) A five to fifteen year follow-up study of infantile psychosis: II. Social and behavioural outcome, *Br. J. Psychiatry* **113**, 1183.

Rutter, M., Lebovici, S., Eisenberg, L., Sneznevskij, A. V., Sadoun, R., Brooke, E., and Tsung-Yi Lin (1969) A tri-axial classification of mental disorders in childhood: an international study, *J. Child Psychol. Psychiatry* **10**, 41.

Rutter, M., and Lockyer, L. (1967) A five to fifteen year follow-up study of infantile psychosis: I. Description of the sample, *Br. J. Psychiatry* **113**, 1169.

Rutter, M., and Mittler, P. (1972) Environmental influences on language development, *in* Rutter, M., and Martin, J. A. M. (eds.) *The Child with Delayed Speech*, Clinics in Developmental Medicine, No. 43, Heinemann, London.

Rutter, M., Tizard, J., and Whitmore, K. (eds.) (1970) *Education, Health and Behaviour*, Longman, London.

Schaffer, H. R. (1974) Early social behaviour and the study of reciprocity, *Bull. Br. Psychol. Soc.* **27**, 209.

Schneider, G. E. (1967) Contrasting visuomotor functions of tectum and cortex in the golden hamster, *Psychol. Forsch.* **31**, 52.

Schopler, E. (1965) Early infantile autism and receptor processes, *Arch. Gen. Psychiatry* **13**, 327.

Schopler, E. (1971) Parents of psychotic children as scapegoats, *J. Contemp. Psychother.* **4**, 17.

Schopler, E. (1973) Current approaches to the autistic child, *Pediatr. Ann.* **2**, 60.

Schopler, E., Brehm, S., Kinsbourne, M., and Reichler, R. J. (1971) Effect of treatment structure on development in autistic children, *Arch. Gen. Psychiatry* **24**, 415.

Schopler, E., and Loftin, J. (1969) Thought disorders in parents of psychotic children, *Arch. Gen. Psychiatry* **20**, 174.

Schopler, E., and Reichler, R. J. (1971a) Developmental therapy by parents with their own autistic child, *in* Rutter, M. (ed.) *Infantile Autism: Concepts, Characteristics and Treatment*, Churchill, London.

Schopler, E., and Reichler, R. J. (1971b) Parents as cotherapists in the treatment of psychotic children, *J. Autism Child. Schizophrenia* **1**, 87.

Schopler, E., and Reichler, R. J. (1972) How well do parents understand their own psychotic child? *J. Autism Child. Schizophrenia* **2**, 387.

Schurman, D. L., Bernstein, I. H., and Proctor, R. W. (1973) Modality specific short-term storage for pressure, *Bull. Psychonomic. Soc.* **1**, 71.

Shankweiler, D. (1966) Effects of temporal lobe damage on perception of dichotically presented melodies, *J. Comp. Physiol. Psychol.* **62**, 115.

Shapiro, M. B. (1966) The single case in clinical-psychological research, *J. Gen. Psychol.* **74**, 3.

Sheldon, W. (1968) *Report of Working-Party on Comprehensive Assessment Centres for Handicapped Children*, DHSS, London.

Sheridan, M. D. (1960) *The Developmental Progress of Infants and Young Children*, Ministry of Health Reports on Public Health and Medical Subjects, H.M.S.O., London.

Sheridan, M. D. (1969) Playthings in the development of language, *Health Trends*, 1, 7.

Sheridan, M. D. (1972) The child's acquisition of codes for personal and interpersonal communication, *in* Rutter, M., and Martin, J. A. M. (eds.) *The Child with Delayed Speech*, Clinics in Developmental Medicine, No. 43, Heinemann, London.

Sheridan, M. D. (1973) *Children's Developmental Progress from Birth to Five Years: The Stycar Sequences*, N.F.E.R., Windsor, Berks.

Simon, G. B., and Gillies, S. M. (1964) Some physical characteristics of a group of psychotic children, *Br. J. Psychiatry* **110**, 104.

Siva Sankar (1969) A summary of 30 different biochemical tests in childhood schizophrenia, *in* Siva Sankar, D. V. (ed.) *Schizophrenia; Current Concepts and Research*, P.J.D. Publications, Hicksville, New York.

Skinner, B. F. (1973) *Beyond Freedom and Dignity*, Penguin, Harmondsworth.

Sloan, W. (1955) The Lincoln–Oseretsky motor development scale, *Genet. Psychol. Monogr.* **51**, 186.

Smith, J. J. (1969) Kinesthesia: A model for motor feedback, *in* Brown, R. C., and Cratty, B. J. (eds.) *New Perspectives of Man in Action*, Prentice Hall, Englewood Cliffs, New York.

Smolev, S. R. (1971) Use of operant techniques for the modification of self-injurious behaviour, *Am. J. Ment. Defic.* **76**, 295.

Sperry, R. W. (1968) Hemisphere deconnection and unity in conscious awareness, *Am. Psychol.* **23**, 723.

Sprague, R. L., and Werry, J. S. (1971) Methodology of psychopharmacological studies with the retarded, *in* Ellis, N. E. (ed.) *International Review of Research in Mental Retardation*, Vol. 5, Academic Press, New York.

Stark, J. (1966) Performance of aphasic children on the ITPA, *Except. Child* **33**, 153.

Stark, J. (1967) A comparison of the performance of aphasic children on three sequencing tests, *J. Commun. Disord.* **1**, 31.

Stein, Z., and Susser, M. (1960) The families of dull children: a classification for predicting careers, *Br. J. Prev. Soc. Med.* **14**, 83.

Stengel, E. (1947) A clinical and psychological study of echo-reactions, *J. Ment. Sci.* **93**, 598.

Stutsman, R. (1948) *Mental Measurement of Preschool Children with a Guide for Administering the Merrill–Palmer Scale of Mental Tests*, Harcourt, Brace and World, New York.

Suzuki, T., and Tayuchi, K. (1968) Cerebral evoked response to auditory stimuli in young children during sleep, *Ann. Otolaryngol.* **77**, 102.

Taft, L. T., and Cohen, H. J. (1971) Hypsarrhythmia and childhood autism: a clinical report, *J. Autism Child. Schizophrenia* **1**, 327.

Tallal, P., and Piercy, M. (1973) Developmental aphasia: impaired rate of non-verbal processing as a function of sensory modality, *Neuropsychologia* **11**, 389.

Tate, B. G., and Baroff, G. S. (1966) Aversive control of self-injurious behaviour in a psychotic boy, *Behav. Res. Ther.* **4**, 281.

Terman, L. M., and Merrill, M. A. (1960) *Stanford–Binet Intelligence Scale: Manual for the Third Revision Form L-M*, Houghton Mifflin, Boston.

Thorpe, W. H. (1972) The comparison of vocal communication in animals and man, *in* Hinde, R. A. (ed.) *Non-Verbal Communication*, University Press, Cambridge.

Tinbergen, E. A., and Tinbergen, N. (1972) Early childhood autism—an ethological approach, *Advances in Ethology, J. Comp. Ethology Suppl. No. 10*, Paul Parey, Berlin.

Treffert, D. A. (1970) Epidemiology of infantile autism, *Arch. Gen. Psychiatry* **23**, 431.

Trevarthen, C. (1974) Conversations with a two-month-old, *New Scientist* **62**, 230.

Tubbs, V. K. (1966) Types of linguistic disability in psychotic children, *J. Ment. Defic. Res.* **10**, 230.

Tulving, E., and Madigan, S. A. (1970) Memory and verbal learning, *in* Mussen, P., and Rosenzweig, M. (eds.) *Annual Review of Psychology*, Vol. 21, Annual Reviews Inc., Palo Alto.

Van Krevelen, D. A. (1971) Early infantile autism and autistic psychopathy, *J. Autism Child. Schizophrenia* **1**, 82.

Vaillant, G. E. (1962) John Haslam on early infantile autism, *Am. J. Psychiatry* **119**, 376.

Vygotsky (1962) *Thought and Language*, M.I.T. Press, Cambridge, Mass.

Wechsler, D. (1949) *Wechsler Intelligence Scale for Children: Manual*, Psychological Corp., New York.

Whittam, H., Simon, G. S., and Mittler, P. J. (1966) The early development of psychotic children and their sibs, *Dev. Med. Child Neurol.* **8**, 552.

Williams, M. (1950) *Williams Intelligence Test for Children with Defective Vision*, Institute of Education, Birmingham.

Wing, J. K. (1966) Diagnosis, epidemiology, aetiology, *in* Wing, J. K. (ed.) *Early Childhood Autism (1st ed.)*, Pergamon, Oxford.

Wing, J. K. (1972) Principles of evaluation, *in* Wing, J. K., and Hailey, A. M. (eds.) *Evaluating a Community Psychiatric Service*, Oxford University Press, London.

Wing, J. K., and Brown, G. W. (1970) *Institutionalism and Schizophrenia*, Cambridge University Press, London.

Wing, J. K., Cooper, J. E., and Sartorius, N. (1974) *Description and classification of Psychiatric Symptoms: An Instructional Manual for the PSE and Catego Systems*, Cambridge University Press, London.

Wing, J. K., Leff, J., and Hirsch, S. (1973) Preventive treatment of schizophrenia: Some theoretical and methodological issues, *in* Cole, J. O., Freedman, A. M., and Friedhoff, A. J. (eds.) *Psychopathology and Psychopharmacology*, John Hopkins University Press, Baltimore.

Wing, J. K., O'Connor, N., and Lotter, V. (1967) Autistic conditions in early childhood: a survey in Middlesex, *Br. Med. J.* **3**, 389.

Wing, L., and Wing, J. K. (1971) Multiple impairments in early childhood autism, *J. Autism Child. Schizophrenia* **1**, 256.

Wing, L. (1969) The handicaps of autistic children—a comparative study, *J. Child Psychol. Psychiatry* **10**, 1.

Wing, L. (1970) Observations on the psychiatric section of the "International Classification of Diseases" and the "British Glossary of Mental Disorders", *Psychol. Med.* **1**, 79.

Wing, L. (1971) Perceptual and language development in autistic children: a comparative study, *in* Rutter, M. (ed.) *Infantile Autism: Concepts, Characteristics and Treatment*, Churchill, London.

Wing, L. (1975) A study of language impairments in severely retarded children, *in* O'Connor, N. (ed.) *Language, Cognitive Deficits and Retardation*, Butterworths, London.

Wing, L. (1975a) *Autistic Children: A Guide for Parents*, revised edition. Constable, London.

Withrow, F. B. (1964) Immediate recall by aphasic, deaf, and normally hearing children for visual forms presented simultaneously or sequentially in time, *Asha Monogr.* **6**, 386.

Witmer, L. (1922) Don: A curable case of arrested development due to a fear psychosis in a 3 year old infant, *Psychol. Clinic* 1919–22, **13**, 97.

Wolff, S., and Chess, S. (1964) A behavioural study of schizophrenic children, *Acta Psychiatr. Scand.* **40**, 438.

World Health Organisation (1973) *The International Pilot Study of Schizophrenia*, Vol. 1, W.H.O., Geneva.

Wundt, W. (1896) *Grundrisse der Psychologie*, Engelmann, Leipzig.

Yarrow, L. J. (1961) Maternal deprivation, *Psychol. Bull.* **58**, 459.

Yoshie, N., Okudairn, T. (1969) Myogenic evoked potential responses to clicks in man, *Acta Otolaryngol. (Stockh.)* Suppl. 252, 89.

Yule, W., Berger, M., and Howlin, P. (1974) Language deficit and behaviour modification, *in* O'Connor, N. (ed.) *Language, Cognitive Deficits and Retardation*, Butterworths, London.

Zaslow, R. W. (1967) A psychogenic theory of the etiology of infantile autism and implications for treatment, Paper given at meeting of California State Psychiatric Assoc., San Diego.

INDEX

Aarhus survey 69
Abnormal behaviour 199
Adolescents 47, 117, 279, 304, 312, 313
Adults 312, 313
  prevalence 306–7
Aetiology 20, 72–92
  organic 81
  psychological 72
  theories 126
    concerning basic causes 72–80
Affective contact 17, 22
Amphetamines 275
Anti-convulsants 279
Anti-depressants 277
Anxiety 276
'Aphasia' see Developmental
    receptive speech disorders
Arousal, abnormalities 85
Articulation, defects in 95
Asperger's syndrome 39, 74, 81
Assessment 271, 295
Assessment centres 271, 295, 297
Attachment to objects and
    routines 32
Attention 219
  problems of 90
  seeking 254–5
  to perceptual input 207
Auditory-verbal sequences 156
Autism
  Bleuler's 11
  concept of 9, 12
  definition and use of term 3, 10–11,
    21, 136, 291–2
  temporary 79
  see also Early childhood autism
Autistic psychopathy 39, 74, 81
Autonomic function 29
Aversive therapy 255–7

Barbiturates 275, 277
Behaviour disorders see Behaviour
    problems
Behaviour management
  expertise in 296–7
  in severely retarded autistic children
    253–9
Behaviour modification 312
  see also Aversion therapy;
    Behaviour management; Behaviour
    problems, treatment
Behaviour patterns 16, 18, 22, 264
  after five years of age 34
  first year of life 24
  one to five years 25–35
Behaviour problems 34, 36, 199,
    221–45, 253, 274
  clinical and research data 223
  drugs in 275
  fluctuations in 283
  hierarchy of 230
  historical perspective 221–3
  in education 200–1
  interaction model 227
  relativity 228–30
  secondary 31, 51–2, 80, 132, 269
  threatening family existence 231
  treatment 274–8
Behaviour therapy 167, 200
Binary patterns 151–2
Biochemical abnormalities 86–8
Biological factors 48, 227–8
Blindness 27, 42
  partial 90
Brain damage 41, 81, 82, 248
  echolalia following 128
  sub-cortical 83
Brain dysfunction 48, 199
Bufotenin 87

335

Butobarbitone 277
Butyrophenone 276

Camberwell, survey 292–3
Case histories 53–64
Cerebral dominance, lack of 127–8
Change, resistance to 32, 262
Child-rearing myths 225
Child-rearing practices,
    abnormal 75–8
Childhood psychosis 21
Chloral 277
Chlordiazopoxide 277
Chloropromazine 276
Choice(s)
    of alternatives 213
    repetition of 212
    series of 212
    series of binary 213
Classification 20
Clifford, case history 53, 62–4
Clinical description 22, 49
Coding of sensory stimuli 135–68
Coeliac disease 87
Cognitive development, abnormalities
    of 89
Cognitive impairment 168
Cognitive pathology 167
Cognitive potential 17
Cognitive schemata 206
Cognitive skills, teaching 205–20
Collections of objects 32–3
Communication 91, 95–8
    definition 95
    development in autistic
        children 103
    development in normal children 98
    gestural see Gestures
    goal-directed 96
    impairments in 117
    lack of 260–2
    non-verbal 96, 98–9, 103, 113, 130–1
    problems affecting 49–50
    symbolic and non-symbolic or
        concrete 97
    verbal 113, 130–1
Comprehension
    mental age 183–4

non-verbal 107–8
Concepts 122
    definition 93
    formation of 117–18
Co-operation, developing 216
Counselling 266
Crises 242–3

Dancing 201
Day hospital 64, 272
Day nurseries 299
Deafness 8, 41
    partial 90
    see also Hearing
Delusions 37
Dental care 284, 313
Depressive illness 313
Deprivation experiments 158
Development
    concept of 226
    difficult phases in 45
Developmental 'aphasia' see
    Developmental receptive speech
    disorders
Developmental receptive speech
    disorders 18, 42, 90, 112, 119,
    130, 164–5
    differential diagnosis 42–3
Developmental Therapy Program 226,
    241
Diagnosis 15, 17, 19, 20, 35–7, 49
    differential 37–46
    operational 36
    services 294
Diazepam 277
Diets 283–4
Differential diagnosis 37–46
Difficult phases in development 45
Distance reproduction 147
Distress 27
Division TEACCH 224
Dizziness, lack of 29–30
Doctor, role of 285
Don, case history 6–7
Down's syndrome 108, 124, 290, 291
Drinking 29
Drugs and drug therapy
    psychotropic 274, 275–8

Drugs and drug therapy (*cont.*)
  systematic evaluation 275
Dysarthria 60, 63
Dysmenorrhoea 281
Dyspraxia 175, 185, 193
Dystonia 276, 277

Early childhood autism
  comparison with normal children and
    adults 124
  comparison with severely retarded
    children and adults 123–4
  dealing with problem 20
  definition and use of term 3, 10–11,
    21, 136, 291–2
  hyperaesthetic or Hölderlin
    variety 11, 12
  partial form of 74
  prevalence 71, 293, 306–7
  symbolic functioning problems and
    full clinical picture 129–33
  temporary 79
Eating 29
Echoing 110–11, 128, 207
Echolalia 26, 44, 62, 94, 110–11, 115,
    118
  characteristics of 128
  clinical phenomena 129
  following brain injury 128
Education 43, 57, 197–203, 231, 237,
    299–305
  adolescents 304
  aims of 197, 267–70
  behaviour problems in 200–1
  comparison of approaches 197–9
  content of programmes 199–202
  evaluation of results 202–3
  parents in 202
  remedial 5–6
  see also Schools
EEG 81, 85, 174, 272, 278–9
Elective mutism 44
Electric shock treatment 255, 256
Electro-convulsive treatment 278
Emotion, expression in sounds 99,
    103
Emotional development, abnormality
  of 88

Emotional reactions 33
Emotional response 16
Employment 61, 305–7
Encephalitis 133
Environmental pressures 79
Epidemiology 65–71
Epilepsy 47, 48, 69, 272, 275, 276,
    278, 282
Erroneous expectations of
  parents 235–8
Eye poking 257–8

Facial expressions 104, 107–8
Family
  practical help required 297
  role of 318
Fascination 27
Faulty conditioning 77–8
Fear 25, 33, 61, 79
Feature extraction 153
Feeding problems 284
Feral children 221–3, 225
Fits 248, 278
Fitting and assembly tasks 190
Follow-up studies 243, 256, 298
Frostig test of visual perception 154

Games 34
Gaze avoidance 88
Genetic abnormalities 75, 81
Gestural stimuli 259
Gestures 98, 105, 107
Glucose 87
Grammar 101–2, 112–13, 119–20

Hallucinations 37
Haloperidol 277
Head banging 34, 255, 256, 260–1
Hearing
  disorders 41
  investigation of 273
  see also Deafness
Heterogeneity 274
Hilda Lewis House 312
Hormones 280, 282
Hospital placements 308–10

Hostels   308–11
Humour   115, 124
Hysterectomy   283

Illness   260, 283
Imagination   33–4, 43
    see also Language, inner
Imitating movements   106
Imitation   207
    deficiency of   91–2
    of body motion   185
    problems of   29, 50
    training in   261
Immaturity   30
Indifference   27, 31
Infantile psychosis   38
Infections   260
Information processing   139, 140
    and perceptual impairments   137–8
Information reduction   138
Insulin   87
Intelligence   169, 170, 247–53
    see also IQ
Interaction matrix   228
Interaction model   227
IQ   38, 40, 47, 48, 67, 77, 109, 124,
    140, 170–1, 174, 175, 181, 190, 193,
    235, 238, 243–53, 290
    see also Intelligence

Jig-saw puzzle task   154

Kamala, case history   222
Kanner's criteria   20
    problems in applying   17
Kanner's syndrome   3–21, 35, 87
Kinaesthetic information
    experiments   144–8

Language   56, 89, 259
    abnormalities in autism   18, 26,
        49–50, 103–17
    acquisition in autistic
        children   121–3
    acquisition in normal children   120,
        125

components of   94–5
definition   93
delay   45
development in normal children   125
development of, teaching cognitive
    skills underlying   205–20
gestural   *see* Gestures
inner   94, 102, 116, 120, 122, 269,
    292, 296
rules of   207
sign   97, 261–2
teaching   201, 205–20
verbal and non-verbal   97
visual analogies   217–19
    see also Communication; Gesture;
        Speech
Learning by conditioning   121
Learning problems   90–1
Left to right rule   210
Leisure   314–15
Lithium   277
Location reproduction   147
Lynestrenol   282

Malabsorption   87
Management
    aims of   267–70
    medical   271–86
Masturbation   279, 280
Matching
    and sorting, choice in   211
    from cues   150
    of similar items   211
Maturation, retardation of   86
Medical examination   272
Medical treatments   274
Memory   163, 164, 206
    for visual patterns   31
    immediate visual   150
    of temporally distributed series of
        events   148
Memory-dependent skills   30–1
Memory-storage abnormalities   122
Memory tasks   214–16
Memory test   150, 215
Menstruation   280–3
Mental retardation   18, 40, 117, 123,
    132, 244, 245, 250, 269

Methylphenidate 275
Middlesex survey 65–9, 293
  parents 67–9
  siblings 68–9
Miming, difficulty in 29
Mood fluctuations 264
Motor control, problems of 29, 51
Motor imitation, problems of 29, 50
Motor performance 185
Motor skills 124
Movement reproduction 146
Music 30, 56, 59, 113, 163, 164, 314
Mutism 105, 109
  elective 44

National Society for Autistic
  Children 309, 315, 317
Nature-nurture controversy 227
Negativism 199
Nembutal 277
Neurobiological dysfunction 87
Neurological involvement 82, 172,
  251, 252
Nine Diagnostic Points 21
Nitrazepam 277
Nursery schools 299

Obsessions 32
Occupational therapists 314
Operant conditioning 78, 109,
  199–200, 220, 225–6, 262
Oral contraceptives 281
Organic conditions 92
Orphenadrine 276
Over-activity 276
Oxygen, over-sensitivity to 85

Paget–Gorman system 261–2
Parent-child interaction 227
Parent counselling 232–5
Parent-professional
  relationship 235–42
Parent-teacher relationship 231
Parental confusion 233
Parental pathology, abnormalities
  exacerbated by 78

Parental psychopathology and
  mismanagement 240
Parental responses 78
Parents
  abnormalities in 72–5, 80
  access to results of diagnostic
    evaluations 234, 237
  and skills acquisition 268
  as cotherapists 229
  effect of abnormalities in their
    child 80
  erroneous expectations of 235–8
  estimation of child's level of
    functioning 236
  guidance for specific
    problems 241–2
  in education 202
  Middlesex survey 67–9
  practical advice for 296
  psychotherapy 298
  reasonable intervention by 242
  role of 318
  shielding 234
Partial sightedness 42
Partial syndromes 35
Pattern perception 139
Paul, case history 53, 58–62
Perception, problems of 90
Perceptual impairments and
  information processing 137–8
Perceptual-motor performance 185
Performance profile 185
Pericyazine 276
Perphenazine 276
Personality 18
Phenobarbitone 275
Phenothiazines 276, 277
Phenylketonuria 133
Phenytoin 279
Photo-sensitivity 276
Physical attractiveness 30
Physical development 29
Physical education 201
Physio-therapists 314
Piperazine 276
Play 33–4, 42, 102, 116
  see also Language, inner
Play groups 299
Posture 29

Premenstrual tension   281
Pre-school unit   299
Prevalence   71, 293
    adults   306–7
Primidone   275
Prognosis   20, 46–8, 252–3
Pronunciation, problems of   116
Psychological environment,
        abnormalities of   72
Psychological functions   88–92
Psychologist in behaviour
        management   296–7
Psychophysiological functions   88–92
Psychosis, childhood   21
Psycho-social deprivation   44
Psychotherapy   298, 312
Psychotropic behaviour   39
Psychotropic drugs   274, 275–8
Puberty   279

Rating scales   274
Reading   60, 117, 251
Reciprocity   151
Recreation   314–15
Regression   264
Regressive techniques   197, 198
Relationships between objects   209
Remedial education   5–6
Repetition of same choice   212
Repetitive speech   43, 62
Residential accommodation   231,
        307–12
    short-term   310
Residential units   231, 312
Resistance to change   32, 262
Reticular system, abnormalities   84
Reversibility   151
Rituals and routines   32, 126, 249, 305
Rocking   276
Romulus and Remus   222
Routines and rituals   32, 126, 249, 305
Rubella   81, 90

Sally, case history   53, 54–8
Schizophrenia   21, 70, 86, 250, 278
    and autism   11
    differential diagnosis   37–9
Schools   57, 60, 232

ESN   302–4
    special   267, 300–2
    see also Education
Screaming   54, 58, 59, 283
Screening   65, 274, 293
Self injury   34, 78, 248, 252, 253–8
Self stimulation   258
Sensory experiences   25
    abnormal responses to   27, 28, 50,
        89–91, 131
Sensory modality   135
Sensory stimuli, coding of   135–68
Sequencing from left to right   210
Seriation test   150
Serotonin   87
Services
    areas lacking provision of   285–6
    calculations of needs   292
    diagnostic   294
    integration of   316
    plan for   293
    principles governing the provision
        of   290
    problems in providing   289–90
    provision of   287–318
    specialist   311–14
Severity of the disorder   23
Severity of impairment and treatment
        aims   242–5
Sexual behaviour   279
Sheldon report   271
Sheltered community   309
Sheltered workshops   *see*
        Employment
Siblings   228
    Middlesex survey   68–9
Side effects   276, 277
Sign language   97, 261–2
Skills   30, 57, 61
    acquisition of   268
    cognitive, teaching   205–20
    memory-dependent   30–1
    motor   124
    non-language-dependent   30
    practical   201
    resistance to learning new   262
    special   30, 51, 133
    splinter   190
    visuo-motor   124, 209

Sleep 29, 277
Smell 28
Social adjustment 47
Social aloofness 31, 35, 57, 198
Social conduct 108, 126
Social interchanges 32
Social relationships 47, 91
Social responses 22
Social withdrawal 37, 79, 173, 234, 237
Social worker, role of 297–8
Sorting tasks 213
Sound, response to 27
Sound-labels 109
Spatial coding 166
Spatial location 141–4, 166
Spatial ordering 157–62
Spatial patterns 166
Spatial sequence 215
Special schools 267, 300–2
Special skills 30, 51, 133
Specialist services 311–14
Speech 259, 261
  abnormalities 26
  'aphasic' 174
  comprehension of 100
  content of 113
  definition 94
  delayed development 26
  development 108–17, 100
  echolalic *see* Echolalia
  lack of interest in 114
  non-verbal 106
  onset of 100
  problems in comprehension of 26
  pronunciation problems 116
  repetitive 43, 62
  spontaneous 94, 111–13
  understanding of 114–16
Speech disorder 37, 47, 128, 130
  developmental receptive 18, 42, 90, 112, 119, 130
  expressive 95
  receptive 95
Speech therapists 313–14
Splinter skills 190
Staff training 315–16
Stereotyped behaviour 91, 132, 248, 252, 258, 276, 305

Stimulus-response theory 225
Sub-cortical lesions 82, 126
Sulthiame 279
Surgery 284
Swimming 201
Symbolic function
  impairments of 205
  problems of 129–33
Symbols 89, 90, 118–19, 214, 217, 220, 231
  definition 93
  difficulty in handling 120
  system of 94
Syndrome
  as separate entity 18
  identification of 15
  partial 35
  use of term 10

Tactile sensations 28
Taste 28
Teaching
  cognitive skills underlying
    language 205–20
  techniques 207–9
Temper tantrums 7, 25, 32, 34, 58, 78, 283
Temporal ordering 157–62
Temporal sequences 166, 208
Terminology 20–2
Terry, case history 236–7
Thioridazine 276
Toys 33
Tranquillisers 276, 277
Treatment 20, 274
  aims of, and severity of
    impairment 242–5
  at home 266
  settings 265–7
Trifluoperazine 276
Tryptophan metabolism 87

Understanding of speech 114–16

Verbal abstraction abilities 184
Verbal profiles 176–85

Verbal subtests   180
Verbal tests   176
Vestibular control   29
Vestibular system, dysfunction of   83
Victor, case history   4–6, 13
Vision disorders   42
Visual cortex   141
Visual information   27
Visual inspection, abnormalities
   of   28, 50
Visual-motor performance   185, 191,
   192
Visual patterns, memory for   31

Visual perception, Frostig test of   154
Visual sequence experiments   148
Visuo-motor skills   124, 209
Visuo-motor task   208
Visuo-spatial sequence   215
Vitamins   277–8
Vocabulary subtest   183
Vocalisation, goal-directed   98
Voluntary organisations   289, 317–18

Wisconsin survey   70
Word-labels   205, 219